The Archaeology

OF

Christianity in Africa

THE ARCHAEOLOGY

OF

CHRISTIANITY IN AFRICA

Niall Finneran

TEMPUS

First published 2002

PUBLISHED IN THE UNITED KINGDOM BY:
Tempus Publishing Ltd
The Mill, Brimscombe Port
Stroud, Gloucestershire GL5 2QG

PUBLISHED IN THE UNITED STATES OF AMERICA BY:
Tempus Publishing Inc.
2 Cumberland Street
Charleston, SC 29401

British Library Cataloguing in Publication Data.
A catalogue record for this book is available from the British Library.

ISBN 0 7524 2510 2

Typesetting and origination by Tempus Publishing.
Printed in Great Britain by Midway Colour Print, Wiltshire

Contents

List of illustrations

Note on illustrations

Every effort has been made to track down the original copyright holders of the photographs where it is known that the copyright has not lapsed, but in some cases this has proved to be impossible. Where possible, copyright holders are credited. All line drawings have been redrawn from primary sources. They are acknowledged below: Figures **5**, **6**, **7**, **8**, **9** from Ennabli, 1997; figures **22**, **24**, **26**, **27**, **30**, **31** from articles by P. Grossman, *Coptic Encyclopedia* 1991; figures **38**, **39**, **40**, **41** from M. Krause (ed.), 1986; figures **44**, **45**, **46** from Welsby and Daniels, 1991 and Welsby, 1998; figures **47**, **48**, **49** from Shinnie and Chittick, 1961; figures **50**, **51**, **52** from Anderson, 1999; figure **57** from Munro-Hay, 1991; figure 58 from Munro-Hay, 1989; figure **60** from Buxton and Matthews, 1971, *Rassegna di Studi Etiopici* 25; figures **64**, **65** from Buxton, 1971; figure **69** from Matthews and Mordini, 1959; figures **74**, **75**, **76** from Redman, 1986; figure **77** from J. Kirkman, 1974; figure **78** from C. Clark and M. Horton (unpub.) *The Zanzibar Archaeological Survey, 1984-5*; figure **80** from Mortelmans and Monteyn, 1962.

Cover

Afternoon sunlight catches the rooftop cross of an ancient Ethiopian church in the countryside west of Aksum

Text illustrations

Colour plates

Acknowledgements

I would like to record my gratitude to the following individuals who have commented upon aspects of this work, given help and advice and have generously provided illustrations (the latter are also acknowledged in the picture credits). Any errors remain my sole responsibility.

For comments and criticisms on specific chapters, I would like to thank: Dr Paul Lane (chapter 1), Reverend Professor William Frend (chapter 2), Dr Okasha El Daly (chapter 3), Dr Jacke Phillips (chapter 4), Professor David Phillipson (chapter 5), Dr Andrew Reid (chapter 6) and Professor John Picton (chapter 7). My thanks also go to Mr Adrian James who undertook the proof reading of the manuscript, and to Mr Peter Kemmis Betty of Tempus Publishing who has commented at various stages on the manuscript, and has been a paragon of patience!

The following have also helped with advice, illustrations and in general with the manuscript: Dr John Alexander, Dr Christopher De Corse, Dr Joseph Elders, Ato Girma Elias, Mr David Morgan Evans, Mr Edwin Johnson, Dr Geoffrey King, Mr Tony Lock, Dr Kevin MacDonald, Ms Sarah Mulligan, Mr Glenn Ratcliffe, Dr Andrew Reynolds, Mr Simon Roffey, Mr Geoffrey Tassie, Mr Richard Thorne, Dr Tania Tribe, Professor Frank Willett, Ms Stephanie Wynne-Jones and a number of undergraduate students at SOAS who have helped, during the course of my seminar sessions on African art and archaeology, to develop some of the themes in this book.

I would also like to record my thanks to the staff of the following libraries for dealing so patiently and effectively with my requests for material: SOAS library, University of London, the Institute of Archaeology library, University College London, the library of the Society of Antiquaries of London, the Haddon Archaeology and Anthropology library, University of Cambridge, the Africa Studies Centre library, University of Cambridge and the library of the British Institute in Eastern Africa, Nairobi. For financial work with fieldwork connected with this book, I would like to record my gratitude to the British Institute in Eastern Africa, SOAS and the Society of Antiquaries of London. This book was written whilst the author was employed as a British Academy Post-Doctoral Research Fellow at the Department of Art and Archaeology, SOAS, University of London.

Introduction

Christianity has had a foothold in the African continent for almost two thousand years; as Britain, and much of Europe, still maintained an essentially pagan outlook, Egypt, Nubia, Ethiopia, and Roman north Africa all were home to thriving and diverse Christian communities, the homes of dynamic Christian thinkers too, people who shaped the philosophical and theological outlook of Christianity in its formative years. Africa was not a cultural or intellectual backwater. This book looks at how the arrival of Christianity in different parts of Africa has left its mark in the archaeological record, from the earliest times up to the impact of European colonialism in the later half of the nineteenth century.

This book has developed out of a personal perspective; a work of this nature cannot claim to be all-embracing, there is too much to say. I am an archaeologist, not a historian in the strictest sense of the word. Besides, there is no room, I feel, for such a descriptive or synthetic work. This book, although written within a certain historical framework, is from an archaeological perspective – it is a culture history. Nor do I wish to synthesise what amounts to a great deal of relevant archaeological data; recently many new challenging theoretical directions and concepts have emerged in archaeology, orientations which seek to put new perspectives on the study of humanity, culture and religion. These questions need to be faced, and here is an immediate justification for this present work.

This book has been a long time in the making, and surprisingly the idea was not initially conceived in Africa. Some time ago, in Jerusalem, I revisited the Church of the Holy Sepulchre after an absence of five years. To be honest, this church – one of the holiest sites in Christendom – is something of a depressing place. Jerome Murphy O'Connor, one of Jerusalem's most influential biblical archaeologists, had this to say about it:

> One hopes for peace, but the ear is assailed by a cacophony of warring chants. One desires holiness, only to encounter a jealous possessiveness. The frailty of man is nowhere more apparent than here; it epitomises the human condition.
>
> (*The Holy Land: an archaeological guide from the earliest times to 1700*, 2nd ed. 1986, Oxford: Oxford University Press, 46)

The place has a ramshackle appearance; bits and pieces have been added on to this church over centuries, seemingly without any thought of architectural improvement. The air is heavy with incense and the chants of the Roman Catholic, Greek Orthodox, Armenian, Syrian, Egyptian Coptic and Ethiopian clergy who share, awkwardly, this most sacred space. From time to time national rivalries and shared hatreds arise; disputes are frequent, and it is no surprise that the keys of this church are in the hands of a local Muslim family who have been entrusted with this role for centuries.

The Copts and Ethiopians, Africa's representatives in this uneasy league of Christians, have traditionally never seen eye to eye. The Ethiopians, once a numerous and important element of Christian Jerusalem, have now been relegated to a small compound on the roof; a disparate collection of small mud huts that would not look out of place in the Ethiopian highlands. This small outpost of ecclesiastical Ethiopia is manned by a steadily diminishing number of tall, thin, but graceful and dignified monks who like to keep themselves to themselves. From this eyrie, in the cool fragrance of a very early Jerusalem morning, one can hear their fellow Africans, the Copts, intoning their sombre matins in a language that is not so far away from ancient Egyptian, the language of the Pharaohs.

I had never given any thought to the antiquity of Christianity in Africa; most archaeological students will be familiar with the Copts, but what of these mysterious, stately Ethiopians? What of the disappeared glories of Roman north African Christianity, or those of Nubia? This contrast was heightened upon stepping out of the cool church into the dry heat of the Via Dolorosa; here a Roman Catholic priest from Kenya stopped to chat to a colleague from Senegal, and a large Anglican delegation of black South Africans pushed past into the Church. This brought home not just the varieties of Christianity present in contemporary Africa, but also led my thinking into another, rather more disturbing, direction.

The squabbles in the Church of the Holy Sepulchre were obviously a symptom of inter-denominational point-scoring; church – if not national pride – was at stake in the greater game for control of holy places. Religion, or any form of ideology, can always serve a more useful purpose than making the masses feel contented and helping them understand their place in the greater scheme. Religion can exercise a definite degree of social control. This line of thought has recently been developed among the newer breed of theoretical archaeologists – frequently prehistorians – who see the emergence of cultic or ritual activity in the past in terms of social control; we shall discuss this in more detail in chapter 1 when we consider the relationship between archaeological interpretation and religious or cultic behaviour in the archaeological record. Within the strictly defined terms of the African Christian phenomenon we can recognise such patterns.

Religious affiliation can problematically take on a more enhanced role in defining ethnicity, or at the extreme end of the scale pushing nationalist sentiment: for the Copts in Egypt their Christianity is a jealously guarded identity, setting them apart from their Muslim compatriots to the extent that they have become targets for extremist terrorist groups. The Ethiopian Church maintained a vital role in the lives of the people even under the dark clouds of the notorious Marxist military junta – the *Dergue* (1974-91) – yet throughout the centuries has always provided a national rallying point in the face of Muslim incursions; for over a thousand years the Church and the fragmented state lived together in a mutually beneficial symbiotic relationship. More recently we may point to the role of the Dutch Reformed Church in the sinister workings of South African Apartheid; we may even question – from the cynical twenty-first-century viewpoint, perhaps – the motives behind European missionary work in Africa in the nineteenth century and earlier. The competing European nations in the so-called scramble for Africa all jealously pushed their own brand of Christianity, the Protestant or Roman Catholic, and such brands of Christianity went hand in glove with the prevailing systems of enlightened governance of the native.

This idea of social control is fascinating; we can divine the workings of the process from historical texts, but for the vast sphere of the African Christian experience, where textual sources are rare, can we make the same assumptions from the basic material evidence? Other important questions – from this cultural perspective – also spring to mind. Can we divine, from the archaeological record, the nature of the process of conversion? What were the motives of the missionaries, and what perceived benefits were there for the converts? How did the coming of Christianity affect the day-to-day social and economic lives of the newly converted? How did the implanted forms of Christianity subsequently develop in their new homes, how much indigenous shaping of the faith went on? The African archaeological record can offer new perspectives on these questions, perspectives that can also be viewed on the wider global scale.

This then, in very broad outline, is the basis of this book, an investigation of diversity and change on a massive continent – wide scale, the study of a very important stage in humanity's cultural and social development from the perspective of a much understudied source: African archaeology, and African historical archaeology at that. But there are obvious limitations here and the scope of this book needs still to be adequately defined; rigidly defined boundaries or pigeon-holes within academic archaeology are unhelpful – such as being as Egyptologist, or being a Romanist in the case of northern Africa – especially when one thinks of the geographical scope of such a vast continent; this study attempts to see the temporal and spatial whole rather than applying subject or area-specific pigeon-holes.

It may be as well to clearly state what this book is not. It is not a history of Christianity in Africa; although some historical background is discussed, as an archaeologist largely uncomfortable with teasing the intricacies out of historical documents, I limit myself to teasing the intricacies out of a range of excavation reports to provide a synthesis. This is only the first step. The book cannot claim to be the definitive guide to archaeological sites in Africa that show evidence of Christian activity in the past; such a book would require many volumes and a spread of expertise only possible in a large team. I prefer here to deal with a series of case studies, temporally and spatially separate, yet easily inter-linked; and rather than limiting myself to descriptive archaeological evidence for, say, early Christianity in Egypt, I would like to take these data a step further, and ask why? Not what, or where, or when?

The accusation may be fairly made that this study has been spread too thinly; I rather like to think that I have attempted, economically, to deal with a representative sample of the varied manifestations of the archaeological evidence for Christianity in Africa. At this point the structure of the book could be usefully explained. The book divides itself logically into three parts.

The first part, chapter 1, defines the contexts of the study. In the first chapter the geographical and historical contexts of Christianity in Africa are broadly set out. A generalised overview of the historical development of Christianity is presented without touching excessively on the minutiae of theological differences. This historical overview is the important framework for seeking to understand the cultural development discussed in the core of the book. A brief history of Christianity in Africa is then recounted, from area to area, from the earliest times up to the present where the chapter concludes with an overview of African Christianity today, as well as its historical and cultural relationships with indigenous religions, and the other key world religion present in contemporary Africa: Islam. The second part of chapter 1 defines the methodological constraints of the study; a number of key questions need to be addressed here. What is the nature of the uneasy relationship between archaeology and religion? What are the criteria for defining religious behaviour in the cultural, archaeological record? What is the nature of the evidence? How can archaeology be objectively and 'responsibly' used in elucidating the cultural history of religion, and what implications do these questions have in the study of Christianity, especially in Africa? It is not my intention to burden the reader with the detailed arguments of recent archaeological theoretical developments, rather to outline the interpretative frameworks in which the raw archaeological data may be viewed.

The key chapters that form the core of this work deal with regional case studies, working roughly north to south, early to late. Chapter 2 looks at the impact of Christianity on Roman north Africa, a region that was riven by internal conflict between two different strains of Christian thought – how was this conflict reflected in the archaeological evidence? Chapter 3 considers the Egyptian experience of Christianity. Alexandria was an important early centre of Christianity and the home to a dynamic group of radical Christian thinkers. Egypt also saw the emergence of the ascetic, monastic ideal at an early date, a lifestyle that was enthusiastically embraced. Again, how does the archaeological evidence reflect this dynamism and development? Chapter 4 considers the Nubian picture, where, in the sixth century AD, three small states on the Nile adopted, it seems, two different forms of Christianity, and for a short period of time before Arab incursions, flared brilliantly as a beacon of Christian civilisation on the middle Nile. In chapter 5 we meet the remarkable Ethiopian Christians, who high in their mountain home resisted total conquest until 1935, and even then the brief Italian occupation did little to dim the glories of a Christianity of high antiquity and remarkable powers of survival and adaptivity.

The next case studies present a slightly differing perspective. Chapter 6 looks at the earliest European contacts and their impact on the native peoples. The

Europeans, adventurers and slave traders, all left their mark to varying degrees, but their impact was noticeably nebulous, and their intermittent activities along the African seaboards did little to further the Christian message in the interior. In fact, their activities were markedly un-Christian, as thousands of peoples were forced shackled into the sweltering decks of Atlantic slave ships never to return. Was there, we ask, a veneer of Christian respectability here, and did it manifest itself archaeologically? We then take the story southwards, to the Cape of Good Hope, where the establishment of a small victualling station by Dutch merchants in the seventeenth century had moral ramifications for centuries afterward. As colonisation proceeded, the single glue that held these strangers in a strange land together was their unshakeable faith in God and themselves as a chosen people. Here, more than anywhere, we see the mask slip to reveal motives of domination, social conditioning, and oppression. The Church was an instrument of such actions. Stretching this thread further, in the last part of the chapter we look at the archaeological evidence for nineteenth-century missionary activity in the rest of sub-Saharan Africa, and consider the motives behind the proselytising process, the national and inter-denominational rivalries, and their reflection in their European cultural roots. In the final chapter – the last of the three sections – we draw the threads together to consider the emergence and development of Christianity in Africa against the macrocosmic, global perspective, the contrast and comparisons, with special reference to understanding the modern material culture picture of Christianity in Africa from the dynamic African perspective.

To end this chapter, I offer a few personal images that have shaped this study and also reinforce that motif of socio-cultural diversity in African Christianity. A Coptic wedding in Cairo at the height of summer, the smell of the street competing against the haze of incense. An eighth-century AD wall painting of Saint Anna from the walls of the now lost Faras cathedral in Nubia, peering from the pages of the excavation report, mournful looking, beautiful, unmistakably northern African in appearance, reminding us of glories – religious and archaeological – now long disappeared. Sitting among the deacons at the back of the Old Cathedral in Aksum, Ethiopia, at festival time, banging drums, shaking sistra, creating a mighty din in clouds of heavy incense, all competing with the senses. An all night service too, the most important time of the Ethiopian liturgical year, fighting drowsiness and the soporific beat of the drums and chants to emerge into the early dawn with the sun rising above the eucalyptus and bare hillsides beyond. Driving down rutted tracks in western Uganda, through tiny villages, on a Sunday morning, passing long human crocodiles of people coming from miles around to worship at a small, neat, simple, yet beautiful boarded church with a corrugated iron roof. The incongruity of a German Lutheran cathedral against the clear blue sky and raw harsh brightness of a Namibian day. It is this intriguing cultural diversity that we shall be considering here.

A note on further reading

At the end of each chapter, I have included a small list of further reading. I have not referenced the text throughout in order to keep the thread of the narrative and for the sake of economy. Credit is given within the text for ideas of other scholars, and the key sources are to be found within the further reading section. I have for the most part selected works that are informative and accessible to the non-academic reader; many are still in print or may be easily obtained through second-hand book dealers, while selected journals may be found in any good university library. These readings effectively represent the tip of the iceberg, but any readers wishing to take their research further are urged to begin with these key sources and work outwards from there.

1 African Christianity: a historical and archaeological framework

According to the latest figures, there are estimated to be some 400 million Christians in Africa – approximately one-fifth of the total global Christian population. These figures can only be a vague approximation, for in many areas so-called traditional religions still retain a great deal of importance to the average man or woman. As such, Christianity is only a thin veneer over traditional socio-ideological concepts. This is one of the key points that we will encounter time and time again in this study: socio-cultural and 'westernised' conceptions of Christianity have been moulded through years of contact within the African milieu. Some facets have been borrowed from other religions, in terms of belief, liturgy and cultural elements. This borrowing of symbols of other religions and belief systems is known as syncretism.

A question of syncretism

> It was the old riddle of the dying god made carnate and sacrificed miraculously to appease his own bloody godhead. Is it any wonder that the African ancestors of these worshipers, with such traditions of their own, had accepted also the Hebrew–Syriac version of this age-old riddle taught them by the early colonial priests?
>
> (William Seabrook, 1929, *The Magic Island*)

A number of key examples will be cited here to clarify this concept of syncretism. Voodoo, alluded to by the American writer William Seabrook (above), is a richly symbolic belief system prevalent in Haiti in the Caribbean; it is essentially the grafting of Roman Catholic belief to traditional west African concepts of god and magic. Voodoo – along with its other Caribbean variant Obeah, and its Brazilian counterpart Macumba – is the result of centuries of mixing of belief systems in a fundamentally oppressive society built upon African slavery. Voodoo participants looked back to their homelands, resurrected ancestral memories, and moulded them to fit in with their essentially Roman Catholic daily life. The principal Voodoo goddess Erzulie represents an amalgam of sexual and compassionate characteristics, a sort of

Venus combined with the Virgin Mary. Within the Voodoo temple, representations of Roman Catholic saints are commonplace; the Virgin represented by Erzulie, Damballah, the serpent god as St Patrick and the god of thunder and rain, Shango, is frequently represented as St John the Baptist. The sinister undercurrent of Voodoo necromancy – divination through the dead – reaches its fevered apogee on one of the most important Roman Catholic feast days – All Souls Day – with dancing in cemeteries. In a similar vein, adherents of the collective Brazilian Afro-American spirit religions known under the umbrella term of Macumba seek intercession through the African sea goddess Yemanja – a figure who could be identified with the Roman Catholic conception of the Virgin Mary.

Going further back in time, Roman religion borrowed symbols and identities freely from other religions, Greek, Egyptian and Persian; the Roman pantheon was clearly based on that of the Greeks, while changing fashions often saw the addition of Egyptian elements. The Persian cult of Mithraism, a dualist belief that saw a strict dichotomy of good and evil, was enthusiastically embraced by legions in the east and brought back to the western Empire where its emphasis on comradeship found a ready supply of potential converts. The Ethiopian Orthodox Church – which we will encounter in chapter 5 – has within its recognisably oriental Christian framework a number of liturgical and social beliefs which are Judaic in character, and the traditional beliefs of animism have left their mark in a number of ways, not least the use of charms and amulets and the belief in the evil eye. One can even argue that modern conceptions of Paganism or Wicca – the New Age beliefs – are merely packages of amalgamated and borrowed beliefs from a variety of pre-Christian western sources and reflective eastern religions. This amalgam is readily recognisable in the history and development of the Christian church in Africa.

The African perspective

In this chapter, we will consider the historical development of Christianity in Africa, and in the last section of the chapter consider how archaeological research – as distinct from text-driven, historical research – can elucidate the complex picture of this development. We can conveniently divide the developmental process into three key phases. The first area to consider is the Church in antiquity. Northern Africa and Egypt came under the aegis of the Roman Empire, and key developments here mirror those in Europe and the Levant. The presence of a large Jewish community in Alexandria, for instance, made it a key focal point for the development of this new sect from Palestine, and in time the fabled city became a hot-bed of intellectual Christian debate. Over to the west, in Roman north Africa – roughly taking in the modern states of Tunisia, Algeria and Libya – Christians looked more to Rome for direction. This region was an important economic cog in the Roman system, and was settled extensively by ex-soldiers of the Empire; it proved to be a fertile breeding ground for the emergent faith, and a focal point for some of the worst excesses of internecine feuding. Within this scope of the Church in antiquity comes Nubia and Ethiopia, peripheral areas of the Roman imperial system, but important economic players nonetheless.

Over a thousand years, Christianity in Africa had its foothold along the Nile Valley and within the Ethiopian highlands. The second phase of Christian development comes with the formative stages of European colonialism, and the most important group on the scene at this stage were the Portuguese: indefatigable traders and bold explorers. The first European contacts did not seek actively to promote the Christian faith, but inevitably over time, as contacts and trust were built up with African rulers in the interior, so some element of missionary activity developed. Finally, the third developmental phase sees the orchestrated European scramble for Africa, where the concepts of civilisation-bringing, national self-interest and the process of missionary work went hand-in-hand. In the following discussion we will consider the salient historical framework of the development of Christianity in Africa, but with the goal of considering in more detail the socio-economic elements that made the emergence of the new faith such a success, and with special reference to viewing the cultural developments that form the core of the present study against this framework.

In the beginning...

At the beginning of the first century AD – but that, of course, was not what it was yet known as – the Roman Province of Palestine (modern Israel and Jordan) was in ferment. The Roman administration had always followed a policy of live and let live with the largely Jewish population. During this time, Judaism was rent by intellectual feuding. Large numbers of disaffected religious splinter groups or sects such as the Pharisees, Sadducees and Essenes emerged, all competing with each other to decide who was the closest to the Judaic ideal. It is against this uneasy backdrop of debate and feuding that Christianity emerged as a fundamentally rebel Jewish sect that appealed to the disaffected masses, but it took time to develop. Initially, from the cultural point of view, there would be little here to distinguish the nascent faith from its Jewish progenitor; the Roman writer Suetonius famously described Christianity as being a Jewish cult. Undoubtedly the new faith found its fertile recruiting grounds within the Hellenised (or Greek-speaking) Jewish communities of the Levant; it was here that the missions of St Paul met with great success in the decades following the crucifixion.

Events, however, soon took a savage turn. The first organised action against the adherents of this new and challenging faith was orchestrated by the emperor Nero in 64, and at regular intervals Christians were made to suffer for their beliefs: the Aurelian persecutions 161-80, Severus' persecutions 193-211, Decius' persecutions 249-51, Valerian's persecutions 253-60, and finally in this macabre list the infamous and brutal persecutions of Diocletian from 303-5. The rationale behind these orchestrated and brutal purges was complex, but it bred a climate of fear. For early Christians it paid not to draw attention to oneself, and this is reflected in the relatively low archaeological visibility of the formative stages of Christian development: the first churches, for instance, were merely simple houses.

In 306, Constantius –the former Caesar of the western division of the Empire who had served under the Emperor in the west, Maximius – died at York in Britain. His son, Constantine, seized his moment to reunite politically the Roman Empire. His victory at the battle of Milvian Bridge, allegedly inspired by a vision of the Christian Chi-Ro symbol, saw a sea change in the Roman ideological world view. Although Constantine's edict of Milan issued in 313 sanctioned Christianity, it is arguable whether Constantine actually embraced the faith, but at least Christianity was now on a firm footing, and in time would become the official religion of Rome's ruling classes as well as of the proletariat.

With Christianity now freely operating within the broader Roman political framework, and at least enjoying a degree of protection, it was now possible to begin to resolve a number of nagging theological disputes that had long dogged the Church. One radical Christian thinker, the Alexandrian Arius (c.250-336), held views on the nature of Christ that did not square with the official – or orthodox – line of thinking. In suggesting that there was an overarching supreme god with a subordinate Christ, he set himself up for excommunication at the extraordinary council of Nicaea in 325. But other stresses began to emerge. While such scholars as Nestorius (d. c.451) argued for a Christ with two distinct and separate natures in his make-up – the human and divine – others such as Eutyches (c.378-454) argued that Christ had only one nature, the divine alone. The Orthodox view, however, disagreed with both and saw Christ having two distinct natures in one person. Thebattle-lines between the dyophysites of the Orthodox persuasion and those who followed the monophysite outlook as championed by Eutyches were drawn.

The Council of Chalcedon, called in 451 to resolve the complex dispute about Christ's nature, failed to reach a consensus and the Churches of Armenia, Syrian Jacobites and Egyptian Copts broke away as a monophysite bloc, a line also adopted by the churches of medieval Nubia and Ethiopia. So, apart from the Christians of North Africa, who traditionally looked to Rome for leadership and guidance, the other established African Christian churches of late antiquity went on their own doctrinal path, heedless of the threats from the Orthodox, dyophysite churches, who were referred to by the monophysites semi-contemptuously as Melkites – men of the king. We should now consider the history of the development of Christianity in north and northeast Africa during the first seven centuries AD by area, starting with Egypt and working outwards in rough chronological order of conversion.

We do not know when Christianity made its presence felt in Africa, but it is inconceivable that the faith was not gaining a considerable foothold in Egypt during its formative years. The geographical proximity to Palestine is one obvious criterion, but social conditions were ripe too; the fabled city of Alexandria was home to a sizeable Hellenic Jewish population, grouped in an informal structure called the Politeuma, a corporation for resident aliens. This population formed an ideal recruiting ground for the new faith, and Alexandria subsequently played an important role in the development of African Christianity; intellectuals such as the Jew

Philo (*c.*20 BC–AD 50) had long dominated the city's social fabric, and in time it would become a centre of Christianity's early intellectual elite: doctrinal philosophers such as Panateus (d. c.190), Clement (*c.*160-215), Origen (185-254) and Dionysus (d.264) who formed the fabled Alexandrine Catechetical School. Alexandria became an important see in the eastern church, but often found itself at odds with its neighbours – especially Antioch – although in St Cyril, its archbishop of the early fifth century, it found an orthodox champion. But Egypt was not immune from the worst excesses of the early persecutions. Christians suffered horribly at the hands of Diocletian; Bishop Peter the Martyr (305-12) met his end at this time and became the first Egyptian saint and the Coptic calendar commemorates this event by beginning from the date of Diocletian's accession in 284.

According to Egyptian Christians, St Mark was the first apostle of Egypt, and according to legend he ordained the first Alexandrine bishop Annianus in 62, but this is only stated in Eusebius' *Church History* of 320. Sources from the New Testament (Acts 18:24) mention an Alexandrine Jew named Apollos who began preaching in Corinth at around this time. What we do know from fact was that Egyptian Christians were ready to embrace innovative and sometimes controversial ideas. The discovery in 1945 of a set of fourth-century Christian texts (codices) at the village of Nag Hammadi have thrown light on the workings of a mysterious group of Christians known as the Gnostics. Gnosticism – the word is based on the Greek idea of self or inner knowledge – saw the world in a dichotomy of good and evil, its supporters were dualists in their outlook and led an essentially reflective way of life in stark contrast to the more staid, introspective religious mainstream. Dualism was not a new concept; these Gnostics had borrowed heavily from the neo-Platonist philosophers of Alexandria and their Hellenic inheritance, and also developed ideas propounded in the popular Roman military cult of Mithraism, which was originally a Persian religion that developed from Mazdaism via Zoroastrianism, and formed the basis of later Manichaeistic beliefs. Gnostics had a belief framework outside mainstream orthodoxy, and they saw their faith in terms of the individual. Reaction to the Gnostic path was not slow in coming, and persecutions and intimidation saw their hold in rural Egypt wither, although their influence permeated western European Christianity in the middle ages, when so-called heretical sects such as the Cathars could almost claim a Gnostic intellectual inheritance.

In the meantime, other Christian groups in Egypt were developing different personal approaches to their faith. St Anthony (251-356), a former soldier, believed in a rigorous code of self-discipline, and he espoused the idea of solitude and asceticism. He was a hermit – or anchorite – whose beliefs laid the basis for Egyptian monasticism. Living in isolation in the desert, resisting temptation and living a life of extreme poverty, Anthony was the impetus behind the movement of the 'Desert Fathers'. A contemporary of Anthony, St Pachomius (286-346), approached Anthony's ideas in a different way. He espoused a communal lifestyle dedicated to God; his so-called coenobitic, or communal monastic settlements, would initially have developed from the cell or cave of a hermit into a fully-fledged, self-reliant religious community, a monastery in every sense of the word. The Pachomian ideal, at least in Egypt, reached its zenith in the founding of the White Monastery at Sohag by Pachomius' disciple Shenoute (d. c.450) in the mid-fifth century. Although the monastic concept had emerged initially in the Levant, it was its development in the Egyptian sphere that brought it to maturity. In the eastern church, these developments influenced St Basil the Great of Caesaria (c.330-79) to formulate coherent rules for monastic communities. In western Europe in the fourth century this movement found its adherents with St Ambrose at Milan, St Martin at Tours in France, and in the fifth and sixth centuries in the British Isles with the distinctive brand of Celtic monasticism developed by St Patrick, St Columba and St Ninian.

Clouds were beginning to gather on the horizon; soon massive social and ideological changes would be felt across northern Africa. By the beginning of the seventh century, Arabia was in social turmoil. A charismatic religious leader, Mohammed, had fled to Medina from Mecca in 622; his followers embraced a new creed of self-discipline and devotion. Islam had emerged among the Arab tribes, and soon became an unstoppable force. The eastern Roman Empire now felt itself in a threatened position; Egypt fell to Muslim armies in 639, north Africa a few years later, but Egyptian Christians were guaranteed a role in the new Islamic state framework, they were favoured as administrators and civil servants – positions which offered them a chance to settle old scores with Melkites – and good relations with their conquerors, perhaps allied to a vital monastic tradition, ensured the survival of Egyptian Christianity up to the present day.

In another part of Rome's African empire, Christianity was also beginning to find fertile ground. The line of provinces on the southern Mediterranean seaboard – Mauretania, Numidia, Africa Proconsularis, Tripolitania – had a key role in the Imperial economy: they provided grain for the Empire, and produced the emperor Septimius Severus who ruled from 193-211. In 180 we have textual evidence from the *Acta Martyrum* of the earliest Christian martyrs in the region: on 17 July that year seven men and five women from Scilli were put to death for their beliefs. All through the second and third centuries, a common theme re-emerged: persecution, denial of faith, and schism, but the church maintained a dynamic growth. By the third century Christianity was perhaps the dominant religion amongst the urban poor, and the city of Carthage was the focal see in the region; its theological school rivalled that of Alexandria, producing such brilliant scholars as Tertullian (c. 160-225) and St Cyprian, who was martyred during Valerian's persecutions in 258.

Diocletian's persecutions of the early fourth century had a wide-ranging impact on the ecclesiastical history of Roman north Africa; a disaffected, largely conservative and mainly rural population felt unable to stand with the predominantly urban Christian populations who had so readily renounced their faith under duress. This disaffected and unforgiving grouping – who labelled their Christian colleagues under the bishop Caecillian as collaborators and traitors (*traditores*) – were led by a charismatic bishop called Donatus, and his followers became known as Donatists. With their exceptionally violent cohorts the Circumcellions, Donatists maintained an extensive powerbase in southern Numidia centred on the city of Timgad and were implacable in their hostility to the tarnished reputations of the mainly urban, Catholic Christians whose organisation and strictures they held in contempt. Donatism has been seen as the movement of a disaffected rural populace or a vehicle for aboriginal Berber national aspirations; but they had a broad appeal and it took the intervention of St Augustine of Hippo (*c.*354-430) to bring the Donatists to their knees.

Donatism remained in the shadows, although the raw wounds of the schism were really never satisfactorily healed. In 429 north Africa was attacked by the Vandals under Gaiseric, a central European people responsible in no small part for the destruction of the western Roman Empire, and a people traditionally regarded by Romans as barbarians. Donatism enjoyed a small resurgence, but the reconquest of north Africa by the eastern Roman Emperor Justinian's able general Count Belisarius in 533 saw it back again in the orthodox fold. In 697 Carthage finally fell to the Arabs who had thrust westwards from Egypt, and Islam began to usurp the Christian faith among the people. Historical texts indicate that Christianity held on in some rural areas until the eleventh century, and it is probable that a small Christian community survived in Carthage until the sixteenth century. But for the rural Berber population, Islam now held sway. The departure of the upper echelons of the Church – and with it perhaps an intellectual orientation towards Rome – had marginalized the rural peoples, and from now on there could be no challenge to the vigorous rise of Islam. In other areas of Africa not directly under Roman control, Christianity now began to spread through the efforts of missionary activity.

To the south of Egypt's borders lay Nubia, historically a region that had always enjoyed mixed relationships with its northern neighbour. Although in close geographical proximity, the socio-cultural outlooks of the two areas were markedly different. At the end of the fifth century, the Merotic state which had dominated the region collapsed; into the vacuum stepped large groups of itinerant cattle herders, but soon three clear political units emerged: in the north, with its capital at Faras was the state of Nobatia, to its south, roughly in the middle of Nubia was the state of Makuria with its capital at Dongola, and to the far south the state of Alwa emerged centred on its capital at Soba.

According to the ecclesiastical historian John of Ephesus (516-86), the conversion of these three Nubian kingdoms was the result of a doctrinal power struggle between the then eastern Roman Emperor Justinian (483-565) and his wife Theodora (500-47), although we should be cautious about his account as he was clearly a zealous monophysite. Justinian (**colour plate 1**) was a Melkite, or dyophysite; he had already intervened in north Africa to defeat the Vandals, but was now clearly turning his attentions to the southern borders of his Egyptian province. He had already invited the pastoral Nobatian groups to settle on the border to act as an effective buffer zone, and in 539 forbade pagan worship at the Temple at Philae near Aswan in southern Egypt. His wife, Theodora, was an Egyptian-born monophysite who also had her own plans for the Nubian states. Theodora had met an exiled monophysite Egyptian priest called Julian, and she proceeded, through a degree of subterfuge, to undermine Justinian's missionary groups through the machinations of the Duke of Thebaid. Julian and the Bishop of Theodorus of Philae got their monophysite ideals through to the Nobatians first, in about 543, although Justinian's mission succeeded in beating them to Makuria, which became a dyophysite – or Melkite – outpost. After the death of Theodora in 547, Nobatia briefly lapsed, but the monophysite Patriarch Theodorius consecrated Longinus as bishop, and he returned to Nobatia and thence to Alwa, avoiding Makurian attempts to stall him. Another story related in the New Testament Act 8: 26-39 tells of an official of the court of the 'Kandake, or queen of Ethiopia' who was converted in Egypt and brought Christianity to Nubia (there is confusion in earlier texts with the use of the word Ethiopia; Kandake was a recognised Nubian term).

Soon structured sees and bishoprics were established, and Longinus himself became the first bishop of Soba. In time, each capital saw a massive degree of ecclesiastical building, although at first pagan temples were converted – such as happened at Qasr Ibrim. Despite their theological differences, which may have been less marked than they seemed, the kingdoms of Nobatia and Makuria merged between about 690 and 710 with their new capital centred on Dongola, although King Merkurious began an ambitious building programme at the former Nobatian capital of Faras in the early eighth century which remained important as capital of the administrator, the Eparch. But Nubia remained geographically and socially isolated. Politically fragmented, it could not offer resistance to Muslim incursions during the seventh century, although a treaty (*Baqt*) signed between the Muslims and Christians did stabilise the situation to some extent. While in Egypt Christians were on friendly relations with their Muslim overlords, Nubia was always going to be an easy target. Ayyubid armies attacked from Egypt in the twelfth century, and in 1173 Turan Shah, brother of the famed Saladin, took the frontier town of Qasr Ibrim in response to Nubian provocation, turned the church of St Mary into a mosque and being a Muslim promptly slaughtered all the pigs he found there. As Egypt fell under Mamluk domination in the thirteenth century, Nubia's position became even more precarious, and after a series of military campaigns, the region came under the aegis of Islam, and although it may have lingered on dying a slow death in rural areas, Christianity in Nubia finally disappeared, only enjoying a small resurgence under the efforts of nineteenth-century missions.

The Aksumite polity, which had dominated the northern Ethiopian highlands since about the first century AD, was essentially internationalist in outlook. Utilising a coinage system based on imperial Roman values, Aksum was locked into the eastern Mediterranean/Red Sea trade dynamic. With such an outward-looking view, Aksum and its rulers were open to new ideas and influences. According to Rufinus' emendation of Eusebius' *Church History*, Christianity arrived in Aksum in the following way. In the early fourth century, a Christian from Tyre, Syria, called Meropius was on his way to India with two charges: Frumentius and Aedesius. Having been shipwrecked in the Red Sea, Frumentius and Aedesius were brought to the King Ella Amida, where they soon found themselves in the employ of the King. After Ella Amida's death, Frumentius as the former King's secretary and treasurer acted as regent before Ella Amida's son Ezana was old enough to take the throne. Evidently Frumentius had exerted a profound influence on Ezana's thinking and development, for although free to return to his homeland, Frumentius went straight to Alexandria and after consultation with the then Patriarch Athanasius, found himself ordained bishop and then returned to his adoptive home where Ezana received him in the spirit of a fellow Christian.

During the fifth century, and again according to legend, the so-called nine saints from Syria entered Ethiopia to continue the missionary work begun by Frumentius, and soon Christianity was an integrated part of the Aksumite world view. Few textual sources can adequately elucidate the nature of the formative years of Christianity in Ethiopia; certainly it was linked implicitly to the Alexandrine, Coptic sphere of influence, and maintained a monophysite outlook, albeit with some liturgical and doctrinal idiosyncrasies – discussed in more detail in chapter 5. Christianity survived the collapse of Aksum, and essentially remained the glue that held the successor states together in the face of attack from the legendary queen Gudit (or Judith) in the eleventh century. Monasticism, as traditionally defined by the teachings of the Syrian nine saints, played a key part in the conversion of the southern peoples such as the Shoans, and in the twelfth century the ancient Solomonic imperial lineage was broken by a new dynasty from the southern margins of the old Aksumite sphere of influence: the Zagwe dynasty from Lasta were responsible for perhaps the most remarkable testaments to Ethiopian Christianity – the rock-hewn churches of Lalibela. With the revival of Solomonic fortunes, the Ethiopian political powerbase shifted perceptibly southwards, and although from time to time Muslim armies tried to take the highlands, the Christian court of Abyssinia, as it was now known, was beginning to attract interest from others far beyond the shores of the Red Sea.

This then, is the picture of the formative development of Christianity in northern and north eastern Africa. Initially, the great north African and Egyptian sees played a dynamic role in shaping early intellectual approaches to liturgy and doctrine, but by their geographical position, they were always occupying a precarious toehold. The only survivors of the African churches of antiquity are the Egyptian Copts and Ethiopian Orthodox Christians. Beyond their homeland, the Christian church evolved and splintered; the great Schism between the western and eastern churches in the eleventh century, the fall of Byzantium in 1453 and the end of the last vestiges of the glories of imperial Rome, and then the reformation and the emergence of the Protestant churches. All these events had consequences for Christianity in Africa, but for the next stage in our story, we should consider the *deus ex machina*, the god from the machine that started to take a cynical interest in the resources of Africa. The clouds of European colonialism were gathering, and with them a new chapter in the history of Christianity in Africa.

Europe's African aspirations

Portugal is geographically orientated towards the sea; with a single land frontier with Spain, Portugal always looked outwards, beyond the horizon, for new economic opportunities in much the same driven way as the traders of the Dutch Republic of the seventeenth century and the British Isles of the eighteenth and nineteenth centuries. In the fifteenth century, Portuguese ships ranged far and wide; explorers such as Vasco de Gama sought new economic markets along the African coasts. Portugal, at various times, had contact with western Africa, the gold fields of south-eastern Africa and the Islamicised Swahili coastal settlements of the eastern African seaboard. The romantic ideal of a priest king in the eastern Indies who bravely held out against Muslim pressure – the so-called Prester John – brought them into contact with the Ethiopian court. Any story of modern European-driven colonialism in Africa must start with the Portuguese.

A brief time-line gives some indication of the relative rapidity of Portuguese expansion within Africa: the first African foothold was gained at Ceuta (modern Morocco) in 1415; Fort Elmina was established on the Gold Coast (modern Ghana) in 1481; Vasco de Gama completed his African circumnavigation in 1498, and by 1510 Portuguese influence had reached the southeastern African interior with contacts with the goldfields of Zimbabwe and Madagascar. The first emissary to the Ethiopian court of Lebna Dengel arrived in 1520. This was a remarkably dynamic and swift process of expansion, but as ever was not based on altruistic motives. Africa offered a host of economic benefits, both material and human.

It would be impossible at this juncture to generalise about the nature of African society at the time of the first contacts with the Portuguese, but a few examples indicate the relatively patchwork nature of African social development at the time. Ethiopia possessed a comparatively large and integrated state framework headed by an emperor with the full force of tradition behind him. To the south, the Swahili towns of the Indian Ocean coast were to all intents small-scale polities driven by mercantile ambition. Gold could be had from the region around Great Zimbabwe (modern Zimbabwe) via the Portuguese trading post at Sofala, and here in the interior was a patchwork of integrated, small-scale 'chiefdom' societies rather than states. Monarchies in western Africa, such as Ife, Ijebu, Kongo and Benin offered good opportunities for exploitation, and good relations were pursued with the inland Islamicised state of Songhay. The Saharan trade – principally focusing on gold, salt and slaves – allowed for a free cultural and ideological interchange with the northeastern African sphere of Islam, especially as Cairo attained a great reputation as a centre for learning in the fifteenth century. The unspoken aim of Portuguese colonisation – which was actively supported by Papal authority – would have been to neutralise and outflank the threat of Islam in northwest Africa. In this respect, some degree of missionary activity was built into the grand Portuguese design.

Between 1485 and 1487 the Portuguese set up a colony in the Kongo (modern Congo), baptised the local chief or Mani Soyo and burnt tribal artefacts they found there. Essentially the Portuguese brand of Christianity had to weave in elements of local beliefs in order to prosper: a classic case of syncretism. The efforts of the Portuguese were less successful in Benin, but the process of conversion certainly helped foster good economic relations when and where it worked. In this regard, the Kongo scenario may be seen as a good case study. Under the patronage of the Portuguese, the King of Kongo named Afonso – note the Portuguese name – allowed Christianity to flourish in the early sixteenth century. Efforts at conversion, however, were hindered by a lack of trained priests, and those that did go to west Africa soon succumbed to disease. Another key problem in the conversion process was the signal failure of priests to learn the vernacular language of their potential congregations; such a stratagem smoothed the path of the conversion of the rural Egyptians and Ethiopians in earlier times. Indeed, as the late Adrian Hastings – an important historian of the Church in Africa – has pointed out, the missionary in rural Egypt reached out to his potential recruit by taking his language seriously. In a few cases indigenous clergy did become active; a formal see was established in the Kongo in 1596 and Dom Manuel the Mani Vunda of the Kongo visited Pope Paul V in 1608, and made such an impression that on his death in Rome his exploits were recorded on frescoes in the Vatican Library.

From ecclesiastical centres based on the island of São Tomé – the site of an important seminary – the Portuguese reached out to the mainland; the conquest of Angola brought into being an important mainland centre at Luanda, but by the end of the seventeenth century little concrete progress had been made. In Kongo, local rulers took on meaningless ducal titles, and began to lapse into traditional ways. Now the Vatican began to take a keen interest, and Spanish Jesuits turned up in Luanda, much to the chagrin of the Portuguese who resented outside interference in their spheres of influence. Now concerted efforts went into translating the bible into local languages, and the establishment of a small mud brick and thatched cathedral at Sao Salvador saw the emergence of a concerted missionary effort.

Other interested parties now step into the picture; Capuchin friars entered the Portuguese sphere of influence to begin a structured programme of conversion and biblical translation – a high mortality rate among them indicates the lengths to which they went to carry the message into the inhospitable interior. Syncretic concepts had no place, there was only one type of Christianity, and missionaries energetically suppressed traditional local religions. Kongo still remained the focus of action, and an outbreak of miracles and visions in the early eighteenth century shows just how far the local people had absorbed the mystique of the Roman Catholic Church. In southeast Africa, along the important Zambesi river, Dominican friars were gaining a foothold. Here, in the Mutapa kingdom, the capital at Dambarare already had a fort and church in the mid-seventeenth century, although it was wiped out in 1693. The whole reason for this presence however was not in furthering the progress of Christianity; slaves and gold were brought to Luanda in Angola, and before being sent across the Atlantic to Brazil, the human cargoes were baptised in the cathedral at Luanda before sailing off into bondage. Although Jesuits had been at work in Ethiopia – indeed a detachment of 400 Portuguese musketeers was credited for saving Ethiopia from Islamic invasion – the prime Portuguese focus remained on furthering and developing their slave trade.

The seventeenth century saw a mini-scramble for the African spoils; the British, Danish, Dutch and French all established small forts along the western coast of Africa, although they only made religious provision for themselves, and there was no attempt at concerted missionary activity. However, the tide was beginning to turn against slavery; a freed London slave Olaudah Equiano (1745-97) led anti-slavery agitation and by the 1780s political talk in high London circles considered the establishment of a state for freed slaves in western Africa; when Britain abolished slavery in 1807, the colony of Sierra Leone came into being with a ready-made population of western-ised, Christian returned Africans. Sierra Leone became a Britain in microcosm, even down to names of towns and socio-political ideology. In a similar vein, freed American slaves set up the neighbouring state of Liberia along similar Christian lines.

In southern Africa events had taken a different turn. In 1652, the Dutch East India Company established a victualling post at what is now Cape Town. Over the years, this small corner of Holland became the focus of settlement for Protestants fleeing persecution in Europe – Calvinists and Huguenots – who had a particularly conservative and dour frame of mind. These peoples – who would be later known as Boers, or Afrikaners – settled down to a predominantly farming existence sup-ported by an extensive cadre of local slaves. At the end of the eighteenth century, two events of varying magnitude began to change the shape of Christian develop-ment in southern Africa. In 1792, a small religious sect known as the Moravians arrived, and they began within the Dutch Reformed Church framework to reach out to the indigenous pastoralist KhoeKhoe (formerly known as Hottentot) peoples of the Cape. The British occupation of the Cape in 1795 introduced a more open missionary ethos to the region; small, self-supporting mission villages – essentially small-scale monastic communities – such as Bethelsdorp, Genadendal and Kuruman began to flourish. These missions took total control of the inhabitants' lives, and began a process of social conditioning. A natural extension of the local, traditional household, these spiritual communities were initially discouraged by the national churches in so far as they blurred the distinction between the religious and secular spheres, but they attracted potential converts by offering some form of employment, and flourished openly in the more marginal rural zones.

Missionary activity and colonial ideology in the nineteenth century

Into the nineteenth century, missionary movements burgeoned in Africa against the background of European colonial self-interest. Formal mission organisations had exist-ed under the aegis of the Roman Catholic Church, but now Protestant groups began to take an interest. The Society for the Propagation of the Gospel had been founded in 1701, and by 1752 the first Anglican missionaries became active. Although the mis-sionaries sought converts, their progress could only be assisted by active governmental involvement. A number of disparate missionary groups of many nationalities and per-suasions now sprung up. The Baptist Mission Society, founded in 1792, sought work in the Congo, the London Missionary Society (incorporated in 1795) focused on southern Africa, while the Swiss Basel Missions looked for converts on Ghana.

What kind of people were attracted to this sort of arduous and dangerous work? Missionaries came from a broad range of backgrounds; evangelical missions sought links with commercial organisations, while others followed a more basic, if not ascetic, existence. The Church of Scotland Mission at Blantyre in Malawi was an example of the more vigorous, muscular form of missionary work. A strong work ethic was encouraged, and offenders against the rules of the Society were often ruthlessly flogged. In every sense, these first mission stations were an extraordinary sociocultural mix of people and ideologies; they also represented the spearhead of the operation to spread the holy word to deepest Africa. Roman Catholic missions enjoyed a resurgence in the nineteenth century, and in South Africa the Cape Dutch voortrekkers, who had escaped British rule in 1838, opened up new branches of the Dutch Reformed Church in the interior lands of the high veldt. From Natal, missions penetrated the Zulu kingdom, then north to the Shona and Tswana peoples. As a reaction to this overtly European interpretation, a number of indigenous Christian churches emerged in the late nineteenth century; calling themselves Ethiopian Churches, these groups offered a focus to disaffected indigenous Christians with a well-developed sense of their own African-ness.

In east Africa, the Portuguese influence had long disappeared, and although the coast remained steadfastly Muslim, the interior offered scope for exploitation. A missionary by the name of Johan Krapf had begun work at Mombasa as early as 1844, but with the impetus of exploration and colonial exploitation others came, none more famous than David Livingstone whose travels opened up new colonial vistas; indeed the Malawian mission station of Livingstonia was endowed by the Free Church of Scotland in his honour. In Buganda (modern Uganda), the Church Missionary Society and the Roman Catholic White Fathers went to work, and the fruits of their enterprise provided martyrs when King Mwanga ruthlessly persecuted his Christian subjects in 1886. In west Africa, while the Christian outposts of Sierra Leone and Liberia thrived, the European scramble for Africa was bringing new converts into the fold; the Niger mission established a station at Bonny in 1865, and soon missionaries of all nationalities joined the secular scramble for territory and subjects.

Of course not all the progress was smooth; as mission groups competed to gain new brethren, the traditionally solid Muslim areas firmly resisted attempts at conversion. The Maghreb fell under French influence in the mid-nineteenth century, but the efforts of such vigorous players as Charles Lavigerie notwithstanding, Islam remained a constant in the daily lives of France's new subjects. The situation was scarcely better in Egypt which although detached from the Ottoman sphere of influence, offered no better possibilities for missionaries; both Egyptian Christians and Muslims saw their presence as being indicative of an erosion of their privileges. Ethiopia offered no comfort either; after the expulsion of the Portuguese Jesuits, Capuchin friars and Church Missionary Society groups tried their luck, and were initially encouraged in their efforts by the canny Emperor Tewodorus, unaware that they were being played off against each other in a greater political power game. Some missions had success in re-establishing Christianity in the southern Sudan, but the north remained steadfastly Muslim, a situation that is sadly mirrored today in a bitter war.

Here we must leave this narrative; we could have taken the story of African Christianity up to the present day, but it is not central to our theme. We have considered the story of the Church in Africa over three distinct phases of development, and in each case a similar theme emerges: syncretism. African Christianity of early and recent vintage was a thin veneer laid over centuries-old belief systems; to make the new message palatable, it was inevitable that some form of incorporation of symbols would have taken place, so elements were mixed to form a dynamic and vigorous brand of Christianity. Yet Christianity still evolves in its African context and a new dynamic force is emerging; in recent years the President of the Ivory Coast, Felix Houphouet-Boigny, invested vast amounts of money in erecting a bigger version of Saint Peter's Basilica of Rome in his country. In Rome, the controversial Zambian Archbishop Milingo plies a charismatic mix of traditional African-style exorcism ceremonies and traditional conservative Catholicism to an appreciative congregation and a sceptical, disapproving Vatican. These are but two examples of the dynamism, vigour and elemental nature of Christianity framed in an African social milieu. Soon we may not be speaking of how Christianity may change Africa, rather how Africa will change world Christianity.

We have now placed the historical narrative in a broad socially-orientated discussion; we see the motives of the players emerging, we have seen the wider developmental process rather than the narrow history. It is a complex tale that for necessity is kept brief here, but we have the framework in which to view the cultural developments which, as archaeologists, are our primary source of evidence. Let us now consider the nature of the evidence, how as archaeologists, primarily working in the African milieu and broadly aware of the historical contexts of our research, we can recognise – if it is possible – what constitutes cultural evidence of Christianity.

Archaeological perspectives on Christianity

Reconstruction and the understanding of ideological systems in the past has always been a challenging issue to archaeologists; it is obviously far more difficult in the prehistoric part of our discipline to decipher what is going on in people's minds: rock art is rich in symbolism, but what does it mean? Similarly burials with grave goods may be indicative of some form of belief in the afterlife, or could merely represent a useful way of disposing of the dead with their effects. Piecing together the nature of Classical (i.e. Greek or Roman religion), ancient Egyptian or Mesopotamian belief systems becomes easier with the benefit of historical documentation.

Of late, prehistoric archaeologists of the so-called post-processual orientation – who are naturally working without the confines of an historical framework – have sought to see ideological patterns in prehistory; they are seeking to get into the minds of the people they study, be it through applying new techniques to reading structures in rock art styles or seeking patterns in bone deposition in megalithic tombs. The noted archaeologist Colin Renfrew has attempted to deal with these issues in defining a number of key ideological components that would leave recognisable archaeological evidence of 'cult': redundant (recurring) symbols that refer to a deity or deities, the act of communal worship or ritual and the maintenance of a physical or symbolic barrier between the secular and religious realms. Surely when dealing with the archaeology of Christianity we can take these assumptions for granted.

Here we run into a number of problems. The relationship between Christianity and archaeology is complex in terms of concepts of motivation. In the loosest sense of the term, what is called 'Biblical Archaeology' embodies a multitude of shades and meanings. Are we using archaeological techniques to verify biblical facts, or conversely does the bible supply an invaluable textual back-up in which to frame our archaeological data? At the level of Old Testament archaeology we have countless instances of misinterpretation, deception, and even downright fraud: interpretation of destruction layers in late Bronze Age Canaanite cities taken to indicate the accuracy of the traditional conquest story of Joshua; Jewish and Christian fundamentalist groups seeking to excavate the remains of Solomon's Temple in the emotionally highly charged and incredibly sensitive area of Jerusalem's Haram-as-Sharif; and at the extreme end of the scale the search for the Garden of Eden, or the quest for the remains of Noah's Ark under the glaciers of Mount Ararat in eastern Turkey.

In most cases, such grandiose and eccentric schemes can be guaranteed a level of funding and public interest that would make conventional, academic archaeologists green with envy, and in some cases, recent 'New Testament' archaeology cannot consider itself to be immune from such flights of fancy: from General Gordon of Khartoum using psychic sources to locate the real Golgotha, to ongoing and continuous discoveries of the room of the last supper or Jesus' house, to the interminable saga of the interpretation of the radiocarbon dating of the Shroud of Turin. There is perhaps no other area of archaeology that can be tinged with such self-interest, greed and at times extreme eccentricity. It should not be forgotten that in recent times, Frederick Bligh Bond, the architect responsible for the conservation of Glastonbury Abbey in Somerset – itself a site of considerable significance for understanding early Christianity in Britain – sought extra interpretative assistance by contacting the spirits of former abbots via a ouija board, and this under the eyes of some of the most august British antiquarian societies who were sponsoring his endeavours.

In many cases, then, we must look harder at the motives and directions behind the basic archaeological research design. What are we trying to prove and how are we going about it? In the absence of contact with the dead, there are a number of methodological problems to be faced. From an African perspective, written records for most of sub-Saharan Africa do not go much further back than five hundred years, and these are written from a European or Arab perspective. We can utilise oral history approaches, where we reach into the past through folk memories of our informants, but this approach can also be unreliable.

African historical archaeology is a new discipline, albeit one that is hard to define satisfactorily. At an arbitrary level, we could suggest that it begins with reconstructing societies at the interface with initial contact from elsewhere, such as the colonial period. In this regard, and with this narrow definition, the archaeological search for early colonial-period contact may not readily find favour with the rulers of African states trying to assert their own identity through archaeology and heritage management. Would state-funded archaeological projects in Libya, for instance, see the worth in the study and preservation of Christian-era Roman remains? Would different research priorities in, say, Ethiopian archaeology see the possibilities of studying the remains of Portuguese mission settlements? Secondly, and a more universal problem, how do we recognise Christianity in the cultural record? What could constitute a 'typical' Christian cultural assemblage? Let us assume we have a check-list for such an assemblage: firstly, find the church building, and secondly find the burials which we assume to be of Christian pattern. As we will see in this section, these are risky assumptions to make.

A church building would appear to be the most obvious indicator of a Christian community. The first churches were merely ordinary houses for clandestine meetings, and only occasionally would the presence of a secret symbol, such as a fish painted on a wall, indicate that it was a Christian meeting place. (The fish acted as a covert symbol for early Christians; the initial letters of the Greek words for 'Jesus Christ Son of God Saviour' spelt in acronym *Ichthys*, Greek for fish.) The key focus for the celebration of the Eucharist would be an altar, but again a simple wooden table could suffice, and would this be interpreted as an altar? As Christianity became an established state religion over the next few hundred years, so the design of the church itself evolved to reflect the changing social situation of the religion.

In early Christian architecture, a single form of building predominates: the basilica. The basilica – which may take its name from a Greek term meaning house of the king (or *basileus*) – is essentially an outgrowth of Roman civic architecture developed by designers working under the Emperor Constantine. The basic form of the building is broadly standardised to the point that the basilican form of a church is one of the most readily recognisable plans, archaeologically speaking: a rectangular building is subdivided into three parts on a longitudinal axis, the nave at the centre flanked by two aisles separated by a line of columns. At the western end of the building a narthex, or basic portico, may be found, while the ritual focus is at the eastern end, where a semicircular projection from the nave, the apse, contains the holy sanctuary and altar. The apse is occasionally flanked by two sacristies to provide robing facilities for the priests and storage of equipment required for the service. The emphasis is therefore on communal worship, involving the congregation, rather than acting, as pagan temples frequently did, as closed-off, secretive houses of the gods. The church of St John Lateran in Rome remains an archetypal and excellent example of this form of building.

Although smaller chapels commemorating martyrs (*martyria*) were also utilised, it is the basilican form that dominates early church architecture in northern Africa and Egypt, and found its zenith in the eastern or Byzantine church, where its walls were often decorated with a brilliant array of mosaics depicting important biblical scenes. The Haghia Sophia in Byzantium (latterly Constantinople, now Istanbul, Turkey) was perhaps the greatest church in eastern Christendom, but after the fall of Byzantium it was converted into a mosque, and this brings us back to that problem of syncretism. Earlier pagan temples and sacred sites were often appropriated by the new faith as a means of economy, as well as emphasising a symbolic dominance over the old religion.

The siting of a church itself is an important factor. Churches are perhaps the most recognisable features within a cultural landscape, and the significance of their situation reflects the need to dominate their surroundings. According to the church historian Bede, Pope Gregory urged the Archbishop of Canterbury Mellitus in 601 to appropriate sites sacred to earlier beliefs: 'if those temples are well-built, it is necessary that they should be converted from the cult of demons to the service of the true God'. Again it is a question of pragmatics as well as symbolism. In a similar vein, water and springs have been venerated for centuries by animist cults across the world, but with the importance of the baptismal rite within Christianity, such symbolic parts of the landscape could be freely appropriated. In Derbyshire, England, wells are still 'dressed', or decorated with flowers at Easter; St Winefride's well in north Wales has become a centre for pilgrimage and votive offering. Again, the syncretic thread is a global phenomenon, and one which will be recognisable within the African milieu. So much for meanings behind the place, what of the building itself?

Church archaeology has recently become a key component in the study of medieval archaeology in Europe. The church is frequently the dominant cultural feature as well as being the most conservative in terms of architectural development; the fabric of the building embodies a multitude of meanings. The design of the building clearly reflects its liturgical function, so as liturgy changes, so do certain architectural elements. Certain zones within the church building, be it a classical basilican form or a Victorian Anglican church, have special spatial meanings. At the top, the altar, often screened from the main church body, is a symbolic separation of the holy and secular zones. A baptistery and font provide for one of the key Christian sacraments – baptism. A pulpit provides the focus for the congregation to listen to the sermon, while side chambers provide for extra chapels and storage space.

At the time of the Reformation, for example, as monasteries were destroyed in England and Wales, so too did ecclesiastical architecture lose certain key elements: statues were smashed, cross heads broken, Marian veneration (praying to Mary as mother of Christ for intercession) stopped. Later nonconformist Protestant churches tended to be sparser in decoration and embellishment, and their design acted to emphasise the act of the sermon, while High Church Anglican elements retained an essential Roman Catholic flavour. Vernacular architectural design served as the archetype for the new mission churches in Africa, a transplanted European phenomenon, with its own set of spatial rules in the traditional African dimension. The Nonconformists, however, had different conceptions of space; Baptists would use streams, pools or outdoor tanks for their baptismal rites, but the baptistery or font as a discrete architectural element only became a real feature of the Baptist church fairly recently. Other groups abandoned any fixed notions of church architecture and embellishment, almost playing down the visual impact of their buildings. Such is the variety of Christian denominations that we cannot make simplistic assumptions about the reflection of liturgy in the use of architecture and space.

What of northern Africa? Could we recognise, say, a Donatist church in Numidia, or in Nubia discern the difference between a church dedicated to the Monophysite rather than the Melkite rite? This is a moot point and a complex one. Churches are also a social phenomenon: they are multi-faceted and subsume a number of different meanings to the people whom they serve. In Dover Street in the west end of

London, for example, a former Victorian church has been converted for use by the capital's Ethiopian Orthodox community. Now there are different perceptions of space, a change of role, still Christian, yet playing to a different set of spatial rules. How would this converted Victorian church be recognised as a centre of Ethiopian Orthodox worship by a future archaeologist if merely the foundations remained? These are just a few examples of how different architectural elements combine to reinforce the Christian message; there is a huge variation in design, there is no ideal.

Symbolic meanings within this cultural, architectural record are everywhere, and we have to attempt to disentangle them. An ordinary building may serve as a church, but in a specialised place of worship, symbolic referents are required to focus on the basic nature of the message, breath life into a blank canvas; in most cases one would use paintings, statues or crosses. The early Christian thinker Tertullian was against the use of depictions of Christ for worship; he was perhaps rightly worried that such a practice directly broke the commandment about worshipping graven images, and any pagans recently weaned off their old ways may have been tempted to lapse. It is noticeable that Muslims and Jews still condemn the artistic depiction of God (and in the case of Muslims, depictions of Jesus too). There are other ways of symbolising; many motifs crop up again and again in Christian churches: the lamb, the dove, the fish, vines, all symbolic of Christ's passion, not to forget the Ichthys symbol (born of religious repression) or the recognisable Chi-Ro monogram. And of course there is the most recognisable Christian symbol of all: the cross. These are all extra elements which we could bring into our hypothetical archaeological check-list for Christianity.

A sub-discipline – or rather sister-discipline – of church archaeology is monastic archaeology. Monasteries, which played a vital part in the Christian dynamic of north Africa, Egypt, Nubia and Ethiopia, are a distinctive and valuable source of cultural information in their own right. Monasteries are communities dedicated inwardly to Christianity, while outwardly serving missionary, teaching or charitable works. Monastic communities have been the seed-bed for the propagation of Christianity, a dynamo in the process of conversion, development of training and philosophy and as repositories of knowledge. Traditionally, whether in the western or eastern Christian context, monasteries have been large wealth holders, and this has often left them open to attack and pillage. Viking raids largely obliterated the monasteries of north-ern Britain, with severe social and economic consequences. Similarly, Henry VIII saw them as a key power-base of the Roman Catholic Church in Britain, both spir-itually and financially, and dealt with them ruthlessly.

As a community serving a number of members, certain key elements would be required: at the centre a church, with associated communal living areas and habita-tion zones for monks and nuns. On the more practical level one would recognise areas for food storage, repair shops, mills, guest houses to service pilgrims (a key rev-enue source) and in some cases defensive works. The monastic ideal developed by St Anthony and St Pachomius influenced subsequent developments in Europe; from the small, spartan hermits' cells on the bleak wind-swept island of Skellig Michael off the southwestern coast of Ireland to the great monastic estates of western Europe, and the self-governing communities of the Greek Orthodox monasteries of Mount Athos. All these communities share several key facets in common, and the archetypal 'ideal' monastery as defined by the ninth-century bishop of Basle Haito at St Gall has its echoes in the great houses of Cluny and Tours. Away from the architectural and associated symbolic attributes that may betoken Christian belief, there is another problematic indicator.

Conventional archaeological wisdom would suggest that Christian burials might be recognisable by three key factors: an east-west orientation with the head to the east, an extended, supine body position and absence of grave goods – the latter regarded as being a 'pagan' motif. Cemeteries are notoriously hard to disentangle archaeologically. In many cases societies regard digging up their dead with a great deal of mistrust; Jewish cemeteries, for example, are an ideologically charged battleground. Assuming we can excavate the cemetery areas, what ideological information can we gain? Pagan and Christian cemeteries are not always easily distinguishable. In western Europe, grave goods are still found in recognisably Christian contexts, and conversely there are Iron Age burials that would confound the criteria for a pagan burial. The question of alignment is also difficult; burials will follow the axis of the nearby church rather than a strict 'compass' east. And surely the practice of burial with grave goods has not entirely died out today? How many times are loved ones buried with an item of special meaning to them? These are not for use in the afterlife, rather a recognition of the intrinsic meanings of certain goods to that individual during life.

The locus of burial is also important; few early churches would have had discrete cemetery areas set aside, and in most cases familiar, age-old burial loci would have been re-used. Socio-economic aspects would also have played a part; wealthier individuals and those high up in the religious hierarchy would have had preferential access to burial zones within the church precinct or indeed beneath the floor, whilst 'lower-class' burials would have been sited farther away and more at risk from later disturbance or destruction, thus skewing our overall picture. Certainly during the formative stages of the Christian expansion, the majority of recruits to the new religion were indeed drawn from the lower classes, and as such it is unlikely that their burials would have been highly distinctive, rich affairs. This picture would also have been reflected during the nineteenth century missionary efforts in Africa, where by and large the main source of converts was from the more marginal areas of traditional African society. Yet again our criteria and neat boundaries are blurred.

From the global archaeological perspective, we have seen that there are no hard and fast rules in defining Christianity from a purely cultural perspective; there are too many variables. The picture becomes more obscure the earlier we go back; at the formative stages of a hypothetical process of conversion, there would be little in the way of large-scale monumental evidence. The arrival of a few missionaries over a long time period would have an immediate impact; the missionaries would have to work within a two-way relationship, the potential converts would need to see a benefit for themselves. Perhaps with the co-operation of the ruling elites, the cultural picture would become clearer. At the top of the hypothetical society, with control of exchange and ideology, more Christian symbolism would become apparent as the mission work was consolidated. But it would be many years down the line, with full state backing and wealth to support the new faith, that we would see concrete, cultural manifestations, and even then some form of pre-Christian cultural survivals would be expected, or even tolerated within the framework of Christianity. We need to be aware, as archaeologists, of the variety and hidden meanings to be found within our data, and it is this factor that makes the study of the cultural remains of African Christianity such a rewarding – and occasionally exasperating – exercise.

Further reading

One of the best and most detailed histories of the development of Christianity remains W.H.C. Frend (1984) *The Rise of Christianity* (London: Darton, Longman and Todd), and another useful source is R. Peterson (1999) *A Concise History of Christianity* (London:Wadsworth). M. Gough (1961) *The Early Christians* (London: Thames and Hudson) presents a brief and readable overview of the key developments of liturgy and architecture of early Christian communities.

Three key sources are important for understanding the history of African Christianity: A. Hastings (1994) *The Church in Africa 1450-1950* (Oxford: Clarendon Press), E. Ischei (1995) *The History of Christianity in Africa* (London: SPCK), and B. Sundkler and C. Steed (1998) *A History of the Church in Africa* (Cambridge: Cambridge University Press).

Aspects of the relationship between archaeology and the definition of cultic behaviour are dealt with in C. Renfrew and E Zubrow (eds) (1994) *The Ancient Mind: Elements of Cognitive Archaeology* (Cambridge: Cambridge University Press). More detailed relationships between archaeology and Christianity are discussed by P. Lane in T. Insoll (ed.) (1999) *Case Studies in Archaeology and Religion* (Oxford: British Archaeological Reports international series 755), while specific problems in church archaeology and the archaeological study of monasteries are addressed by: P. Addyman and R. Morris (1976) *The Archaeological Study of Churches* (Council for British Archaeology Research Report 13), J. Blair and C. Pyrah (1996) *Church Archaeology: Research Directions for the Future* (Council for British Archaeology Research Report 104), M. Aston (2000) *Monasteries in the Landscape* (London: Tempus) and R. Gilchrist and H. Mytum (eds) (1989) *The Archaeology of Rural Monasteries* (Oxford: British Archaeological reports 203). The issue of the journal *World Archaeology* no. 18 (1987) is devoted to the archaeology of Christianity, whilst a good history of archaeological research into early Christianity is W. H. C. Frend (1996) *The Archaeology of Early Christianity: an Introduction* (London: Geoffrey Chapman).

An excellent comparative study worth reading is T. Insoll (1999) *The Archaeology of Islam* (Oxford: Blackwell). Insoll has also edited the volume *Archaeology and World Religion* (2001, London: Routledge); of special interest is the paper by P. Lane entitled 'The archaeology of Christianity in global perspective', pp.148-181.

2 North Africa, the granary of Rome: martyrs, rebels and philosophers

The Phoenician peoples of the eastern Levant – roughly the area of modern Lebanon – were great travellers, and the Mediterranean Sea was their playground. From the second millennium BC, these adventurous peoples penetrated the far west of the Mediterranean, and indeed beyond round the northwest African coast; they established a line of colonies along the southern littoral of the Mediterranean Sea, from Leptis in the east, to Hadrumetum, Carthage, Littica, Hippo, Siga, Lixus, finally ending up on the shores of the Atlantic at Mogador on the coast of what is now Morocco.

When the Phoenicians made landfall on these bleak coastlines, it is debatable whether they encountered any organised, centralised social groups. This region was home to transhumant pastoral peoples, probably forbears of the modern Berbers (from the Latin *barbarii*, or barbarians), who ranged across the Sahara in chariots, and buried their brethren under large, stone dolmens. In essence, these Berber peoples acted as economic go-betweens for Phoenician traders on the coast and the peoples of the interior mountain massifs; salt, ivory, glass and metalwork were among the luxury items traded, and aided by a well-developed agricultural base, these coastal entrepôts thrived.

To the east, the Greeks were expanding into Cyrene (modern Libya), but it was the rise of the Roman Republic during the third century BC that threatened the settled Phoenician lifestyle. With help from Berber allies, and over a series of three protracted military campaigns, Rome became master of the region by 150 BC with the defeat of the dominant city state of Carthage, home to a prosperous Phoenician (or Punic) population and of the fabled general Hannibal, who had inflicted so many key defeats on Rome, and who had famously crossed the Alps on elephants to attack the heart of the Roman Empire. From the coast, Rome's influence encroached southwards, and this region, with its fertile soils and potential for agricultural productivity, became the granary of the later Roman Republic and Empire.

Roman north Africa (excepting Egypt, for the purposes of this chapter) was centred on the region known today as the *Maghreb* – meaning west in Arabic – comprising the modern states of Morocco, Algeria, Tunisia and Libya. By the third century AD, the whole of this coastline had become firmly locked into the Roman political system, and an unprecedented building programme saw the rise of magnificent new cities in the desert hinterlands and along the coast. For the Romans, northern Africa retained a key strategic and economic significance. From the west, a line of provinces formed the political framework of the region: Mauretania Tingitana (roughly the northern portion of modern Morocco), Mauretania Caesarensis (western Algeria), Mauretania Sitifensis (middle Algeria), Numidia (eastern Algeria and western Tunisia), Africa Proconsularis (northern Tunisia), Byzacena (southern Tunisia) and Tripolitania (the north-western coastline of modern Libya).

Huge economic significance was invested in Rome's African empire: a complex series of irrigation works attests to the importance of farming in the economy of the region, and this agricultural wealth underpinned a massive settlement building programme. By the third century there were a large number of major cities across the area; all were formally planned along the strict Roman urban model, with the forum at the centre where the basilica – or court of justice – was to be found, housing was segregated into delimited urban quarters and the presence of baths in these settlements shows that the Roman way of life had permeated all aspects of north African culture. It was not all a one-way dynamic; culturally the natives of northern Africa felt themselves in no way inferior to the Romans across the Mediterranean Sea: the famed author of the *Golden Ass*, Apuleius, was north African, as indeed was the Emperor Septimius Severus who ruled from 193-211.

The religious background of Roman north Africa shows ample evidence of rich syncretic borrowings. In many rural areas, Berber beliefs – often associated with evil spirits or genii focused on sacred places within the landscape – survived, and indeed the Romans were not averse to borrowing certain Punic elements, much as they had done with the native religions of the Greeks and the Egyptians. The Punic Kohanim priests still could practise child sacrifice as late as the second century AD, and whilst

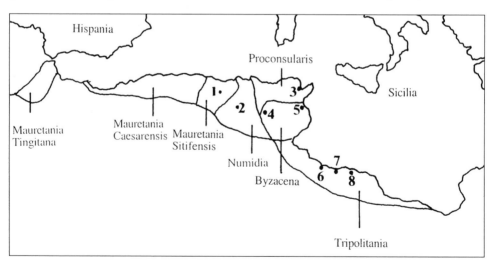

1 *Roman north African provinces in the fourth century. Key to principal sites with ancient names first and modern names following: 1. Sitiflis/Setif, 2. Thamugadi/Timgad, 3. Carthago/Carthage, 4. Theveste/Tebessa, 5. Hadrumetum/Sousse, 6. Sabratha/Sabrata, 7. Oea/Tripoli, 8. Leptis Magna/Lebda*

the Romans may have felt shocked by this, they freely adapted the Punic god Baal and identified him with Saturn – who was perhaps the most widely worshipped of deities in pre-Christian Roman north Africa – and Melkart became Hercules. Even after the emergence and formal acceptance of Christianity, Saturn worship was still being practised in the fourth century; the stelae at Ain Tonga, dedicated to Saturn, are dated to around 323, but this became a relatively rare occurrence after the last decades of the third century. By and large most Saturnalian inscriptions have disappeared by the late third century – a mere hundred years after the deaths of the Scilli martyrs – a factor that attests to the widespread and relatively swift acceptance of the Christian faith in the region.

Further to the east, in Tripolitania, the gradual acceptance of Christianity had relatively little impact on the rural population. Mausoleum (tomb) dedications to the Egyptian god Amon and ancestor cults were especially popular, and some Libyan tombstones pay homage to Punic deities. Animism was also important in the fringes of Roman north Africa; of special note are the Koubba, or shrines dedicated to offerings for evil spirits. Even after the death of Christianity in the region – which in the fringes of Tripolitania may have survived into the tenth century – and the dominance of Islam, these age-old folk beliefs still surfaced. In the fourteenth century, the cult of the holy man was especially important; followers of 'Maraboutism' sought mystic truths from these sages, and dedicated sacred stones and small, stone-built enclosures to them. It is into this rich syncretic ideological background that Christianity emerges, as with the rest of the Roman Empire amongst the lower classes initially, before formal acceptance and integration within the Roman political system.

The Christian period in Roman north Africa may – as a generalisation – be considered as beginning in the late second century. Initial cultural indicators are few, but the adoption of Christianity by the Roman Empire in the late fourth century saw the establishment of permanent places of worship, and of structured sees and bishoprics to administer the new church. The fifth-century Vandal (a European barbarian people and followers of the Arian heresy) interregnum witnessed another progression in the cultural development of the church, as does perhaps the most profound political shift, the re-integration of the region into the Roman sphere by the Byzantines in the mid-sixth century. Orientations shifted too; from the early Christian and Vandal periods, which looked to the west and Rome, the whole cultural outlook leaned towards the eastern Mediterranean and the core of Byzantine political and ideological power.

As we have seen in chapter 1, the history of Christianity in this area presents a traumatic picture. In this chapter we will consider how the archaeology may mirror the Donatist versus Catholic struggle, how schisms and martyrs are represented, how the Vandal incursions may be defined, and above all how the eastern Byzantine influence had an effect on a predominantly Catholic, rural, Romanised population. Before considering the nature of the archaeological record, it would be as well as to outline the history of archaeological research on the Christian antiquities of northern Africa.

During the early part of the nineteenth century, the coast of western north Africa gradually came under stronger French political influences; this imperialist ethos was partly based on economic as well as political demands, and by 1847 Algeria was formally incorporated into the French state. The key antiquarian impetus came largely through French army officers who, when not subjugating natives and concluding treaties, found themselves fascinated by the splendour of the departed imperial glories of the Romans. To some extent, the French identified themselves as the heirs to the Roman Empire, especially in regard to the ideal of civilising the local population. As an overwhelmingly Roman Catholic country, the Roman and Byzantine Christian archaeological legacy was especially attractive, and great efforts were invested in the excavation and recording of the magnificent basilican churches of Algeria and later Tunisia.

As early as 1832, the basilica at Rusguniae (Cap Matifou) was cleared by a French army unit, and by 1856 archaeological investigations – again mainly army led – were commencing at the important Christian site of Tebessa (Théveste). The new demands and responsibilities of empire saw the gradual development of an integrated programme of Christian archaeology, which culminated in 1856 with the founding of the journal *Révue Africaine*, an important source for understanding not just the nature of Christian antiquities in Algeria, but also the socio-political ideas that underpinned their excavation. Formal French intervention in Tunisia in 1881 saw the archaeological focus switch to the famed city of Carthage; a new museum was established, and there was even briefly talk of completely reconstructing the city in the image of the new imperial power, albeit with heavy Roman undertones. Two key figures dominated archaeology in this area during the nineteenth century: Charles-Martial Lavigerie (1825-92) and Stéphane Gsell (1864-1932). Gsell excavated the martyr's centre at Tipasa, as well as producing the monumental eight-volume *Histoire Ancienne de l'Afrique du Nord* (1913-28), a work that remains relevant and enormously useful today. During the twentieth century, the fascination of the archaeological evidence for northern African Christianity waned somewhat, but with the efforts of the UNESCO-sponsored Save Carthage Campaign in the 1960s, interest has again centred upon this intriguing corner of the Roman Empire. The deep thread of French imperial contact with this region has resulted in an unparalleled database for early Christian archaeology, and although some of the early excavation methodology may be regarded now as being deeply unsatisfactory, it is possible that we know more about the archaeology of African Christianity in this region than anywhere else.

Some 500 church buildings have been excavated and published in the region that covers the former Roman north African provinces, so it is perhaps best when considering the archaeology of Christianity here that we begin with that most obvious indicator of the religion: the church building. Before discussing key examples of north African church archaeology, we should perhaps outline a few broad generalisations regarding the local architectural development of the building. In some cases – and as we have seen in chapter 1 – the most obvious model for the building would have been the judicial basilica, and in some of the larger cities, it was a

2 *A view of the 1939 excavations at Bir Djedid, Algeria.* W.H.C. Frend

simple matter of adapting a pre-existing civil building for Christian worship, or, if economics permitted, building a new building in the basilican style. The basic pattern of the basilican church in Roman north Africa remains stable even after the Vandal incursions and the Byzantine restoration, and it is often very difficult without the aid of historical texts to differentiate a Catholic basilica from a Donatist version. One of the key features of these north African basilican forms is the addition of another apse directly opposite the original one (which may or may not contain the altar); we will consider the meaning of this architectural facet later on in the light of the following discussion.

Algeria

It is convenient to begin this overview by considering the churches of the area covered by modern Algeria, and subsequently working eastwards through Tunisia and Libya, a broad geographical swathe where the majority of Christian-period archaeological research has been conducted. (**3**) One of the greatest Roman cities to be found in Algeria is Timgad. This city, established by the Emperor Trajan in 100 as a colony for retired soldiers, was based on a strict Roman urban grid plan, and offers some of the finest standing Roman buildings in the Maghreb. In the northwestern area of the town, a basilica measuring 39m long by 17m wide (128ft by 56ft) is sited amongst a courtyard complex with a baptistery, whilst nearby a smaller basilica was constructed within the earlier House of Julius Januarius; again there is an associated baptistery and in the former atrium – or hallway – of the original house are a num-

3 *Oued R'zel. A fragment of pillar from a chancel arch depicting a dove from Noah's Ark.* W.H.C. Frend

ber of burials obviously associated with the Christian-period settlement. The size and nature of these buildings clearly hints at a fairly large and active Christian population in this area of the town, and this too is reflected in the buildings of the so-called Donatist quarter. Here the large basilica is of cathedral proportions, and is recognised as being the seat of one bishop Optatus; near the baptistery with an unusual hexagonal font, a large house is to be found, and it has been suggested that this may be some form of episcopal residence. In addition to the obvious Christian settlement quarters, there is an extensive necropolis (literally city of the dead) with over 10,000 tombs and two funerary chapels.

The site of Tebessa represents one of the key themes in the Christian archaeology of Roman north Africa; the site is dedicated to the memory of the martyr Crispina who met her death during Diocletian's persecutions in 304. Martyrs' shrines represented an important spiritual focus for the area's Christians simply because of the large number of people who were put to death for their faith and who formed the foundations for the vigorous expansion of the faith during the first four centuries AD. The basilica, which measures 81m by 22m (265ft by 72ft) and has an 8m-wide (26ft) nave, is built atop a podium, which includes a crypt. The whole complex is enclosed by a walled precinct into which some 65 cells are built. The additional presence of a putative refectory, kitchens and library would suggest that this was some form of pilgrimage centre, although subsequently the sacred nature of the place was ignored, and it was pragmatically converted into a prison.

The spiritual focus of this community would have been the shrine of the martyr, and this was probably located in an adjacent small, trefoil-shaped building. The desire to be buried close to the martyr is another theme which we shall investigate later in this chapter, and at Tebessa this is reflected by the presence of eleven inlaid sarcophagi including the remarkably well-preserved wooden coffin of the Bishop Palladius. Evidently, at this stage, it was only the religious hierarchy that were able to enjoy the privilege of burial in the proximity of a martyr saint.

Other important sites in Algeria include Cuicul, where the fourth/fifth-century Christian quarter possesses two quite similar basilicas with circular baptisteries and associated episcopal residence, the northern one being noted for its fine animal mosaics, and the southern basilica possessing unusual double side aisles. In the town of Cherchel, the basilica is situated at the northern end of the Forum area, and incorporates extensive masonry portions from the older civic buildings. The apse is built from concrete, and the basilica as a whole lacks side aisles. The graffito hints that this building may have been a Vandal construction, as indeed may the basilica at Rusguniae (Tametfoust), which in the Vandal phase represented a simple tripartite construction, but which was subsequently enlarged during the Byzantine period with an additional apse being built.

Tunisia

Moving eastwards in to what is now Tunisia, we come to perhaps one of the most well-known of the classical cities of northern Africa: Carthage, at one time the third largest city of the Roman Empire and home to a distinguished line of theological thinkers. Founded originally by the Phoenicians as *Kart Hadasht*, or new capital, Carthage was one of the greatest of the Phoenician ports. Excavation here as part of the UNESCO Save Carthage project (instituted when it became clear that modern building works were encroaching heavily on the remains of the ancient city) by a number of international teams has thrown light on the development of the town as

4   *View of the port area of Carthage in the nineteenth century*

a principal religious centre from Punic times – when the goddess Tanit demanded child sacrifice – through to the Greek takeover in 480 BC and the mixing in of Hellenic elements, the Roman takeover of 146 BC right up to the development of the city as one of the key centres of early Christian thought and debate.

By the end of the 1990s, excavations at Carthage had uncovered a large number of Christian remains, often in a wide variety of forms. In the most up-to-date list, the archaeologist Liliane Ennabli identifies the following structures. Within the city walls themselves the largest basilican churches are represented by: the Basilica of Carthagenna, the Basilicas of Dermech I and II, the church within the civil basilica in the forum area, a church associated with the circular monument (see below), and a church destroyed during the construction of the college at Carthage. A small oratory on Junon's hill and Gauckler's chapel at Douïmes complete the picture. Outside the walls, and associated with cemetery areas, are the churches of Bir el Knissia, Damous el Karita, Bir Ftouha, Mcidfa, and the Basilica of St Monica. Baptisteries are usually associated with some of these structures. Specialist Christian monuments include the martyria of the circular monument to the northwest of the theatre and that of the rotunda at Damous el Karita. Three small oratories or funerary chapels have been noted, as well as the two probable monastic structures of St Etienne and Bigua. This list probably only represents a small sample of what may be expected to be found in the future, but the range of monuments listed above certainly gives some indication of the importance of Christianity in Carthage. We shall now consider a few of these monuments in a little more detail.

The probable fourth-century basilica of Carthagenna – adjoining the so-called House of the Greek Charioteers – was originally a relatively small and somewhat basic construction measuring only 16m by 8m (52ft by 26ft), but on top of this is a Byzantine construction measuring 38m by 25m (124ft by 82ft), and containing a profusion of fine mosaic work set out along five naves, six aisles and the familiar double-apse or opposed-apse layout. The presence of a baptistery complex nearby also helps place this building firmly into the Byzantine period. The basilica of Dermech I is set out along a similar pattern; here the building has five naves, nine aisles and an apse to the east. The whole structure measures 35m by 21m (115ft by 69ft). The walls are covered with an exceptionally fine range of different coloured marbles and porphyry along with fine stucco work. The baptistery too is especially fine; the feature measures 12m by 10m (39ft by 32ft), the tank is hexagonal and is accessed by a flight of steps. The whole tank area is covered by a baldoquin (canopy) supported by a number of columns.

Special attention attaches to the vast Christian complex at Damous el Karita outside the city walls. Here we have the foundations of a truly huge basilica area which in its final phase measured 200m by 60m (656ft by 197ft). Flanking the massive nave are ten aisles, and beneath the floor is a large rotunda – a probable martyrium – with the roof supported by granite columns. The sheer scale of this building implies a degree of importance; it is clear that this church was a cathedral, the seat of a bishop, and it is perhaps not beyond the realms of possibility to envisage this church as being the venue of the important Council of Carthage in 411.

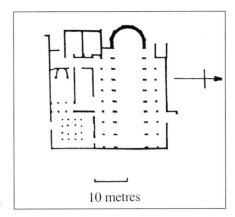

10 metres

5 *Plan of the Dermech 1 basilica*

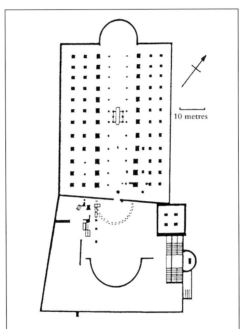

10 metres

6 *Plan of the* Basilica Maiorum, *Mcidfa*

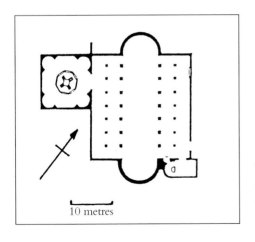

10 metres

7 *Carthage. Plan of the basilica of Carthagenna with flanking baptistery building to the north-west*

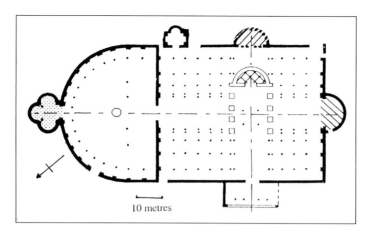

8 *Carthage. Plan of the basilica of Damous el Karita*

One of the most enigmatic Christian monuments is the so-called circular monument. This building probably represents the rebuilding of a fourth-century *memoria* building, not quite circular (38m long, 31m north-south axis; 125ft by 102ft). Two concentric circular areas delimited by trapezoidal pillars enclose a central area measuring 8m by 12m (26ft by 39ft), and it is fairly clear that the extant building –which survives to a height of 3m (10ft) – is largely a sixth-century reconstruction.

Outside the main metropolis of Carthage lie other important Tunisian Christian sites. At La Skhira there are four large Christian necropolis areas, but the focus of worship was the basilica. Measuring 24m by 21m (79ft by 69ft), this is a rather simple construction with an associated baptistery with blue schist flooring and finely stuccoed (plastered) walls. During the sixth century, the building was reconstructed and more mosaics were added – indicative perhaps of a heavier Byzantine influence. The building was also extensively re-floored, and sockets were built into the altar table possibly to prevent the spilling of the communion wine. Another obvious Byzantine feature is the development of the baptistery complex; here the tank is shaped like a cloverleaf, and it is richly decorated with mosaic work. A small funerary chapel (29m by 11m; 95ft by 36ft) completes the Christian complex.

The site of Sufetula has yielded four basilican structures. The fifth-century Basilica of Bellator contains the apse burial of Jucundus, who was martyred by the Vandals. The Vandals themselves built the Basilica of Vitalis, a structure that probably served as their cathedral and is noteworthy for the fact that the construction technique is based on alternate brick and stone courses rather than being built entirely of one material. The Basilica of Servus and Basilica IV are both late fourth-century constructions, and it is possible that the former served as the centre for Donatist worship. The Basilica at Macomades is an obvious Byzantine construction; measuring 78m by 35m (256ft by 115ft), the interior walls are covered in stucco, and the building unusually possesses a triple apse rather than just the two. At Ammaedara (Haïdra) there are five basilicas dating between the fourth and seventh centuries. Basilica I, of the Bishop Maleus (568-9) contains the reliquary of St Cyprian, and the ideological meanings behind the presence of these holy relics is reflected in the large number of

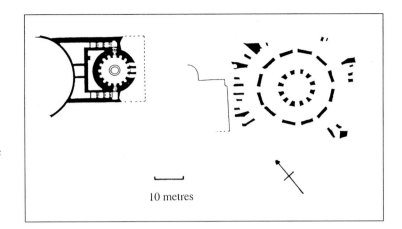

9 *Carthage. Left: plan of the Damous el Karita rotunda. Right: the round building adjacent to the theatre complex*

10 metres

associated burials: some 148 tomb inscriptions, mainly clergy, have been recorded nearby. Perhaps the most unusual architectural feature of this building is the use of flying buttresses to support the exterior walls; buttresses where used are often flush against the wall acting as a direct support rather than the stronger, architecturally more complex, but visually more satisfying arch-like flying buttresses.

Tripolitania and Cyrenaica

Further eastwards, we come to the area of western Libya, known in Roman times as Tripolitania. Most of the archaeology conducted here has, through the consequences of colonialism, been dominated by the Italians and the British, and even now, despite the uncertain political climate of Libya, archaeological research flourishes there still.

10 *Reconstruction of one of the Byzantine church complexes at Haïdra*

11 *The ambon, or pulpit, in Church I, Leptis Magna.* Society of Antiquaries of London

Arguably the most famous settlement on this coastline is that of Leptis Magna. This large, well-developed Roman city (complete with luxurious baths and theatre) had its first bishop – Archaeus – as early as the late second century, and by the fourth century was the home to five bishoprics. The city was the centre of a large Donatist population, and the fact that Tripolitania was on the edge of the Roman frontier may help explain why Christianity survived in the region even as late as the tenth century.

Six basilicas – two of them Byzantine – have been found at Leptis Magna. The first large church was constructed on the site of the Severan Basilica, a third-century secular construction. Three aisles were already present in the building, and the altar itself was placed in the southern apse – being marginally more eastward than the facing northern apse. The floor level here was also raised up, and a decorated pulpit on an ambon approached by four steps was added, along with a cruciform baptistery. Another church was built upon the site of a temple podium; here the floor level was built up in the corner of the building, and a simple apse was added. The remaining pillars here suggest that the roof, rather than being of a barrel-vaulted type, was probably cross-vaulted. The associated baptistery tank is cruciform-shaped, in common with many northern African examples, and the floor of the tank is accessed by three flights of four steps.

The city of Oea, just along the coast, has yielded little in the way of Christian architecture, although there is an extensive Christian cemetery area where all the graves are orientated east-west. At Sabratha, the picture is a little clearer. Church 1 is situated in the western part of the former civil basilica to the southern side of the forum, and parts of the older building are often utilised in the Christian struc-

ture. The church takes the standard pre-Byzantine form, i.e. three aisles, and a baptistery situated within a set of rooms behind the western apse. Byzantine architects
evidently re-embellished the building with extensive mosaic work, and as was the
usual practice enlarged the baptistery; here this took the form of a completely new
tank with access steps making in plan a cruciform shape. It is also interesting to
note the presence of footings for a screen in front of the altar. Hitherto, the altar
had always been placed centrally, allowing for maximum participation by the congregation. Within the Byzantine rebuilding episodes of the traditional northern
African church formats, a trend towards closing off the congregation emerges; this
is a theme that we shall pick up in the following two chapters on Egypt and Nubia.
This facet is also noted at church 3, where a simple three-aisled construction with

12 *Aerial view of Church I,
Sabratha* Society of
Antiquaries of London

13 *Mosaic work on the floor
of the of the apse and nave,
Sabratha, Church I.* Society
of Antiquaries of London

a western apse and central altar is considerably remodelled in the Byzantine peri-od. Church 2 at Sabratha re-used Roman architectural elements, and its rough exterior belies an exceptionally well-decorated mosaic interior, which betrays clear Byzantine characteristics.

Moving away from the cities of Tripolitania, we see a similar pattern of architec-tural change between the Vandal and Byzantine periods. At Breviglieri (Hr-el-Aftah), a simple basilica is enlarged during Byzantine times, whilst at El Asabaa the three-aisled basilica (measuring 28m by 18m; 92ft by 59ft) possesses a baptistery directly behind the apse, again indicative of Byzantine remodelling; the date of this may also be further confirmed by a buried associated coin hoard dating to the time of Justinian. The small three-aisled basilica at Wadi Crema clearly illustrates another Byzantine architectural trait; the apse here is on the same level as the nave, in contrast to the basilica at Ain Wif – built from rubble and masonry and faced with limestone blocks – which has a raised apse above the nave floor. The above facets were also noted at the church at Souk el Oti/El Awtry in the Wadi Buzra. From the largest urban churches to the smallest rural desert churches, there occur repeatedly a number of key architectural traits which mark out clear Byzantine re-building episodes.

To conclude this broad survey, we need to go further east still, into Cyrenaica, where perhaps we begin to gain a more Egyptian flavour to the church architecture. This stretch of coastline was the home of the five cities, or Pentapolis of Cyrene, Apollonia, Ptolemais, Teuchira and Berenice (latterly becoming the Hexapolis with the addition of Hadrianopolis). Of these cities, it is only really Cyrene (modern Shahat) that has produced the best evidence for the evolution of church building in the region. The eastern basilica, or cathedral, shows two clear building phases that may conform to the basic pre-Byzantine/Byzantine patterning. The earliest phase sees a basilica measuring 40m by 30m (131ft by 98ft), with a broad nave and eastern apse. The second phase may be Byzantine; an apse is added to the west into which a throne was placed, and the complex is enclosed by a wall. The mosaics again show a clear Byzantine influence with the emphasis on depictions of nature motifs. The baptistery, intriguingly, seems to have been largely ignored in the grander scheme. Instead of a richly decorated cruciform tank, a re-used pagan sarcophagus upon which crude crosses have been carved has been utilised, and was situated under a six-columned canopy. The design and layout of the church building is but one line of evidence we have for understanding the development of Christianity in Roman north Africa. Mention has already been made in the preceding discussion about inscriptions, mosaics, burials and martyria. Let us now consider each of these facets in a little more detail.

Church decoration, burials and martyr dedication

Perhaps the most decorative embellishment to be considered, and certainly the one that breathes most life into a plain church building, is the use of mosaic. The Romans were undoubtedly the masters of this craft; from northern England to Palestine we can see many examples of Roman mosaic work, the construction of mythical scenes, human depictions, nature scenes from tiny pieces of coloured tile set in concrete. In terms of the Christian mosaics from northern Africa, we are dealing with a rather narrow repertoire. In comparison with the work of the pagan Romans, it has been said by the author Katherine Dunbabin that we are dealing with a degree of 'iconological poverty' within the Christian milieu. It seems at first that such an overtly pagan method of depiction could only have aroused a degree of mistrust, if not downright hostility amongst the followers of the nascent faith. At the site of Sakiet es Ziet in Tunisia, for example, a fine mosaic of Orpheus has had its face destroyed. In certain cases, such actions may have had more to do with the widespread proscription of depicting humans or gods, or the very action of destroying the face may have represented a means of defaming the old religion.

Christian mosaic motifs were generally selected from a very narrow range of devices, but by the Byzantine period it is noticeable that there is a general improvement of quality and broader spread of themes. Geometric and ornamental motifs predominate, floral depictions being particularly popular, but by Byzantine times the general flavour is more adventurous. At Sabratha, the Byzantine church has a magnificent set of vine-leaf decorations in mosaic, and a pair of colourful peacocks flank the entrance. In the baptistery of Kelibia in Tunisia the mosaic decoration on the baptistery is especially fine, and here a number of themes combine to form a harmonious design; we have the traditional natural elements such as vine leaves and bees, combined with recognisable Christian symbols – such as the Chi-Rho monogram and Alpha and Omega device – within the font as well as Old Testament scenes including Noah's Ark. Old Testament scenes are also recognised on mosaics at Tipasa, and another widespread motif – which is also noted on later wall paintings in Egypt and Nubia – is that of the three Hebrew boys being saved from the fires of Hell by the intervention of the Archangel Michael. The basilican church at Hergla (Tunisia) has also yielded exceptionally fine mosaics; with the town being originally a coastal settlement, a large number of the scenes are clearly dominated by fine maritime imagery in a variety of different tile materials.

Not all mosaics necessarily show religious or quasi-religious motifs; those from Oued Ramel show a building scene, whilst a fifth-century tomb mosaic from

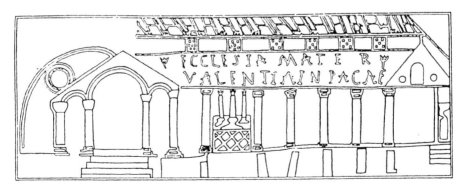

14 *Tabarka. The fifth-century Ecclesia Mater mosaic representing a church building*

Tabarka shows what is generally held to be a church. The building itself appears to be the basic pre-Byzantine form; a façade is shown with a raised apse to the left and a central altar; the roof would appear to be pitched and seems to have a raised clerestory level above, with a line of supporting pillars within the actual building. The words *Ecclesia Mater* (church mother) and *Valentia in pace* (an obvious funerary invocation for the buried – Valentia – to rest in peace) are added at the top. By and large, the selection of motifs for the mosaics within the churches reflects those from elsewhere in the Byzantine world; this will become clearer when we consider the wall paintings of the churches of Egypt and Nubia. The relative paucity of depiction of humans is a similar trait, but the naturalistic depictions are themselves loaded with Christian symbolism: the vine representing the wine of communion, the lamb as Son of God, the fish and the more obvious monograms all contribute to the ideological schema. These symbols are also to be found on small African red-slip ware (*terra sigillata*) oil lamps that abound in this region.

Another key source of information is inscriptions. A chance find of parchment discovered near Tebessa after World War One threw light on the prevalence of dualistic Manichaean beliefs within mainstream Christianity, a facet reflected in the discovery of the Nag Hammadi codices in Egypt (see chapter 1). The Tablettes Albertini, found in 1928 and now in the Algiers Museum, have also helped elucidate the nature of religious teaching and belief in the fifth century, but it is the most widely found inscription, the funerary inscription, that frequently provides us with the best data. These inscriptions are often brief and very formulaic, but undeniably Christian. The words *in pace* (in peace) are often at the top of the stone. There are usually invocations to local martyrs and perhaps a Chi-Rho device; all very Christian, yet at the same time essentially pagan Roman in style. The name or identity of the deceased is also given, usually with the word *fidelis*, or faithful, signifying a believer. Dates of birth and death are rarely given, but usually there is some form of depiction that hints at Christian symbolism in the natural world; birds or fruit alongside a cross, perhaps.

In chapter 1, it was suggested that burial evidence would be a key indicator of Christian belief, and perhaps more than any other type of archaeological evidence, it is the burial rites that are the most sensitive to syncretic traits; this theme is something that will be continually encountered in the course of this book. Most of the putatively earliest Christian burials, such as those from Cherchel in Algeria, show little difference from pagan Roman funerary rites. Romans never buried their dead within the walls of towns, always extra-mural cemeteries were set aside for this purpose. As much as any ideologically-loaded explanation for this custom may be advanced, the obvious concerns for hygiene would also have come into consideration. The burials at Setif in Libya/Tripolitania actually show few signs of recognisable Christian traits much before 471, something that may have been dictated by the need for discretion. The burials here are all extra-mural, and it is also noticeable that there are no burials in the actual Christian basilica.

Other strangely pagan concepts survived; one was the notion of the feast for the dead. Here, it was customary, following earlier practice, to commemorate the deceased with lavish banquets over their tombs, and with the pouring of libations over the grave. Large numbers of inscribed funerary stones give ample evidence of the prevalence of this custom. A grave stone on view in the Louvre Museum in Paris is a clear example of a Christian version of a pagan Roman *mensa* (table) for such feasts. This large tablet from Tebessa in Algeria is engraved with crosses and the Chi-Rho device, but clearly also served as the table from which the celebratory commemorative meals were eaten.

The dedicated extra-mural cemetery areas of Roman north Africa have provided some of the best evidence for the development of Christian burial rites. The vast cemetery area of Timgad – excavated between 1900 and 1911 – comprises some 15,000 graves; most of the bodies are covered in tiles and laid out in a plaster cocoon, as if to preserve them for the Day of Judgement. Large subterranean tunnels, or catacombs, were also used for the disposal of the dead. Those of Sousse/Hadrumetum in Tunisia stretch over 1.5km (1mile), with 105 different tunnels containing over 10,000 burials. Each burial niche is often simply decorated with a dove or fish motif, or a monogram and cross. Similar structures may be seen at Sabratha in Tripolitania. Sarcophagi or coffins were also utilised; at Carthage some burials near the basilica are only simply covered by an amphora, or large wine jar, whilst one of the most beautiful fifth-century coffins from the same city – exhibited now at the Louvre in Paris – has a bas-relief model of the Good Shepherd on the lid.

It is in Tripolitania (Libya) that we see some of the strangest – and indeed latest – manifestations of the Christian burial tradition. The cemetery of En Ngila may have been in use up until the tenth century; 28 Christian tombs have been noted, one of which may belong to a monk, but only two have been excavated. These graves contrast sharply with those of the local Libyan pagan tradition, which are mainly cairns, and those of the modern Muslim population whose graves are marked with a stone at head and foot, and are often covered with broken pottery. At the Ain Zara cemetery, all the graves are clearly orientated east to west, a probable Christian indication, it will be recalled. This cemetery seems to span the period 451-1021; the graves are rectangular in shape, with a stepped plaster-covered superstructure often covered with symbolic Christian motifs such as the cross, fishes, or peacocks. The bodies were buried beneath these structures at a depth of about one metre. The complex seems to be surrounded by a wall, and there is an associated funerary chapel, which is thought to be of the Vandal period. Another example of a late-surviving Christian rite may be found at Kairouan; here three Christian epitaphs give the date as being 397 *Anno Infidelium*, i.e. year of the infidels, or the Muslim Hejira date. This date would approximate to the eleventh century AD.

It is now important to touch upon another significant theme in the archaeology of north African Christianity, that of the martyr cult. The importance of being interred near to a holy martyr has already been touched upon; perhaps nowhere is this more clearly seen than in the massive basilica church at Mcidfa to the north-west of Carthage. Within this huge seven-aisled church, which measures 160m by 140m (524ft by 459ft), is a martyr's shrine centred over a small chapel in the nave containing the sarcophagus of the martyr. In close proximity is a large pit filled up to 30m (98ft) deep with bodies, indicating the popularity of the martyrs and their cults. In many cases, the wording of the funerary inscription indicates the desire of the deceased to be associated with the dead saint; the formula *ad Sanctos* – towards the saints – is usually given on the funerary slab.

Relics of the martyr could take many forms; a piece of clothing or an entire body. These relics, placed inside a container or reliquary, effectively gave a degree of spiritual cachet to the church in which they resided. In many cases, the martyr need not be local. A Byzantine inscription from Henschir Akrib in southwestern Numidia records the names of the Byzantine saints Pastor and Julian alongside those of local origin: Felix and Cassian. It is hardly surprising, given the blood-soaked history of the development of Christianity in northern Africa, that the cult of the martyr should have such a strong hold over Christians of all classes. As such, martyria – shrines dedicated to the memory of martyrs and often containing a reliquary of the saint – became rather big business.

At Tebessa during the fifth century, the cult surrounding the burial of the martyr St Crispina attracted large numbers of burials, and gradually a large dedicated complex grew up around the tomb, including a large basilica, a martyr's chapel all enclosed by a wall and a series of courtyards. In essence, a subtle shift in attitudes towards the place of burial was also occurring. In their desire to be associated with the body of the saint – *ad Sanctos* – people were often now buried within the church which itself would frequently have been located within the walls of the city; the long-held Roman taboo was gradually being eroded. We can recognise similar urban martyr centres at Sbeitla – which had two large basilicas with a baptistery and a bishop's residence – as well as Djemilia. At Guelma, the seventh-century inscription of Massa Candida marks the martyr's reliquary.

Perhaps the best known martyr's centre in northern Africa is that of Tipasa, a coastal site west of Algiers. The dedication here is to St Salsa, and the complex itself is exceptionally rich in burial evidence. Attention centres on the fourth-cen-

15 *Tipasa. Tomb from a pagan cemetery transformed into the tomb of the martyr Salsa.* W.H.C. Frend

tury Great Basilica, a structure measuring 52m by 45m (170ft by 148ft) and possessing an unusually wide (13m; 43ft) nave. Approximately 500 sarcophagi have been found in the vicinity of this structure. Nearby, and within the western area of the town, we find large baths and tanks, evidence perhaps for the ritual ablutions that would have preceded entrance to the holy ground. A baptistery and episcopalian residence are also present. Within the eastern area of the town is located the basilica dedicated to SS Peter and Paul; this structure, originally of a mid-fourth century date, was considerably enlarged by the Byzantines. Three reliquaries were placed near the ambo, thus conferring a degree of spiritual authority, and to the right of the pulpit, a sarcophagus containing a headless skeleton was found. The identity of this person is not clear, nor is the significance of the find. The corpse may be that of a martyr, but is more likely to have been the body of a senior member of the clergy.

In all cases, the body or relics of the saint had to be accessible to all people, not just the privileged clergy. People would make extensive and often arduous pilgrimages across the Empire to visit the graves of favoured martyrs, and these spiritual needs had to be provided for. But the accumulative weight of numbers, perhaps allied to the need to maintain a degree of control of access required a certain distancing. The solution was to place the body or relics within a tomb and allow a small opening within the wall to admit the hands of pilgrims who wished to touch these relics. A typical *fenestrella confessionis* (confessional window) may be seen in the Louvre; this example, from Ain Fakroun, Algeria, during the fifth century, consists of a series of limestone fragments containing two small, arched windows divided by a small central pillar. The only decoration is a simple cross and herring bone patterning. This window would have been placed at the front of the tomb, and in this way access to the body of the saint could be restricted and controlled. The cult of the relic is still vital today; a special department of the Vatican deals with hundreds of enquiries from all over the world for relics of favoured saints. The grading system is subtle; for a lesser saint, perhaps, it is easy to come by

16 *Azron Zaouia. Martyrs' tombs and relics beneath the church altar.* W.H.C. Frend

a scrap of clothing. Relics of the more famous saints in the Roman Catholic world are considerably harder to come by.

Seeking the Donatists

An important question connected to the archaeological history of the Church in Roman north Africa still remains to be addressed, however. Can we recognise from the archaeological record the presence of Donatist communities? A brief outline of the activities of the Donatists has been presented already in chapter 1. It will be recalled that the Donatist community, fiercely anti-Catholic, was born amidst the trauma of persecution. This 'rebel' sect, disowning the besmirched sacraments of the mainstream Church, became a remarkably dynamic and vigorous socio-religious force in the region. The movement has been mainly interpreted as being a vehicle for Berber nationalism; to some extent this may be true as by and large its power-base was among poor rural populations largely within southern Numidia, but it also attracted disaffected intellectuals and maintained a forceful missionary programme. By 330 there were some 270 dedicated Donatist bishops, a figure that hints at a very large congregational base and clergy.

Donatist activity is generally delimited geographically to Numidia, but we know from textual sources that other communities were active elsewhere. Large-scale church building programmes were instituted by local Donatist bishops and clergy as if to reinforce their new dominance. The church at Tebessa is a fine example of a large Donatist church, and there are no fewer than 17 churches in Timgad, a key Donatist centre. On occasions, Donatists were not averse to deploying rather strong-arm tactics; they seized the Catholic basilica at Cirta in 330, for instance, converting it into a Donatist establishment. Here we now come to the crux of the archaeological problem. What is culturally different about a Donatist church building?

The short answer, and the most disappointing one, is that there are no clear architectural differences, nor is there any shift in the perception and use of sacred space within the building. The key evidence for Donatist ritual activity comes from inscriptions on the building. The most obvious Donatist inscription is *Deo laudes*, meaning praise to the Lord. This formula has been noted on a lintel at the church (latterly a mosque) at Henschir Taglissi in Tripolitania, on the keystone of the church at Vegesela (Ksar el Kelb), and at the churches of Ain Ghorab, Mascula, Madauros and Castellum Tingitanum amongst others. Many of the Donatist church inscriptions tend to quote extensively from Psalms, the accent throughout, perhaps is on self-righteousness. The formulae of Donatist inscriptions tend to be direct, and one might say 'holier than thou'. It is as if they were protesting the righteousness of their faith, the superiority it held spiritually over the Catholics. So, apart from the evidence of inscriptions, historical sources and (broadly speaking) geographical distribution, it is very difficult to recognise any unique Donatist cultural traits.

We have a linked problem with the recognition of the Circumcellions. It will be recalled that the Circumcellions have been regarded as extremist Donatists, but in truth this may be something of an over-simplification. Circumcellions formed an extremist, highly conservative movement, often violent, outwardly devout, but frequently regarded by suspicion by the mainstream Donatist community. This movement was essentially rural, and in some quarters has been described as being terrorist in nature. The very word Circumcellion may betray the origins of the movement, the name may allude to the fact that they used to congregate as pilgrims around (*circum*) the shrines of martyrs' dwellings (*cellae*). As a social movement, the Circumcellions were forceful players during the fourth century, but again the cultural indicators for this mass extremist group are few. The most obvious indicator would, perhaps, be the presence of small houses and storage places grouped around martyrs' shrines in the countryside.

The large-scale upheavals that threatened the fabric of Church and society in northern Africa during the first seven centuries are only rarely mirrored in the archaeological record; the rise of Donatism and the Circumcellions and the Vandal interlude may only be vaguely discerned, whilst the Byzantine period is marked by a fairly obvious change in church layout and decoration. By bringing all these threads together, we can make a few general conclusions about cultural change in the Church of northern Africa.

The Vandal and Byzantine interlude

As a general rule, the scale of the church building, its size, decoration, orientation and indeed internal layout is highly varied. (**17**) This would be expected in such a large area as Roman north Africa, a political zone that subsumed so many different shades of cultural life. The earliest ecclesiastical buildings would have undoubtedly re-used civil, judicial basilica buildings – such as is the case with the large Severan structure at Leptis Magna. This is not a uniquely African trait; this custom was followed throughout the formative years of western European Christendom, and indeed is a theme to which we will be returning in subsequent chapters. The re-use of the civil building may subsume some deeper symbolic need, such as the ideological appropriation of pre-Christian religious space, but more prosaically may be the result of the dictates of economy and availability of suitable building material. As a very general rule, the pre-Vandal churches were set out to a broadly similar spatial scheme. The apse was usually raised above the level of the nave floor, whilst the altar was placed centrally. Another feature of the basilican church buildings at this time is the presence of the contra-apse.

The opposing apse is found in a number of northern African churches. At the basilica of Castellum Tingitanum (Al-Asnam/Orléansville) in western Algeria, the new contra-apse was added during the fifth century opposite a rather primitive-looking original eastern apse. Whereas the original eastern apse was raised from the nave floor, and was positioned slightly askew of the main basilican axis, the new western apse was larger and decorated in rich mosaic. There is an extensive and varied typology of these opposing or contra-apses; they may have been vestiges of an

17 *Guelma. A nineteenth-century engraving of the Byzantine fortifications*

earlier basilican building tradition, or in many cases were later additions. Their function is also unclear; what role could they have played? In one of the key studies on the topic, the French scholar Duval can only conclude broadly that they may have served some vague funerary purpose (some are sited over vaults), may have sheltered reliquaries – it will be recalled that the presence of martyr's relics symbolically imbued the church building with sanctity and importance, such was the strength of the cult of the martyr – or finally may have reflected some now forgotten liturgical concern. The use of an opposing apse along the main axis of the basilica is not, it should be stressed, a solely north African phenomenon. Similar examples have been noted from southern Spain, Portugal, Baalbeck in Syria, as well as the Basilica of Erment in Egypt.

The Vandal interruption has left us little in the way of concrete data to understand how this Arian perspective settled into the northern African milieu, but it is with the coming of the Byzantines that we get a broadly clearer picture, and a whole new set of rules for the apportioning of sacred space within the church building is now adhered to. Within the building itself, the most obvious transformation is now the extensive investment in mosaic embellishment, and another key architectural change is the rebuilding of the eastern apse complex. The floor of this feature is levelled at the nave height, the building of ambons or pulpits becomes progressively rarer, the altar is shifted to the eastern end of the church, and the occasional presence of footings for sanctuary screens would seem to indicate the gradual distancing of the congregation from the act of worship.

18 *Reconstruction of the façade of the Byzantine church of Dar-el-Kous*

Another feature is the addition of small flanking presbyteries or storage rooms to the apse, this is a characteristic that we shall see in the Egyptian and Nubian contexts. Another important motif, both in terms of economic investment and the sacramental meaning, is the addition or enlargement in Byzantine times of extensive baptistery complexes. The baptisteries usually take the form of spacious and extensive rooms; the tank is often cruciform and stepped, and occasionally richly decorated with mosaic work depicting a number of key biblical themes, even if the repertoire – as previously noted – is somewhat narrow. So, in short the general trend from small, three-aisled, single-apsed edifices, with a single central altar towards larger, more richly decorated Byzantine-period buildings is fairly clear. This conclusion is heavily supported by data from Tripolitania, but as a general rule would seem to hold well for elsewhere.

Discussion

In the course of this chapter, we have only really scratched the surface. Perhaps in comparison to anywhere else on the African continent, we have more excavated churches from the Maghreb than elsewhere. It is a comprehensive archaeological and architectural database, but can only tell a small part of the experience of Christian growth and development here. Maybe we have to begin to accept the limitations of the archaeological record in the light of the research questions that we pose. True, we can cast light upon the important role of the martyr cult, and the expansion and development of ecclesiastical architecture in town and country within certain geographical and temporal limits. We can satisfactorily detect the heavy Byzantine influence, very eastern-orientated and many shades away from the original, western Romanised roots of Christianity. But what of the other major social upheavals that have scarred the region, upheavals whose effects are so clearly chronicled in early historical texts? What of the Donatist movement, are we left with inscriptions alone to recognise their presence, or do more subtle cultural traits await further discovery? What too of the Arian Vandal interregnum, a whole code of new and very European cultural rules set down in an African context?

Christianity withered in the face of the expansion of Islam during the seventh century, but the tomb inscriptions of Kairouan and En-Ngila in Tripolitania tell of survivals perhaps as late as the tenth century, a picture reinforced by contemporary historical accounts. As with the earliest Christians, the adherents of the new religion were not averse to re-using the cultural baggage; in Tripolitania we see the conversion of the churches at Suk el Lokli and Gebel Nefussa into mosques, and in the lower Sofeggin valley, the three-aisled basilica had a mihrab (or prayer niche) set into the central nave. Soon Islam predominated, and it was only with the coming of the French during the nineteenth century that Christianity began to re-establish itself in one of the most important and dynamic regions of its birth. The perspective now shifts eastwards to Egypt, where Christianity emerged roughly contemporaneously, but was of a more oriental flavour and which set its roots in a far different syncretic context.

Further reading

Most of the key sources that deal with the archaeology of the Maghreb are in French, but two useful English starting points for understanding the archaeology and history of this region are: P. Mackendrick (1980) *The North African Stones Speak* (Chapel Hill: University of North Carolina Press) and S. Raven (1993) *Rome in Africa* (3rd edition, London: Routledge). The former is a little dated, but deals well with the archaeological evidence. The latter remains a very solid introduction to the Roman Empire in northern Africa. Varied useful syntheses may be found in sections of W. Frend's *The Archaeology of Early Christianity: A History* (1996, London: Geoffrey Chapman). A very useful French work is J. Cuoq's 1984 book *L'Eglise d'Afrique du Nord au Deuxième au Douzième Siècles* (Paris: Le Centurion). The standard work on the history of the Donatist church remains W. Frend's *Donatist Church* (reprinted 2000); (Oxford: Oxford University Press).

The following are useful sources for the Carthage data: L. Ennabli (1987), *Results of the International Save Carthage Campaign: The Christian Monuments, World Archaeology 18/3*; A. Ennabli (ed.) 1997 *Pour Sauver Carthage* (Paris: UNESCO) and L. Ennabli (1997) *Carthage: Une Métropole Chrétienne du IVeme à la Fin du VIIeme Siècle* (Paris: CNRS Editions). The archaeology of Tripolitanian churches is dealt with in a classic paper by J. Ward-Perkins and R. Goodchild (1953) in *Archaeologia XCV* pp.1-84 entitled 'The Christian Antiquities of Tripolitania', whilst D. Mattingley's *Tripolitania* (1995, London: Batsford) presents the wider historical scope.

The standard work on the mosaic tradition remains K. Dunbabin's 1978 book *The Mosaics of Roman north Africa: Studies in Iconography and Patronage* (Oxford: Clarendon). V. Saxer's (1980) *Morts, Martyrs Reliques en Afrique Chrétienne aux Premiers Siècles* (Paris: Beauchesne) presents an overview of the archaeological recognition of the cult of the martyr. The beautifully-illustrated and incredibly informative *From Hannibal to St Augustine: Ancient art of North Africa from the Musée du Louvre* edited by M. Brouillet, 1994, (Atlanta: Emory Museum) gives a fine flavour of the wealth of the region's material culture. The following fairly accessible journals often provide exceptionally useful sources: *Antiquités Africaines* (for mainly Algeria and Tunisia), and *Libyan Studies* (Tripolitania and Cyrenaica).

3 The great survivors: the Coptic Christians of Egypt

The connection between a glamorous winter sports resort in Switzerland and Egyptian Christianity may not seem to be immediately apparent. St Moritz, the resort in question, was named after a third-century AD Egyptian Christian soldier by the name of Maurice who belonged to the Roman Army's Theban legion stationed in the area, and for a while fellow Christian Egyptian soldiers of Rome, far away from their sunlit desert homes, pursued a programme of missionary activity among the heathen tribes of these high alpine valleys. The fame of Egypt's Christians had spread to some of the most obscure corners of Rome's European empire; a testament to the dynamism and strength of a community that can be seen in the wider African context – along with the Ethiopians – as being among the great survivors of history.

According to current estimates, there are some six million active Coptic Christians in Egypt today, but this word 'Copt' presents in itself an etymological problem. In the modern sense, it is taken to mean an Egyptian Christian, although the word itself actually refers to all Egyptians, both Muslim and Christian. The roots of this word are to be found in a corruption of the Greek word *Aigyptos*, and the later Arabic corruption *Qibt,* perhaps pertaining to a native of Memphis, or Hikaptah, which in ancient Egypt referred to Het-Ka-Ptah, or the sanctuary of the god Ptah. Within the context of this chapter, the word Copt will be used in the widely accepted sense as pertaining to the Egyptian community of monophysite Christians. Even today, the Copts have managed to retain their proud independence and indeed maintain an inherent belief of their being the heirs to the legacy of the ancient Egyptian pharaohs. The Coptic community has managed to successfully strike a balance with the majority Muslim population without compromising its own religious beliefs, and has often wielded a political influence out of proportion to its size. For instance, the recent United Nations Secretary General Boutros Boutros Ghali is himself a Copt, and Egyptian Christians have always been noted for their skills in the civil service, state government and in fields of intellectual endeavour. The relationship between Muslim and Christian, however, has not always been so comfortable; during the 1970s the Patriarch (head of the church) Shenoute III was placed under house arrest by President Sadat because of alleged opposition to the Egyptian Government. But the Egyptian Christian community tenaciously holds on and thrives. To understand the roots of this proud Christian Egyptian tradition, we must go back to the second half of the first millennium BC, at a time when the social order of the New Kingdom was on the verge of collapse.

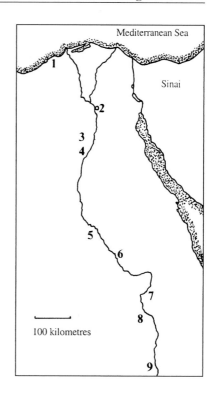

19 *Map of Egypt showing principal sites mentioned in the chapter: 1. Alexandria, 2. Cairo, 3. Fayuum, 4. Bawit, 5. Assiut, 6. Sohag, 7. Thebes/Luxor, 8. Esna, 9. Aswan*

The historical background to the emergence of Egyptian Christianity

During the first millennium BC, the political system of the Ancient Egyptian New Kingdom was reeling under the weight of military and economic pressure from neighbouring states. The key events that were to have repercussions for the development of Christianity in Egypt began with the arrival of large numbers of Jews fleeing Babylonian incursions in the sixth century BC, and the subsequent conquest of the country by the Persians. The famed Macedonian general Alexander the Great now steps onto the scene in the fourth century; in 332 BC he defeated the Persian king Darius III, and all of the middle east was now open to him. In triumph, Alexander set about building his new Egyptian capital on the northern coast of Egypt. Alexandria, as it became known, was soon to become one of the greatest cities of antiquity. Designed by the Greek Deinocrates of Chalcedon, the city was set out on an axial grid system, and the city walls extended some 25km (15 miles) in length. Egypt was henceforth governed from this city by the Ptolemaic dynasty, which was founded after Alexander's death by one of his generals, who claimed the satrapy (or administrative position) of Egypt, and which ruled almost unbroken from 304-30 BC. Ancient Egyptian ideological systems now began to mingle with Hellenic cult, and the foundation of the Serapis Temple at Alexandria – the focus of the Graeco-Egyptian worship – put the city firmly at the centre of the new Ptolemaic dynasty's religious sphere.

20 *A modern mosaic of St Mark, near the Hanging Church, Cairo. Note the Pharos, or lighthouse, of Alexandria to his right*

The famed Kleopatra VII was the last independent Egyptian ruler, and the seeds of Egypt's downfall were sown with her fateful liaison with the Roman Emperor Julius Caesar. After the murder of Caesar, Kleopatra's short marriage to Mark Antony ended in bloodshed at the Battle of Actium in 31 BC, and from 30 BC Egypt was formally incorporated into the Roman Empire. Egypt rapidly became a vital part of the Roman economic system, providing food and manpower, but the pharaonic ideal never quite disappeared. In Alexandria, for instance, the city was given a special status by the Romans, and was governed by its own clique of Archantes, or magistrates. Within the ideological sphere, the city became a hot bed for intellectual debate and religious syncretism. Romans merged their cosmological system with that of the Graeco-Egyptians', venerating Isis and Osiris alongside their own gods; the large Jewish community provided another dimension, and the vital and healthy intellectual pagan tradition flourished in the shape of the magician Hermes Trismegistus, whose philosophy took shape in the mysterious secret works of the *Corpus Hermeticum*, a set of writings which provided some of the fundamental concepts of the later Christian dualistic Gnostic movement. It is into this rich melting pot of religious freedom, intellectualism and syncretism that Christianity in Egypt first appeared.

According to the church historian Eusebius, St Mark introduced Christianity into Egypt around AD 41; his first convert was a shoemaker named Anianus, but the New Testament hints at a much earlier intimate contact between Jesus himself and Egypt when the holy family enjoyed a lengthy sojourn in Egypt when Jesus was a child. What is clear, however, is that Alexandria was home to a large Jewish population, and the prevailing atmosphere of religious freedom and experimentation would have provided a vigorous intellectual climate for the nascent faith to thrive. In time, Alexandria would become one of the most important centres for Christians in the eastern Mediterranean. The Catechetical School flourished there under the great Christian thinkers Clement and Origen during the second and third centuries AD, although the savagery of Diocletian's persecutions briefly destroyed the position of Christianity as a settled force in Egypt. The folk memory of this 'era of the martyrs' when so many Christians died for their faith runs deep in Coptic tradition, and their calendar itself starts from the date of Diocletian's accession in 284.

By the fourth century perhaps as much as eighty per cent of the Alexandrian population was Christian, and within the eastern Mediterranean the city soon began to rival Constantinople as an ecclesiastical centre. This rivalry soon manifested itself in the wider dyophysite versus monophysite intellectual debate. Conditions were especially good for Christians in Egypt; monasticism thrived and individual settlements became wealthy through extensive land holdings, and there was also an officially instituted programme of tax exemption for the clergy. By the late fifth century, the Emperor Zeno declared the *Henotikon*, a scheme designed to effect the unity of church and state, and the fortunes of the monophysite church of Egypt had never been better – notwithstanding perennial quarrels and interminable doctrinal debates with the Melkite religious authorities at Constantinople. Nemesis, however, was not far away, for in the Arabian Peninsula, far over the Red Sea, a dynamic new socio-ideological force was gathering momentum.

The prophet Mohammed's flight, or Hidjra, from Mecca to Medina in 622 signalled the beginning of the era of Muslim dominance of the Middle East. In 639 the Arabs invaded Egypt, and the Byzantine armed forces were decisively defeated at the battle of Heliopolis in 640. When Alexandria itself fell in 642, things looked bleak for the Christians of Egypt, but under the aegis of the Umayyad and Fatimid dynasties of the latter half of the first millennium AD, the Copts were able to maintain a tenuous hold at the centre of the new state machinery. Paradoxically, the real threats to their survival came from fellow Christians; Chalcedonian Melkite patriarchs still maintained a foothold in Alexandria, sharing a common root of popes with the Coptic Church, starting from St Mark until 451 and the Chalcedonian schism. Efforts on behalf of the Vatican to cultivate Egyptian Christians culminated in the foundation of the Coptic Catholic Church in the 1740s, and by the nineteenth century, Protestant missionaries were also hard at work. None of these attentions served to weaken the Coptic Church; they had learned well the art of compromise, and their Muslim overlords were happy to grant a degree of religious freedom within certain defined limits. Two thousand years later, the Copts are still on the Egyptian stage, whilst the other Christian denominations have shrunk to insignificant numbers. Today the Coptic Church is controlled through 21 dioceses in Egypt, with additional ecclesiastical representation in Sudan and Jerusalem.

Having considered the broad historical contexts, we should now turn our attention to the peoples themselves, and consider what marks them out culturally from their Muslim neighbours. It is a dangerous exercise in archaeological studies to attempt to define that problematic term 'ethnicity'; Copts are physically indistinguishable from Muslims, and although they speak Arabic, their liturgy is based on the now extinct language of Coptic. An outline of the development of this language is important in understanding the cultural context of Coptic history and the peoples' sense of self-identity.

Coptic texts as an archaeological resource

For over four thousand years the language of the ancient Egyptians was written in a pictorial script known as hieroglyphs; for writing the language quickly a cursive (shortened) Demotic alphabet was used. As late as the fifth century, hieroglyphs in the form of Demotic graffiti were still to be seen on the walls at the Temple of Philae near Aswan, but with the burgeoning of a large Greek-speaking population in the north, the language of the native Egyptians needed a new medium of writing to help communication. It was clear, however, that the Greek alphabet alone could not cope with the subtle vocal shades of the Egyptian tongue. In order to remedy the problem, seven Demotic letters were grafted onto the 24 letters of the standard Greek alphabet. Now the ancient Egyptian tongue had a new medium of written communication, and literary Coptic now emerged. Although a large amount of Greek vocabulary was incorporated into the language, the ongoing hostility with the Melkite authorities resulted in a widespread reaction in Egypt to Greek-orientated culture as a whole, and the implicit linkage of this Greek culture with paganism resulted in a gradual erosion of the importance of the Greek language; by the eighth century the use of Greek in correspondence had virtually disappeared.

The earliest extant scripts are mainly Old and New Testament writings or biographies such as the *Synaxarion* or lives of the saints, and the favoured writing medium remained papyrus, parchment or pot fragments (ostraka), all of which survive relatively well in the dry climate of Egypt. There is some textual evidence for Christianity before about 300 in the shape of private letters; by the fourth century it is noticeable that more Christian names are appearing and by the fifth century we have lists of clergy; the historical sources, then, seem to indicate a gradual flowering of Christianity and also show, by the sixth century, that the church itself was a very wealthy and influential body. Although these writings are of an obvious Christian character, some syncretic pagan elements remained; the Coptic word for God, for instance was *Nute,* which recalls the ancient Egyptian term *Neter.* This syncretic motif is brought into sharper relief when one considers the case of the Nag Hammadi codices, a strange and convoluted story of alleged international scholarly intrigue and antiquities dealing.

During the early part of the twentieth century, the newly emerging discipline of Coptology was a mainly text-based exercise; the finds of the Oxyrhynchus papyri, and latterly in the 1950s of the Dishna codices provided a broad corpus of written sources with which to work, but perhaps the most intriguing texts were those discovered by a farmer digging for fertiliser near the Upper Egyptian village of Nag Hammadi in 1945. During the course of his work, the farmer stumbled across a red clay jar approximately one metre (3ft) in height. Upon breaking the jar open, he found thirteen papyrus books bound in leather, and recognising their potential financial value – if not scholarly importance – he sold them to an antiquities dealer in Cairo, from where they ultimately came to the notice of the official antiquities authorities. After many twists and turns, the Coptic Museum in Cairo took possession of some of the codices, but one-and-a-half fragments remained to be found, and these were ultimately purchased by the Zürich-based Jung Foundation in 1955. Such were the shady manoeuvrings behind the sale of the manuscripts, it took many years for scholars to study the whole corpus of codices, but when they did it soon became clear that they were dealing with no ordinary Christian texts.

It will be recalled from chapter 1 that a heretical group known as the Gnostics provided a dynamic and controversial dimension to Egyptian Christianity in the fourth century AD. Anathematised and persecuted, the Gnostics – who believed in a strangely dualistic form of Christianity – died out, but not before they had managed to hide their library. The Nag Hammadi codices were part of such a secreted Gnostic library, carefully hidden by a follower for future recovery when conditions were right. Among the strangely titled gospels we find: the Gospel of Thomas, the Apocrypha of John, the secret Book of James, the Gospel of Truth and the Gospel of the Egyptians, but it is perhaps the Gospel of Philip that most challenges the orthodox view of Jesus Christ. In this book, Jesus is imbued with obvious human frailties: a sexual relationship between him and Mary Magdalene is hinted at, the concept of the virgin birth is denied and the story of Jesus' resurrection criticised. The Nag Hammadi texts provided some of the clearest evidence yet of the amalgam of traditional Christian belief with mystic eastern elements within this Gnostic system, yet they were an accident of discovery, and the controversy surrounding their provenance, ownership and ultimate translation does not reflect credit on the academic authorities involved in the whole saga.

Coptic Christian belief and the question of syncretism

Apart from the Coptic literary tradition, we need to look harder at the Christian element, and again see how the syncretic thread makes itself apparent in the day-to-day life of the Copts. The Coptic calendar is reckoned from Diocletian's accession on the 29 August AD 284; the year itself begins on 11 September, and is made up of twelve 30-day months, and one 5-day month (6 days in a leap year). This framework is also broadly mirrored in the Ethiopian calendar. After birth, male babies wait for 40 days until they are baptised, but for females this is 80 days. As they grow up, Coptic children are brought closer to the Muslim world; women wear veils, but frequently may have a cross tattooed on their forehead – a practice prevalent today in Tigray, northern Ethiopia. As with the Muslims, no pork may be eaten, but alcohol is permitted. Marriage – which is permitted for the clergy – is marked by a lengthy festival, and is regarded as a key sacrament, for divorce is very difficult.

Prayers are offered seven times a day; washing of the hands and feet is usual before personal prayer commences, and the supplicant will often pray facing the east, towards the rising sun, the life symbol of Christ. Rigorous fasting and confessions are followed – especially during Lent – but the mystical element of their belief is never far from the surface; use of amulets against the evil eye and belief in the power of holy relics reflect a much earlier folk tradition, and the widely reported mass visions of the Virgin Mary above the church at Zeitoun in Cairo in early 1968 are more redolent of the cult of Mary within European Roman Catholicism than the ethos of oriental churches.

It is perhaps in death that we see the real echoes of the past; 40 days are set aside for the soul to leave the body as a mourning period, and offerings of food are often made to the ghost of the deceased, a theme that may be traced from ancient Egyptian belief. In the New Year families visit graves to offer holy water and palm fronds; another custom that has distant roots in the pharaonic past, a past which to the Copts – the guardians of the glories of ancient Egypt – seems to be only yesterday. How are these syncretic motifs reflected in the archaeological record of Egyptian Christianity? Are we able to define a pharaonic thread running through this evidence? It is this fascinating question of religious syncretism that is more defined in Egypt than in Roman north Africa.

The archaeological perspective

The archaeological remains of ancient Egypt and the study of its texts – traditional Egyptology – have always tended to attract the attention of academics and public alike; the study of anything after the Roman occupation had always been rather neglected. This imbalance of research began to be redressed in 1881, when the then French director of the Egyptian Antiquities Service, Gaston Maspero, urged his fellow workers to turn their attentions to the rich heritage of Christian Egypt; in every sense he may be regarded as the founding father of modern Coptology. With the foundation of the Coptic Museum in Cairo in 1910, the study of the cultural history of the Copts was now firmly established on an academic footing, and the study of Coptic archaeology is now recognised as an important discipline in its own right. In considering the archaeology of the Coptic Church in Egypt, we should start with the most obvious archaeological manifestation: the church building itself.

In common with other areas of the Roman Empire, the earliest churches of Egypt – especially in Alexandria – would have been simple houses, the reason being that it paid not to draw attention to oneself as a follower of an outlawed sect. The fourth century saw the official acceptance of Christianity, and in Egypt this was marked by the newly emancipated Christians with the destruction of pagan tombs, and the appropriation of temples as places of Christian worship (**colour plate 2**). The temples at Thebes were the sites for new churches, and Rameses the Second's mortuary temple at Medinet Habu itself housed three churches. The Temples of Hathor at Dendera, Amon and Ptolemy the Third's temple at Hermopolis, Seti the First's temple at Abydos, the Isis temple at Philae, the Amun temple at Karnak and the Temple of Month at Madamud were all pillaged, variably defaced and adapted to provide building materials and space for new Christian places of worship, but not without reaction. In 391 Theophilus the Patriarch of Alexandria attempted to convert the Serapis complex for use in Christian worship and in doing so sparked a bloody riot. This reaction to Theophilus' actions clearly indicates that even as late as the fourth century AD there was still an active pagan presence in Alexandria.

21 *A cross carved on the surface of the Temple of Isis, Philae*

In most cases, the need to appropriate the cultic space of the old religion could have been a purely economic decision, the availability of building stone being an obvious factor, but there was clearly an additional ideological factor at work, hence the vigorous reaction to Theophilus. It is also clear that the use of the whole temple building for Christian worship would have been itself ideologically unsatisfactory; apart from the obvious pagan connotations inherent within the whole religious space, the Christian act of worship demanded a communal participation which would have been impossible in the rigidly compartmentalised areas of the pagan temples, with their strictly defined control of access for the public within what was considered an actual house of the deity rather than a meeting place for the laity.

The basic form of the church in Egypt followed the ubiquitous basilican plan. The basilica itself, often domed, was usually orientated along the standard east–west axis, although in Upper Egypt it was usually aligned along the course of the river Nile. A number of architectural features of the basilica are more recognisably Egyptian in character. Walls are generally very thick, and the interior and exterior surfaces are broken at regular intervals with niches, a facet that recalls earlier temple architecture, as does the usual presence of an ambulatory or covered walkway around the building. Windows are usually very small, and as bells are forbidden by the Muslims there is no campanile or bell tower. Upon entering the church through the front narthex, one finds usually a baptistery or epiphany tank. These come in a variety of shapes across Egypt, but the usual form is a rectangular brick plaster-lined tank. The *laqqan*, or Maundy tank, for use in Lent, is a later architectural feature, and is rarely noted in churches much before the seventh century.

The nave is usually where men stand during the service, with the women being banished to the side aisles or galleries above, and the division of the nave is marked by an internal line of pillars. Another older Egyptian architectural feature is the construction of a return aisle at the west end of the nave, which usually supports a bridging gallery above. An ambon, or pulpit, is located towards the end of the nave; within excavated churches these are represented by a raised platform, but in active churches the pulpit is often a finely carved wooden box with varied decorative inlays. A chancel area is emphasised at the eastern end of the nave; this space is for use by the church choir – Coptic liturgy heavily emphasises choral participation – and from around the seventh century the chancel tended to be screened off from the sanctuary by a *heikal* screen or *iconostasis*.

The sanctuary area is perhaps the most distinctive architectural feature of the Egyptian church design. It is common to find three sanctuaries in a 'triconch' configuration; the central sanctuary is dedicated to the patron saint of the church, and as the liturgy forbids the use of an altar more than once a day, subsequent daily services will be held in either flanking sanctuary. Unlike the Nubian forms, the apse in an Egyptian church does not project beyond the main body of the church, but the whole sanctuary complex with flanking storage rooms and sacristy is embedded within the overall rectangular form of the main building – the church of St Menas in Cairo is an exception to this rule. Within earlier churches, the sanctuary is separated from the nave and chancel by a basic arch, but by the seventh century a virtually separate room – or *khurus* – develops in front of the sanctuary, perhaps emphasising the gradual distancing of clergy and laity.

Each sanctuary has an altar, cloth-covered with a wooden canopy above. The earliest altars would have often been fully portable wooden tables, and the earliest archaeological examples are restricted to the masonry/block bases of the tables. In the sanctuary of the church of Abu Menas, the altar base is formed by a fragment of re-used Roman column, whilst at the temple of Philae the original pagan altar was itself commandeered for use as an altar for the church. The whole sanctuary area is frequently built atop a crypt – often containing the bones of a saint or martyr, and which may be used for private devotion.

Many of these architectural features clearly differ from the idealised basilican plan, and they reflect changing liturgical concerns over time, especially the gradual isolation of the lay congregation. Not all the earliest churches feature these key facets, and there is no real evidence of a church building in Egypt much before the fourth century. The small churches at Kellia, Kharga Oasis (Shams-al-Din), Amiyrah and the Roman military camp at Abusir (Taposiris Magna) all show clear basilican outlines, albeit on the small scale, but these churches were often destroyed or rebuilt, and we can have few clues about the nature of early church building in Egypt.

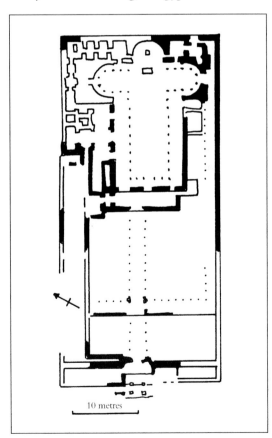

22 *Plan of the transept church at Hermopolis Magna/Asmunin. The tripartite apse arrangement is characteristic of early Egyptian ecclesiastical architecture*

10 metres

Moving from the basic architectural elements of the church building, other aspects of the material culture of early Egyptian Christianity also hint at a continuing syncretic theme. Interiors of churches were often painted using natural pigments on a whitewash and plaster base over the stonework. From around the fifth to seventh centuries we see a gradual increase in the use of recognisably Christian motifs, albeit with a heavy hint of Classical, Byzantine and ancient Egyptian influence. Perhaps the key elements of Egyptian Christian iconography may be noted in figurative depictions: eyes are circular, noses strictly linear. A variety of Old and New Testament scenes may be depicted alongside local saints and wild animals. The ancient Egyptian thread is most readily recognisable in the rendering of the Archangel Michael with his scales weighing the goodness of the dead – virtually identical to the Thoth belief of ancient Egyptian lore, where souls were weighed before entering the afterlife. The seated figure of the Virgin Mary holding the infant Jesus in her left arm presents a striking similarity to the Isis and Horus pose of ancient Egyptian iconography. Other recognisable Christian motifs also appear, including the three Hebrew boys about to be saved from the fires of Hell by St Michael as told in the book of Daniel in the Old Testament – this motif appears too in Roman northern African mosaic work and in Nubian paintings – and of special interest is the Orant, or praying figure with outstretched arms.

Church sculpture too often betrays clear classical motifs; stone capitals are decorated with vines and foliage, and these elements were often painted. Perhaps the most intriguing syncretic element is the re-use of the ancient Egyptian ankh, or cross; in the Coptic milieu this is recognised in the parallel ansate cross with a rounded top. When Theophilus destroyed the Serapeum in Alexandria, the ankh crosses were retained, the only pre-Christian decorative element to survive his purge. The climate of Egypt is especially conducive to the survival of organic material, and the nature of Coptic burial treatment – with its roots in ancient Egyptian practice, the Akhmim burials are a good example – has left us a rich corpus of textiles. As a rule, linen and wool cloth was coloured with vegetable dye, and these early textiles incorporate a variety of motifs including lions, vines and fish; by the seventh century Christian motifs such as crosses were widespread. Let us now consider a little more closely a few obvious archaeological examples.

Within Alexandria, the most important city in early Christian Egypt, we have little concrete evidence for early church building. Here, paganism clearly remained important, as is evidenced by the riots in 391 provoked by the Patriarch Theophilus. Historical sources record the construction of Bishop Thomas' church at the beginning of the fourth century, and we also know that the Patriarch Constantius the Second authorised the construction of a church dedicated to St John the Baptist within the Caesareum building at some point in the mid-fourth century. A church dedicated to St Raphael for the protection of mariners was established on the Island of Pharos at about this time, and during the same period the Temple of Kronos Saturnus was dedicated as a church to St Michael. Perhaps the most intriguing question surrounds the whereabouts of the famed Alexandrine monastic complex or *Enaton*. Located, according to historical sources, on the ninth milestone to the west of Alexandria, this massive complex was sacked by the Persians around 619, and although it has never been satisfactorily located, modern archaeologists suggest that ruins near to Dikhaylah may be the remains of part of this vast Christian complex. Within the broader archaeological context, the ravages of war and ecclesiastical change have all conspired to cloud our picture of the archaeology of early Egyptian Christianity in both city and countryside.

It is perhaps within Cairo that we can get the best overview of the development of church architecture and building within the Coptic Church. In the area known as Old Cairo, in the former walled Roman fortress constructed by Trajan in the second century AD – popularly known as Babylon or Masr el Qadima – a number of important churches, both Coptic and Greek Orthodox are to be found. Probably the earliest churches are those of Deir Abu al Safain and Deir Bablun, but perhaps the best known is the church of Abu Sarga. The church of Abu Sarga was dedicated in the eighth century to the martyr St Sergius, although successive rebuildings and renovations have left little of the original fabric of the building intact. Again the form is clearly basilican, with the usual configuration for segregation of the lay congregation, and a spatial separation between the nave and chancel. Within this church, architectural historians have noted a shift in the location of the baptistery tank; from being sited within an antechamber, it was moved to the side of the narthex until finally finding itself in a position within the church at the end of the aisle next to the altar. The significance of this repositioning is not clear; it may reflect liturgical concepts or more prosaically may be the result of shifting socio-economic fortunes, but the movement of baptistery positions is a common feature within Coptic churches. Also of special note is the presence of an ostrich eggshell hanging in front of the *iconostasis* or sanctuary screen. The egg is a common symbol in pre-Christian Egyptian art as well as featuring iconographically in Nubian Christian painting, and in the use of this motif the Coptic historian Jill Kamil sees a link with the concept of rebirth or resurrection.

The nearby church of Al Moallaqha, or Sitt Maryam is widely known as 'the suspended one' (or more commonly as the 'Hanging Church'); this name reflects the construction of the church building atop two projecting bastions of the older Roman fortress below. The whole building does literally sit suspended between the two supports. Known as a seat of bishops since at least the seventh century, the church has undergone extensive rebuilding since its destruction in the ninth century. The modern church is of a standard Egyptian basilican pattern with a row of eight columns separating the nave and aisle. Of special note is the magnificent carved eleventh-century marble pulpit or minbar, which reflects the beautiful inlaid woodwork within the church interior (**colour plates 3** & **4**). Also of special interest is the church of the nearby monastery of Deir Abu al Saifain, where the church of St Mercurius still shows evidence of the original foundation wall plan and exhibits certain pre-Muslim architectural facets that mark it out as one of the oldest standing churches of Old Cairo. Having now considered the elements of church architecture and their development as revealed through architectural history and archaeology, let us now turn to another key aspect of Christian life and death: funerary ritual.

Early Christian burial rites clearly recall older pagan practices: tombstones are mainly of the traditional monolithic stela form, often with a small cavity carved in the back to allow for incense burning as an offering – again another ancient Egyptian parallel. The burial stelae at the Christian necropolis of Al Bagawat (ancient Hiblis, in the Kharga Oasis, see **colour plate 5**) also have short liturgical texts, or hymns of repose (*trisagion*) carved on the frontal face. The majority of the graves are simple oblong cuts with a small superstructure above and access via a vertical shaft. Of special note within the Al Bagawat complex is an associated large courtyard building, which was latterly transformed into a basilica, and it is suggested that this building was used by mourning families for commemorative feasts for their dead kin.

Another strange Christian burial tradition may be recognised in the Fayuum at the site of Soliman Bayed. Here, in the sixth-century tombs (recently uncovered by a French archaeological team) the bodies are covered by rows of late Roman amphorae. The grave cuts are all simple rectangular ditches, variably aligned north-south or east-west. On the broader scale, it is clear that early Christian burial practices in Egypt were varied and idiosyncratic, and in many cases clearly pre-Christian, pagan funerary rites still survived. Leaving now the basic archaeological motifs of early Egyptian Christian archaeology, we need now to consider the rich wealth of evidence afforded by the study of that most intriguing and far-reaching socio-economic development within the ecclesiastical history of Egypt: monasticism.

The archaeology of Egyptian monasticism

> First I chose to live in a Pharaoh's tomb. But a witchery winds through those underground palaces, where the aromatic smoke of long ago seems to thicken the shade
>
> (Gustave Flaubert, 1874, *The Temptation of Saint Anthony*)

The idea of removing oneself from the daily cares of society in order to devote the whole of one's life to inner contemplation in an ethos of rigid self-discipline is not a feature uniquely associated with early Egyptian Christianity. As early as the second century BC, at the time of the Ptolemies, solitary reclusive ascetics were known at Memphis; these hermits followed the path of *anchoresis*, or withdrawal into the desert. The reasons for doing so varied; around Alexandria these hermits were known as *Theraputae*, or healers, and in Upper Egypt another brand of pagan recluses – Gymnosophists – constituted a vigorous and dynamic movement away from the concerns of secular society to lead a life devoted to philosophical contemplation and an existence of severe asceticism.

Within Christian times, the movement towards solitary contemplation began *c.*234 with St Paul the Hermit, but it was arguably only with the advent of St Anthony that the eremitic, solitary lifestyle really began to develop on a larger scale. Anthony, born around 251, decided when about the age of eighteen to renounce his worldly wealth and he retreated into the deserts in search of a lifetime of disci-

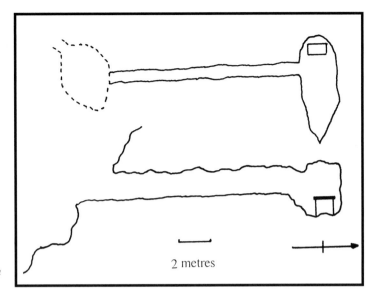

23 *Plan and profile of the cave of St Anthony on Mount Clysma showing the altar within the inner chamber*

2 metres

plined prayer and poverty. In all senses this ascetic way of life sought to focus his mind more upon his relationship with his God, and according to legend his way of life was constantly interrupted by visits from Satan and associated demons seeking to test his faith – a theme developed by Gustave Flaubert in his famous work *The Temptation of St Anthony*.

Initially Anthony retreated into an old pharaonic tomb, but as his fame grew and he was pursued by disciples, he sought sanctuary in a number of other caves and grottoes across lower Egypt, eventually perhaps becoming a victim of his own success. The first kind of small-scale community inspired by the Antonian ideal was Pispir. As hermits such as Anthony became more famous, large numbers of disciples sought them out as teachers, and very quickly loose agglomerations of buildings started to grow up around the central dwelling place of these "desert fathers". These communities did not become centrally organised; they were informal societies with the emphasis placed on the individual, and of course there were no formal rules governing the monastic lifestyle. In time, however, these small settlements began to be enclosed to form *laura* and after the death of Anthony in 356 on Mount Clysma, his tomb would become the focus of pilgrimage and indeed of the wider anchoritic settlement pattern.

The trend towards a more centralised and organised type of monastic ideal was initiated by a near-contemporary of Anthony by the name of Pachomius, or Pachome, but there does appear to be an initial phase where the more group-orientated ideal maiNtains the essence of the raw anchoritic existence. This is especially true of Esna; the underground atrium-style cells or laurum at this site do not seem to lack anything in terms of space or indeed comfort, leading some scholars to suggest that they were clearly modelled on urban upper-class dwellings. This architectural emphasis may reflect the fact that the members of the upper strata of Egypt's society sought the aspects of solitude and asceticism, whereas the lower, poorer classes may have been attracted to the security afforded by the communal, Pachomian ideal.

> In the monasteries derived from Pachomius, the monks did much work, chiefly agricultural, instead of spending their whole time in resisting the temptations of the flesh.

> (Bertrand Russell, 1946, *A History of Western Philosophy*)

In the passage quoted above, we may assume that Russell has his tongue somewhat in cheek; not all the life of the eremitic desert fathers was devoted to self-mortification, but it is true to suggest that they never encouraged any form of communal work. The reaction against the eremitic existence was led by a former Roman soldier by the name of Pachomius (*c.*290-346), who after placing himself under the spiritual direction of a hermit by the name of Palemon started to encourage a more communal way of life among the fellow monks whom he found living at the Laurum of Tabennisi. As Pachomius gradually reorganised the settlement and founded another – or what may be termed a 'true' monastery at Pbow – many converts to this new communal or coenobitic way of life began to join, both male and female.

The basic *modus operandi* of these communes heavily emphasised the group identity rather than the individual; ascetic hermits may have played a small part on the margins of these societies, but it was the strictly ordered world of the coenobium under its titular head or *Hegoumenos* that remained the key focus. This structure may have had its roots in Pachomius' former career as a soldier, and it may be that he consciously modelled his new community on the archetype of an army camp. In a world of strict prayer and self-discipline of the individual, the notion of the communal was enhanced with eating together, worshipping and working together, although the individual could still maintain a degree of choice; monks, for instance, were at liberty to sell their houses if they wished. So successful was the coenobitic way of life that it was subsequently redefined and enhanced by the monk Shenoute (*c.*334-452) who set up his famed White Monastery at Sohag (**colour plate 6**), and the exportation of these ideals to the Levant under St Basil the Great saw the influences of Egyptian monastic Christianity reach a new set of communities.

The key archaeological differences of the two systems would be readily apparent; eremitic monasticism resulting in a less centralised community, frequently with the central focus on the main anchoritic dwelling or tomb. These types of sites, such as Nitria and Kellia, may then have subsequently developed into a more organised *laurum*, or ultimately coenobium. The emphasis on the communal at these types of monastic settlement would see specially organised places of worship, small-scale industrial concerns, communal buildings and guesthouses. Walls, where they existed, served merely to define a settlement spatially within its landscape; with the depredations suffered at the hands of Bedouin desert raiders during later times, however, the walls would take on an enhanced defensive purpose. It is probable that during the fifth century alone in the region around Alexandria there were some 600 monaster-

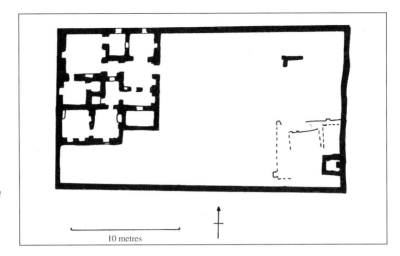

124 *Plan of Kellion mall monks' cells are in the north-western corner*

10 metres

ies, but the number of active inhabited monasteries in Egypt today is only nine. Let us now consider in more detail the archaeological features of Egyptian monasticism.

The spiritual and physical focus of the monastic foundation frequently remained the tomb or dwelling place of an anchorite or desert father; this may have been a simple cave or indeed a re-used pagan tomb as is the case at Nitria, Cellia and the tomb at El Kharga. With the growth of the community of disciples around this focal point, more cells for individual anchorites appeared, and walls gradually appeared to encircle the community. At Cellia, for instance, we see in the fourth century a number of independent cells within their own compounds. By the fifth century, this loose agglomeration of various buildings and dwelling places was enclosed by a wall, and by the seventh century the settlement had enlarged considerably behind a wall that could not be described as being defensive in nature, being only about 70cm (2ft 3in) thick. Clearly, then, the wall served to demarcate the space of the community. At the community of Esna during the sixth century we can recognise two types of dwelling that may be regarded as being semi-eremitic in character; there is as yet no sign of the idealised centralised Pachomian social organisation, rather a sort of transitional phase that may hint at an emerging set of more restrictive social rules designed to give an overall coherence to the community, and perhaps also suggesting an end to the solitary existence and the development of a more companionable way of life. This trend may also be noted at the monastery of St Mark at Qurnat Mari near Luxor; which itself is composed around a re-used pharaonic tomb that served as an anchorite's dwelling. This appropriation of pre-Christian symbol and space can take many other forms. The church of the monastic settlement of Deir Anba Shenouda, excavated by the eminent Egyptologist Flinders Petrie in 1908, contained a hieroglyphic inscription set into the floor. As the congregation entered this church they walked over this stone, and in so doing they were symbolically expressing a disdain for – and rejection of – the pre-Christian religion.

With the development of the ordered and structured Pachomian community, an emphasis on communal rather than solitary acts of worship demanded the presence of

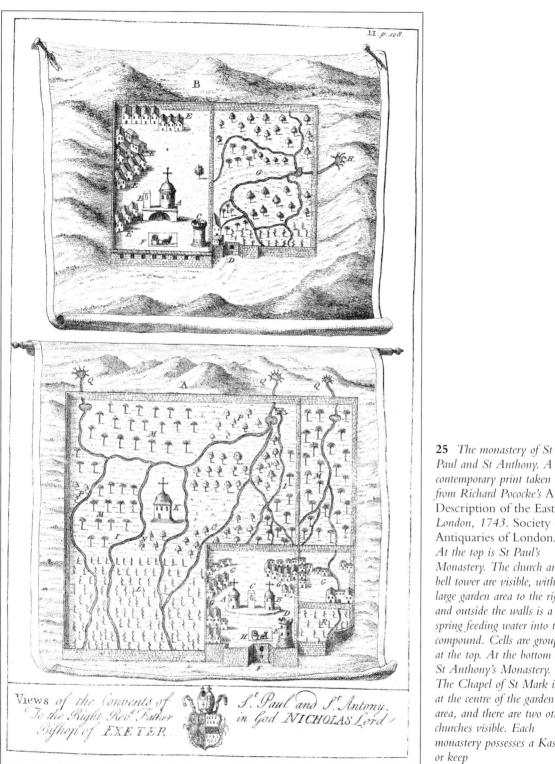

25 *The monastery of St Paul and St Anthony. A contemporary print taken from Richard Pococke's* A Description of the East, *London, 1743. Society of Antiquaries of London. At the top is St Paul's Monastery. The church and bell tower are visible, with a large garden area to the right and outside the walls is a spring feeding water into the compound. Cells are grouped at the top. At the bottom is St Anthony's Monastery. The Chapel of St Mark is at the centre of the garden area, and there are two other churches visible. Each monastery possesses a Kasr, or keep*

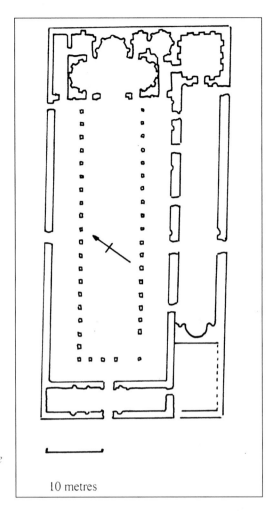

26 *Plan of the monastic church at Deir Anba Sanuda, or the White Monastery. Note the particularly elaborate, buttressed/niched trichonch apsidal configuration*

10 metres

a church. In many cases, monastic churches are close to the usual Egyptian church design, but they have often suffered more architecturally through repeated sackings by marauding Bedouin. Often built from local stone or wattle, daub and plaster, monastic churches often lacked a narthex, and being generally geared to single-sex worship they seldom required the usual gender-based spatial referents inside the church, there was no segregation. A wide variety of monastic church types and internal facets may be recognised, and this fact is partly reflected in the yearly liturgical cycle. Many monasteries have more than one church; some are reserved for daily worship, while others are reserved for special times of the year, such as Lent or Christmas, and the decoration and layout of these churches reflects these cyclic liturgical demands.

The general architectural development of monastic churches may spring from the simple house chapel forms as is noted at the settlement at Dura, and these minor chapels still exist at the Wadi Natrun monasteries. It is only later that the full-scale basilican form emerges, often topped now with beehive or semi-hemispherical domes. Within the framework of the demands of liturgy, a number of key motifs may

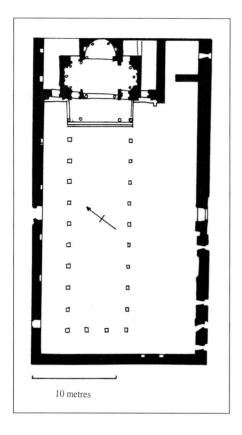

27 *Plan of the church of Deir Anba Bisoi or the Red Monastery. A small flight of steps lead up to the altar*

10 metres

be noted. A feretory is a storage place for relics sacred to the foundation of the monastery, and the sacred use of water is still important within these churches, although it might be thought that there would not be an overtly obvious demand for baptisms in such establishments. The Wadi Natrun monastic churches have large pottery drains set into their floors for washing before prayer, whilst most other churches will contain a Maundy Thursday washing tank and often a separate baptistery area.

Monastic cells, the dwelling places of the monks, are found in a wide variety of forms and sizes. Initially, the basic form of cell for an anchorite would have been a slightly modified cave or old tomb; the monastery of Epiphanius at Thebes, for instance, has a cell (cell A) built within the superstructure of an eleventh-dynasty tomb, to which was latterly added a small vestibule, and perhaps crucially for private contemplation and worship saw the painting of a simple cross on the eastern wall, reflecting the sacred geometry of the standard church sanctuary orientation. More developed cell complexes saw the addition of a number of other basic elements. The cells at Cellia seem to fall into three roughly differing groups of size and complexity, but most possess a discrete sleeping area with bench/bed, a day room with further benches and tables moulded from brick or stone, a kitchen area complete with bread oven and storage facilities within niches set in the interior walls. The dwellings at Bawit are actually multi-storeyed buildings, and the discovery here of pottery vessels set into floors and in niches within the walls shows again the need for storage and the virtually self-contained nature of these dwelling places. The general trend to differentiation of cell size and the presence or absence of certain facilities – as noted at Cellia and Bawit – could appear to indicate the presence of an intra-communal hierarchy and social order; novice monks, for instance, would be expected to have lived communally during their early years at the monastery, whilst more senior figures in the hierarchy attained a larger degree of privacy.

The Pachomian ideal demanded a more integrated social outlook, and this is reflected in the use of refectories for communal meals. Most archaeological examples point to a fairly standardised configuration; the building is usually large, and within it mud-brick benches and tables may be clearly recognised. In some cases, a lectern may be present, emphasising the fact that even while eating the monks of the Pachomian system still had to keep their minds on their whole reason for being there. We know from historical sources that the daily diet of the monks was simple; meat was rarely consumed and the large proportion of meals would mostly have consisted of bread and vegetables. There is little direct archaeobotanical evidence to support this contention, but most examples of kitchens give a clear example of the scale and nature of the daily dietary emphasis. At Cellia, for instance, the bread ovens themselves are built on a very large scale, hinting at a centralised baking organisation to serve the whole community.

The monastery itself needed to be self-sufficient, and as the Pachomian ideal rested on the notion of communal works, it is no surprise that the agricultural work alluded to by Bertrand Russell in the quote at the top of the section should form such a key component of the social lifestyles of a Pachomian monastery, and that Pachomian monastic settlements are always sited within zones of cultivable land. Whilst the anchorites, with the emphasis on the individual alone, could look after themselves by begging, receiving alms, scavenging or by maintaining a small garden, the larger-scale Pachomian communities demanded a more organised economic base. Areas for milling corn have been noted at Cellia, and the utilisation of ceramic pipes as conduits may hint at small-scale irrigation of the main growing areas. Also of importance at Cellia was salt-processing; here this required a small conduit system for water supply as well as an open area for evaporation and the separation of the salt. There is additional evidence from the monastery of Anba Hadra for oil presses and wine presses, but today the consumption of alcohol in monasteries is generally forbidden. A ready source of revenue for these establishments would have been catering for the needs of pilgrims visiting the tomb of the founder, and this concern is reflected in the building of dedicated guesthouses; large buildings with a number of simple rooms and a communal eating area. In short, these were self-contained settlements with extensive land-holdings and homes to monks, who in addition to their spiritual labours, became skilled agricultural workers and artisans in their own right. The military analogy of a regimented, structured existence is again clear, and it is perhaps no surprise that these forms of monastic settlement tended to attract people from much poorer backgrounds.

During the ninth century, the remote and isolated monastic communities of the desert margins became easy targets for Bedouin raiders, and it became clear that new measures would be required to maintain the security of these settlements. Perhaps the most obvious change is the upgrading of the perimeter walls; from merely being thin and occasionally discontinuous means of marking the settlement margins, the walls were rapidly reinforced to incorporate a system of bastions and gatehouses for controlling access. The walls of the Monastery of St Anthony's, for example, are about 10m (33ft) high and 1m (3ft) in thickness, faced with limestone and irregularly buttressed. Another defensive measure that emerges at this time is the Kasr, or central keep.

A Kasr is a large, rectangular, heavily fortified and centrally located building containing cells, storerooms, a well and storage areas for food to cater for sheltering monks; in function rather than form it clearly recalls the round towers of early Irish monasteries. Apart from providing all means necessary to enable the population of the monastery to hold out against attack, the Kasr also incorporates a distinctive ideological motif. All Kasr towers contain a chapel, and these chapels are dedicated to the Archangel Michael, a symbol of protection. St Michael is also recognised in Europe as providing protection against evil, and it is noteworthy that many church dedications are situated on high ground, indicating perhaps some symbolic link between the idea of altitude and protection rather than the obvious functional consideration. At Cellia, there are two keeps, whilst the keep at Epiphanius is over 17m (51ft) in height; this itself is dwarfed in scale and complexity by the Kasr of Deir Abu Maqar, which is over 21m (63 ft) in height, is reached by a drawbridge and has not just one, but many chapels dedicated to St Michael. In some cases, the Kasr would provide an emergency burial ground for monks killed by raiders, and some bodies have been found within these structures, but by and large burial practice was similar to the rites common amongst the laity.

Whilst the solitary hermits were buried alone in their dwellings, which latterly attained the status of shrines, the Pachomian system remained with the ordinary monk through his death, and into the afterlife. At Epiphanius in Thebes we see one of the best examples of a large monastic extra-mural cemetery; bodies are bound up and preserved in salt and juniper – following on from much earlier Egyptian post-mortem customs and rites. Also of interest is the fact that the usual Christian grave orientation is rarely adhered to; at Epiphanius the heads are usually turned to the south-west. By and large graves are simple, but the tombs at Deir Anba Hadra have rectangular superstructures with vaulted roofs. Perhaps the ideal place to see the funerary rites of monastic communities is at the modern monastery of Deir as Surian, the monastery of the Syrians, where the mummies of former abbots are still kept.

How have these concepts survived and developed today? One of the best known of the modern Egyptian monasteries is that of St Anthony (Deir Anba Antunius), a community of some 40 monks located about 18km (11 miles) from the Red Sea coast and with a foundation, according to historical sources, during the fourth century. The monastery itself lies at the foot of Mount Clysma, according to legend the location of the last hermitage of St Anthony. Very little of the original fabric of the community remains; the settlement was enlarged during the fifth century, and again during the eleventh. By the thirteenth century, the monastic establishment was flourishing; the contemporary Armenian traveller Abu Salih noted with pleasure the

28 *Eighteenth-century paintings of St Anthony and St Paul at the Monastery of St Anthony*

wealth of the community and the abundance of its orchards, but in the wider struggle between the Melkites and monophysites, the monastery remained at the centre of the trouble and it is known that the community changed allegiances a number of times. Bedouin attacks in the fifteenth century largely destroyed the monastery, and the extant buildings visible today largely date from the rebuilding programme of the sixteenth century.

The present compound is enclosed by a 10m-high (33ft) wall encompassing an area of about 7ha (18 acres), and the layout is not dissimilar to any neighbouring agricultural village with its own wells and gardens. Five churches cater to the spiritual needs of the community; the Church of St Anthony contains remnants of the sixteenth-century rebuilding work and in some cases smoke blackening is clearly visible, perhaps from the earlier Bedouin raids, which would hint at earlier architectural elements being present within the building. This church is used in the winter season alone, whilst the eighteenth-century Church of the Apostles is host to religious services during the summer. Nearby anchoritic caves recall the origins of this community, and under the south side of the Church of St George at nearby Deir al Maimun is one of St Anthony's habitation grottoes, an indication of the importance in the folk memory of the founding desert father.

Another important group of monasteries may be found in the Wadi Natrun, or Scetis Desert. The monastery of Deir al Barami was largely plundered in the fourteenth and fifteenth centuries, and little of the original monastery survives. This settlement became infamous during the nineteenth century when European visitors noted that the immense and rich manuscript collection was piled up in a decaying state in the library; in some cases these collections were ruthlessly plundered. Many monastic libraries were denuded of their prize manuscripts by avaricious collectors, and this factor – allied to the general state of the libraries themselves in former times, as well as the ever-present risk of raiding by Bedouin groups – has severely affected the survival of important Coptic religious manuscripts. Of additional interest are the nearby monasteries of Deir Abu Maqar – which became the residence of the Coptic Patriarch of Alexandria in the seventh century and latterly turned towards the Melkites – and Deir al Muharraq, with its immense court, Kasr and guesthouse; there is also a church which is claimed to be the oldest in the world, and although largely restored in the twelfth century, the distinct stela-shaped altar is dated to 747. Before leaving the subject of Egyptian monasticism, we should consider briefly one of the most famous monasteries in the world: St Catherine's in Sinai.

Although the Sinai peninsular may be considered as a halfway point, neither Africa nor Asia geographically, this community, which is a Greek Orthodox rather than Coptic foundation, is widely recognised as being one of the great monasteries of the world. The first chapel here was built by the Byzantine Empress Helena in 327 to commemorate Mount Sinai and the story of Moses and the burning bush. St Catherine was an Egyptian victim of the fourth-century Diocletian persecutions, so in a sense, and with the general configuration of the settlement, the monastery has to be considered alongside the Egyptian examples discussed above. In a recent

29 *A fourth/fifth century marble statue of St Menas, Graeco-Roman Museum, Alexandria*

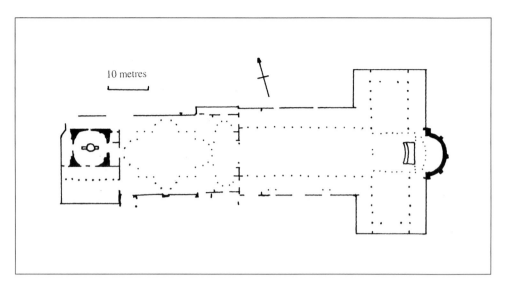

30 *Abu Menas. Reconstruction of the fifth-century basilica. Note the crypt and shrine complex at the western end*

paper in the journal *World Archaeology* in 1994, Coleman and Elsner consider the nature of the manipulation of sacred space at the monastery, especially in the way that the pilgrims are led through nodes in the landscape imbued with a wider allegorical biblical symbolism, to effect a sense of spiritual transformation. For the pilgrim, it is this sense of self-change that is the most important element of the act, and away from the monastic sphere, there is another intriguing Egyptian site that may help us in defining the archaeological perspective on the act of pilgrimage.

31 *The site of Abu Menas today; the modern monastery is in the background.* Sarah Mulligan

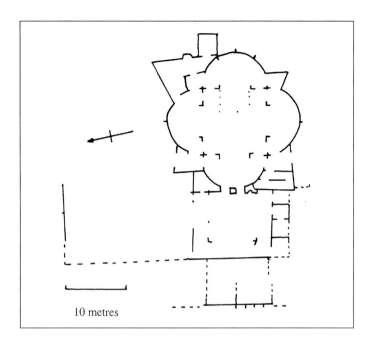

32 *Plan of the eastern church at Abu Menas. The curvature of the walls is especially interesting*

10 metres

The cultural context of pilgrimage in Egypt

Another member of the grisly roll call of Egyptian martyrdom was a soldier by the name of Menas, who met his death in 296. According to legend, Menas' body was transported miraculously from his dying place in Asia Minor to a spot 40km (25 miles) to the south of Alexandria, where it was guarded by two camels who refused to leave the side of the corpse. Menas' remains were subsequently interred in an ancient hypogeum building with lateral burial chambers and access yielded by a long vertical shaft. Very soon, for reasons still unclear, Menas' fame spread throughout the Christian community in Egypt and his grave soon became a pilgrimage centre of some importance. The first act in commemorating the martyr during the fourth century was to build a small limestone church on top of his tomb, but by the fifth century it is possible that the added weight of pilgrim numbers was beginning to have an effect on the tomb itself, and at some stage in the fifth century the church was ringed by a mudbrick wall, which in turn was supplanted by a large tripartite basilica. This great basilica was a truly monumental undertaking; the main structure of the building measured some 60m by 26m (187ft by 85ft), and the internal divisions were effected by 56 monumental columns; the baptistery itself was also on the large scale, measuring 12m by 14m (39ft by 46ft), so it is clear that the scale of the buildings reflected the great popularity of the site as well as the large amount of wealth now being brought in by pilgrims from all over the eastern Christian world. This basilica was destroyed in the seventh century, but the floor plan of the one visible from archaeological excavations by a German team in 1905 – itself an eighth-century re-build – conforms fairly well to the basic outline of the original.

A number of other churches also catered for the pilgrim masses, and not surprisingly the town (now known as Abu Menas) began to attract a number of hermits ready to share in the pilgrim-orientated holy business being developed here. So important was the town that royalty also began to be attracted, and began to build on the grand scale. The Imperial citadel of Zeno, for instance, had its own white marble basilica, a building measuring 20m by 10m (66ft by 33ft), which had depressions let into the floor for holding water, as well as a number of water vessels all bearing invocations to St Menas. This link between water and sanctity is a common pilgrim motif.

Water became the key religious commodity at Abu Menas; rather like an Egyptian Lourdes, this water was held to have strong curative properties, long after the cult of St Mena had declined. For the early pilgrims, the object of the water-based symbolism was a large 150m-square pool, and before leaving town for home, they carefully filled vessels with water to take with them. These vessels, or ampullae, are one of the most distinct indicators of the economic and ideological importance of the town of Abu Menas. The vessels have been found over a large area of northern Egypt, and were mainly locally produced at the site. These containers come in two very distinct forms: the first type is a flat, gourd-like shape with an imprint showing St Menas in military dress; the other type is as a moulded vase in the shape of a man's head – it is not clear if this is meant to be the saint himself. Also popular were female figurines, perhaps indicative of the Virgin Mary.

Abu Menas clearly had to gear itself up to receiving regularly large numbers of pilgrims who had obviously to be fed and given shelter; the massive covered market bears witness to this provision, as do the *xenodochia* or great guesthouses. So successful was the pilgrim centre of Abu Menas, that a specially constructed port was built nearby on the coast at Philoxonite to allow for the swift transit of pilgrims to the town. Within that uneasy relationship between making money and providing the masses with their religious sustenance, it was clear that Abu Menas was something of a success, and in the context of the archaeology of Egyptian Christianity, a unique and intriguing site.

Discussion

Unlike Roman north Africa, where essentially a Romanised brand of Christianity developed during the first three centuries AD, Egyptian Christians still carried a folk memory of their ancient Egyptian religious heritage, and it is perhaps here more than in Roman north Africa that we can clearly identify a deep syncretic motif. Modern Copts still regard themselves as the guardians of this ancient memory. The destruction or re-use of the ancient temples sought to stamp on this idea, but more often than not, especially in the realms of art and the development of Coptic literature this ancient memory could never be fully erased. Another contrast between these case studies is in the general research-orientated biases.

33 *Coptic church furniture: a richly-decorated fan.* Society of
Antiquaries of London

Within the academic scholarly sense, it is probably also true that early Egyptian
Christianity has never really seen the scale of research undertaken in Roman north
Africa; there the Church, state and economic system were all well integrated, while
in Egypt it has too often been the archaeology of earlier periods that has caught the
academic and indeed public imagination, and the development of the early Church

here has never been really viewed as having the same research cachet, or indeed status within the overall Roman socio-economic system. From this chapter we have seen just how much Egypt does have to offer, not just in the African context, but for understanding the formative development of Christianity as a whole: the heritage of monasticism, the dynamism of Alexandria and the intriguing finds of early Christian writings all speak to us down the centuries of a brand of dynamic Christianity almost without parallel in the ancient world. It is this heritage, linked with that of a far earlier, pre-Christian root that gives the modern Copts their identity, and ensures that they will remain amongst the great survivors.

Now, by way of a contrast, we look to the south of Egypt's borders, into Nubia, where political and economic conditions conspired against the brother Christians of these Copts. In Nubia, unlike Egypt, the fight for survival was ultimately lost, and if it was not for the varied range of Christian-period archaeological material, we might never have known that Christianity had existed there at all.

Further reading

For a broad understanding of the historical background to the emergence of Egyptian Christianity, a useful starting point is: A. Bowman, *Egypt after the Pharaohs: 332 BC - AD 642*, (London: British Museum Press). Other useful histories include: O. Meinardus (1999) *Two Thousand Years of Coptic Christianity* (Cairo: American University Press), and R. Bagnall (1993) *Egypt in Late Antiquity* (Princeton: Princeton University Press).

The most useful introductions to the Copts themselves are: C. Cannuyer (2000) *Coptic Egypt: The Christians of the Nile* (London: Thames and Hudson), J. Kamil (1987) *Coptic History and Guide* (Cairo: American University Press) and B. Watterson (1988) *Coptic Egypt* (Edinburgh: Scottish Academic Press). An exceptionally interesting and recent work on the modern Coptic Church, its wider role and outlook is: J. Watson (2000) *Among the Copts* (Brighton, Sussex Academic Press). A good and accessible work for understanding the controversy surrounding the Nag Hammadi texts is E. Pagels (1979) *The Gnostic Gospels* (New York: Random House).

Peter Grossman, a German archaeologist, provides perhaps the most important sources for the excavation of early Egyptian Christian communities, as well as the development of Egyptian ecclesiastical architecture; the majority of his site reports as used here have been gleaned from the bulletin of the German Archaeological Institute in Cairo (*Mitteilungen des Deutsches Archaeologisches Instituts Kairo*); these reports are all in German, so for more accessible, although by necessity more brief reports, the reader is directed to his varied and many contributions to the indispensable *Coptic Encyclopedia*, an eight-volume work edited by Aziz Atiyah (Macmillan, New York, 1991). This really is the standard reference work for Coptic studies, is exceptionally comprehensive and brings together contributions by an excellent range of international scholars.

Two key works present a useful and comprehensive overview of developments in Egyptian monasticism: O. Meinardus (1962) *Monks and Monasteries of the Egyptian Desert*, (Cairo: American University Press) and C. Walters (1974) *Monastic Archaeology in Egypt*, (Warminster: Aris and Philips). A number of individual reports on monasteries are also very useful and fairly accessible, among the most important are: P. Van Moorsel (1995) *Le Monastère de St Antoine* (three volumes, published by the French Institute for Eastern Archaeology in Cairo) and a sister two-volume set on *Kellia* (Cellia) by N. Heinein and M. Wuttman (2000). Both are superbly illustrated and contain comprehensive architectural detail and plans. Although quite dated, the occasionally in-print book H. Evelyn White's *The Monasteries of the Wadi Natrun* (New York: Metropolitan Museum of Art, 1932) represents a thorough survey of the monastic archaeology and modern settlement in this important region of Egypt. The concept of pilgrimage, archaeology and sacred space at St Catherine's Sinai is discussed in S. Coleman and J. Elsner (1994), 'The Pilgrim's Progress: art, architecture and ritual movement at Sinai', in *World Archaeology* 26/1, pages 73-89.

4 Backwaters of the Nile?
The development of Christianity
in medieval Nubia

One of the most remarkable archaeological rescue acts of the twentieth century took place on the southern borders of Egypt in the 1960s. The construction of the New Aswan Dam, while vital for the well-being of Egypt's population, was about to threaten one of the most archaeologically-rich landscapes in Africa; most of what was traditionally recognised as the northern portion of ancient Nubia – or Lower Nubia – was about to disappear under the steadily rising waters of Lake Nasser. As the local animal and human populations frantically sought the safety of higher ground, an archaeological salvage operation – unprecedented in terms of scale and international co-operation – was in full swing. The race was on to rescue Nubia's archaeological heritage from the waters. One of the enduring images of the rescue act was the complete removal of Rameses II's magnificent Abu Simbel temple to safer ground, but other international archaeological teams were busy recording a wide range of archaeological material, from lower Palaeolithic sites to the remains of the ancient cathedral at Faras.

Defining the rather elastic limits of ancient Nubia is a problematic exercise; Lake Nasser now covers the northern (lower) part of Nubia, i.e. that region between the first and second cataracts of the Nile. Moving southwards, through the Dal Cataract and past the third cataract we come to the important early Nubian site of Kerma. Southwards still is Old Dongola, and then the river turns eastwards and slightly northwards, through the fourth cataract, before turning again southwards to the fifth cataract and the confluence with the Atbara river just north of the site of Meroe. Curving again westwards, past the sixth cataract, we come to the confluence of the White Nile – flowing from its source in Uganda at Lake Victoria – with the Blue Nile, which originates from Lake Tana in the far-off Ethiopian highlands. The modern capital of Sudan, Khartoum, sits at the meeting place of these two mighty branches of Africa's longest river. This thin ribbon of land, agriculturally fertile for a short distance either side of a river snaking through the desert on its long journey to the Mediterranean, may usefully define the focus of human settlement in Nubia.

Nubia usually presented a continual thorn in the side to the ancient Egyptians; it was never satisfactorily subjugated, but offered scope for extensive economic exploitation. Racially, the Nubians were noted as being much different from the

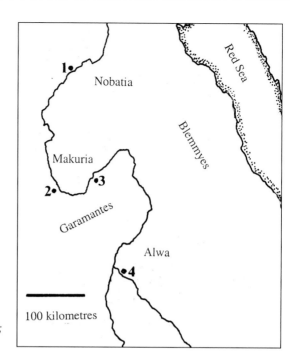

34 *Medieval Nubia showing principal tribal areas and states. Key to sites: 1. Faras; 2: Old Dongola; 3. Ghazali; 4. Soba*

ancient Egyptians, they spoke their own language and had their own world-view. It is difficult to understand the origins of the name Nubia; it may derive from the Egyptian *Nbw*, taken to mean gold, but to the Egyptians it was always *Ta-Sety*, or Kush. Mankind had exploited the fertile river margins from the earliest times; certainly thanks to the work of the salvage archaeologists we have a fairly clear idea of the regional cultural sequence from the first inhabitants onwards. For early Holocene-period hunter-gatherer peoples, this region offered excellent scope for exploitation. After the last ice age, when the climate was much wetter than today, the Sahara took on the appearance of a large interlinked chain of lakes and watercourses. The hunter-gatherers of this region settled on the margins of the lakes, which produced a plentiful supply of fish, and hunted game and gathered plant foods. Widely-spread finds of intensively-settled sites, complete with remains of a broad range of aquatic animals, bone harpoons for fishing and pots decorated with a distinctive wavy-line motif attest to the long-lived economic success of this lifestyle.

Later on, early farming peoples, building on the success of the early economic adaptations, settled in the area. It is one of the key conundrums in African archaeology that plant remains from these sites do not show evidence of the one important local crop that would be expected to have been intensively utilised: sorghum. Today, and certainly in historic times, sorghum was a vital crop to the Nubians; it grows well in all sorts of soil, is exceptionally salt-resistant, and can provide for a wide range of needs, including bread- and beer-making, and its stalks can be used for making fences. In this important area of northern Africa, we may hypothesise that some of the earliest farmers flourished, and in time this thin strip of land to the side of the river was able to provide for large numbers of inhabitants; with the development of successful irrigation technology – such as the *saqia* waterwheel – larger tracts of land could be utilised for agriculture. Already an uneasy socio-economic dichotomy between the river-based farmer and the cattle pastoralists of the adjoining desert zones was developing; this is a theme that recurs throughout the history of Nubia.

The trouble with Egypt

With such a dependable and successful agricultural base, it was perhaps inevitable that some form of a more complex social structure would arise along the Nubian river margins. At around the time of the Egyptian pre-dynastic period – during the fourth millennium BC – the so-called A-Group culture emerged in northern Nubia. The A-Group peoples had a fully agricultural economic base, probably relying on sheep and goat herding, a small cattle herding component, and cereal cultivation. These peoples had undoubted affinities with contemporary Egyptian cultures, but were recognisably Nubian; their distinctive burial practices and imported elements of Egyptian material culture hint at a large degree of contact. Economic relations with Egypt gradually waned, but from around 2300 BC the so-called C-Group peoples emerged in the north, and again maintained extensive cultural contact with Egypt. Egypt maintained a strong interest in Nubia, and during the Middle Kingdom (2000-1600 BC) they garrisoned the north of the country with a series of military forts, although around 1700 BC they retreated from Nubia, at a time when in the south, centred at Kerma itself, the Kerma polity flared brilliantly.

Kerma was a purely southern Nubian phenomenon; having first appeared at around 2400 BC, it maintained a degree of independent and extensive trade contact; its rulers were buried in fabulous, large grave mounds, and the presence of huge monumental buildings – *deffufas* – attests to the overall wealth of the polity. Nemesis arrived – as usual – from the north with the Egyptians, and Kerma, one of the first manifestations of an independent Nubian complex society, was subjugated at around 1500 BC, although it later reasserted itself under the Egyptian cultural yoke when in the ninth century BC the ruler of the resurgent Kingdom of Kush – a polity centred on Napata at the fourth cataract – marched northwards, defeated the Egyptians, and the unthinkable happened: the new pharaohs of the 25th dynasty were foreigners from the south.

In 671 BC the Assyrians invaded Egypt and the Kushite overlords were driven back home southwards, returning to Napata, but later moving upstream to Meroe around 300 BC. Now, far to the south of Egypt's reach, a truly Nubian culture was able to re-assert itself, drawing on a wide agricultural base and a network of regional trade routes, although for the inhabitants of Meroe, Napata retained a certain ideological importance. The rulers of Meroe held coronation ceremonies there, and continued to build temples at their spiritual home.

In popular archaeological parlance, the Meroitic polity has been christened the 'Birmingham of Africa'; this name derives from the evidence of large-scale iron-working at Meroe. The huge slag heaps that are witness to the importance of iron-working in the Meroitic economy probably date from no later than the second century BC, and the finished iron goods were traded to a limited extent throughout Africa and indeed in the Roman political sphere. Culturally, Meroe owed a great deal to Egyptian influence: steeply angled pyramids recall the much earlier Egyptian prototypes; its kingship was held to be semi-divine, and although a key figure in the Meroitic pantheon was the lion-headed god Apedemak, Egyptian cultic elements survived in a remarkable display of syncretism. A Meroitic language also developed; its distinctive cursive alphabet has been transliterated but its script has yet to be translated. Meroe was attacked by the Aksumite King Ezana around the first half of the fourth century AD, and its role as an independent Nubian economy was effectively reduced. These events, described in a fourth-century Aksumite inscription, also mention peoples called the Noba, and it is the Noba peoples who probably formed the basis of the succeeding Ballana culture.

The beginnings of Nubian Christianity

Into this political and cultural vacuum, a new culture – with clear Meroitic antecedents – emerged. The Ballana culture, formerly known as the X-Group, developed in the north during the fifth century AD; the sixth-century Greek writer Procopius mentions disparate groups such as the Nobadae and Blemmyes, pastoralist peoples who originated within the desert zones, and it would be reasonable to suggest that they should be identified with the Ballana culture. The Ballana culture was exceptionally distinctive; burial evidence from the cemeteries at Ballana and Qustul showing a great wealth differentiation among individual graves; some of the more elaborate, probably kingly burials had associated grave goods which included: servants, livestock, jewellery and cooking utensils, and from an ideological perspective it is clear that traditional Egyptian religion remained important alongside the worship of local deities such as Apedemak and the sun god Mandulis. After Justinian's prohibition of pagan worship at the Temple of Philae, it would appear – at least according to Procopius – that the Nobadae were invited by the Romans to settle the border zone to act as a buffer against the aggressive Blemmyes. In some cases they were clearly successful, as is recorded by the actions of the King of the Nobadae (Nobatia), Silko, who boasted of his crushing victories over the Blemmyes.

During the sixth century, the distinctive written Nubian language began to appear, and it may be possible that some degree of small-scale Christian conversion amongst the Nobatians was taking place; although historical sources do not adequately elucidate this matter, some scholars have argued for a settled Christian presence in Nobatia (Lower Nubia) – betokened by very small-scale church remains and limited burial evidence – before the sixth-century events as described by John of Ephesus (who it will be recalled may not be a totally disinterested observer). A Coptic inscription at the temple of Dendur, however, implies that around 550 the local king by the name of Eirpanome had converted the temple to use as a church

35 *The cathedral at Faras in the 1960s*

(much as had been done at Philae) and this gives us a fairly firm date for the emergence of Christianity in Lower Nubia.

The cyclic nature of Nubian cultural development is no better illustrated than by the picture of early complex polities in the region; birth, destruction, rebirth, it is a theme that carries on into the Christian era, and it is against this background of social and economic flux that we see the emergence of the small-scale state polities of the middle Nile that would later embrace Christianity. Nobatia, centred on the area between the first and second cataracts had its capital at Faras or Pachoras, with additional importance attached to the fortress settlement at Qasr Ibrim. Makuria, with its capital at Old Dongola, extended from the third cataract to the Butana, and in the seventh century would undergo political union with Nobatia. Far to the south was the isolated polity of Alwa – as it was known to the Arabs, or Alodia to the Greek speakers – centred on its capital at Soba. The traditional story of the competing missions as described by the monophysite John of Ephesus will be remembered from chapter 1, but it would appear that the problem was far more complex.

Nobatia undoubtedly drew a great deal on the ecclesiastical influence of the monophysite Egyptians, but would also have had extensive contacts with the Byzantine world, so it is probable that both arms of eastern Christianity were represented here; indeed epigraphic evidence from Nobatian tombstones of the Christian period shows clear evidence of a more dyophysite, Byzantine influence, and at any rate the liturgical disagreements could not have been so serious as to threaten the supposedly peaceful union between a seemingly monophysite Nobatia and dyophysite Makuria. The liturgical complexities and shifts may also have had some-

1 *Mosaic at the church of San Vitale, Ravenna, Italy, showing the Emperor Justinian, a main character in the story of Africa's early churches*

2 *Luxor, Egypt. The modern Haggag mosque is situated within a possible former church, itself sited within the massive Temple of Amon Ra*

3 *Cairo: the interior of Al Moallaqha, or the Hanging Church. The ambon, or pulpit is to the left, and note the particularly ornate sanctuary screen*

4 *Cairo: the Hanging Church. An example of Coptic church painting showing Our Lady and an infant Jesus*

5 *Detail of the Necropolis at Al Bagawat*

6 *The external walls of the White Monastery, Sohag. This is the birthplace of the Pachomian monastic ideal*

7 *Old Dongola: view of the churches area under investigation.* Jacke Phillips

8 *Old Dongola, mosque. A Christian fresco of a horseman, now destroyed.* Jacke Phillips

9 *Old Dongola: Church of the Granite Columns..* Jacke Phillips

11 *At the back of the cave containing the monastic churches of Yemrehane Kristos, near Lalibela, are a number of remarkably well-preserved desiccated bodies lying in a heap. Legend has it that these remains are almost a thousand years old, and are the bodies of Coptic pilgrims from Egypt*

Opposite: **10** *Aksum, Ethiopia. The festival of Maryam Zion, 1996. The Patriarch is enthroned before stela 3*

12 *The monastery of Abba Pantaleon on its high rock pinnacle to the east of Aksum*

13 *Modern ecclesiastical church painting: a colourful scene of the temptation of Christ at the church of Webla Maryam, Semema, Shire, Tigray, Ethiopia*

15 *The painted refectory building of the monastery of Giorgis, Shire, Tigray, Ethiopia*

Opposite: **14** *Old Palapye church, Botswana.* Andrew Reid

16 *A west African interpretation of Our Lady: Fadioute, Senegal, carved by Laurent Ndonc.* Frank Willett

17 *The Lutheran church in Cape Town during the early nineteenth century*

18 *A southern African interpretation of Our Lady: Serima, Zimbabwe. Our Lady, carved from jacaranda wood*

thing to do with changing political allegiances and/or expressions of Nobatian independence and nationalism; it is clear that while in the north the picture remains opaque, in the south Alwa was always on the outside looking in. Alwa's population was excluded from the *Baqt*, and its distance from Egypt and proximity to the monophysite Aksumite court may have resulted in a different shade of monophysite Christianity here.

An archaeological perspective

Having briefly outlined the socio-political historical picture, we now turn to a consideration of what the archaeological remains can tell us about the idiosyncratic development of Christianity in these small medieval polities, but before doing so it might be as well to sketch in a brief history of archaeological research in the region. Although we have a number of mainly Arab historical sources to work with, actual archaeological interest in Nubia began in the nineteenth century, but full-scale research did not really become established until the early years of the twentieth century under the aegis of the doyen of Nubian archaeology, the American George Reisner, whose observations and cultural sequences form the basis of the discipline today. It took the building of the High Aswan Dam in the 1960s to bring archaeology in Nubia into sharper focus; faced with the destruction of thousands of square miles of prime archaeological material, an unsurpassed international effort – under the direction of the American archaeologist William Adams and Swedish archaeologist Hans-Ake Nordstrom – raced against the rising waters to provide the best possible picture of cultural evolution in the area between the first and second cataracts since the earliest times.

This intensity of archaeological research has provided a somewhat partial picture of Nubian archaeology, and it should be noted that almost all of the Nobatian polity was submerged. As such, we have a far clearer picture of the archaeology of Nobatian Christianity than anywhere else, although the work of earlier scholars such as Reisner, Griffiths, Mileham and latterly Ugo Monneret de Villard has provided us with a fairly broad database of Christian antiquities in Nubia. Of special importance to this study is the capital of Faras, the excavation concession of which was handed to a Polish team under the direction of K. Michalowski, a move which signalled the continuing involvement of Polish archaeologists in the wider region, evidence of which may be found in the superb range of publications emanating from Warsaw to this day. Another effect of this concession system – and one that in today's archaeological climate may sound unbelievable – was the equal division of spoils between the Sudanese museum authorities and the concession teams' host institutions. Today the Faras frescoes in the National Museum in Warsaw are as magnificent and numerous as those in the National Museum in Khartoum.

Recently attention has shifted southwards, and today Polish teams are active in the former kingdom of Makuria and its capital at Old Dongola, while to the south a British archaeological team has worked in the almost archaeologically virgin territory of Soba, the capital of Alwa. Many gaps remain in the picture; a large archaeological database furnished by the salvage excavations in Lower Nubia, with more patchy coverage further south and east, so before considering specific evidence, let us look – on a general level – at what the extensive Nobatian database can tell us of the archaeology of Christianity in Nubia.

Geographical circumstance has defined the evolution of the Nubian church on a physical as well as social level. Tied into the thin river margins, the socio-economic outlook of the Nubian medieval states was towards the river and the communication potential facilitated by the Nile. On a cultural level, i.e. within the built environment, the inhabitants of the riverine zones had few choices for their building medium. Churches were mainly of mud brick – which survives in the archaeological record poorly – or red (fired) brick with a stone substructure; these foundation courses were often of plentiful local sandstone, or of the more desirable and sturdy granites found in the desert margins.

On the basis of the work in Lower Nubia, William Adams was able to define four key stages in the evolution of church architecture. The earliest churches were probably of the familiar Byzantine basilica type, a rectangular building with two aisles flanking a nave. It is possible that the basilica types, popular from the sixth century, show evidence of more than a cultural contact with the Melkite Byzantine world, and may herald a much earlier dyophysite Christian community in Nubia than the historical sources suggest. Adam's so-called early Nubian style (*c.*650–800) sees a slight shift from the classical basilica form, and it is possible that this shift may betoken a change in spatial perception within the church building brought on either by liturgical change or an individualistic statement by Nubian church-builders.

The classical Nubian style (*c.*800-1150) now sees the apogee of local ecclesiastical architecture; the special feature of this type of church is the addition of an eastern passage to the basic form, leading between the baptistery in the south to the vestry in the north; this passage would have facilitated access across the central axis

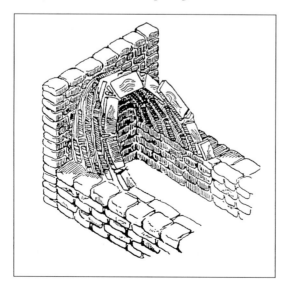

36 *Reconstruction of a typical medieval Nubian brick vaulted roof*

of the church without the clergy having to set foot in the *heikal*, or holy sanctuary. In addition, there began a trend towards separating the nave and sanctuary by means of a brick wall; the obvious conclusion being that now the sanctuary was taking on a far more secretive, spiritual role in the overall spatial perception, whether through a direct liturgical shift or local preference.

Adam's scheme for later Nubian churches (*c*.1150–1400) sees smaller buildings and a general loss of a separate walk-in baptistery tank; the focus now was on the sanctuary area, and it is probable that the congregation was physically kept outside the church, with only the priests allowed inside. The baptism question is also important, implying a gradual separation of the layperson from the actual building; it would seem that baptisms could be easily carried out in the Nile with no special facility set aside for one of Christianity's most holy sacraments. Again, these changes could indicate a liturgical shift, but may also have some degree of socio-economic implication. At this period the status of Christianity was becoming more uncertain in the face of gradual Muslim pressure from the north, so it is possible that economic criteria played a direct role in these physical changes. Adams's typological scheme is perhaps too simplistic to take into account the totality of the Christian archaeological remains across all of Nubia, but his broad conclusions generally hold well, perhaps indicating a shift away from Egyptian influence to a more Byzantine, eastern outlook as Egypt became more inaccessible after the Muslim incursions.

Unlike the Copts or Ethiopians, we cannot ask a Nubian Christian about spatial and symbolic perceptions within these buildings, we just have to guess through analogy with Coptic or Byzantine practice, but there is no doubt that within the church building, many layers of symbolism were embedded in the layout and decoration. Baptisteries in Nubian churches, for instance, are mainly located to the south-east of the nave or narthex, although the tank at Ghazili is outside the main body of the building. Being a monastic church, this may indicate special spatial referents within the coenobitic liturgy. Wlodiemiercz Godlewski, a Polish excavator at Old Dongola, has suggested that broad patterns may be discerned in baptistery development within Nubia; a broad temporal trend sees a development from large, circular tanks to square fonts which after the eleventh century are generally mounted on a pedestal or base (as, indeed is seen in most western churches today). As with the overall development in church architecture, it appears that the emphasis shifts away from the communal and more towards a closed liturgical space; this shift could be mirrored in the baptistery tanks, away from large, walk-in tanks with an emphasis on wider participation towards a more private, smaller scale of baptism.

From the available archaeological evidence, we can deduce that a number of recurring features are present in Nubian church architecture and decoration. Within the nave, it is clear that the roof – be it a vault or flat roof – was supported by granite pillars which, being covered by a layer of paint or plaster, were occasionally painted with frescoes. Stone capitals and stone doorjambs and lintels were richly decorated with a wide variety of motifs that reached a zenith by the eighth century. Granite capitals have been noted in Upper Nubia, but are generally scarce and not surpris-

37 *Frescoes at Faras; note that the eyes have been removed, probably by Muslim peoples*

ingly have often been robbed out in recent antiquity to provide for modern architectural embellishments; fishes, crosses, vine leaves and palm leaves are among the
motifs that feature on these distinctive elements.

Wall paintings or frescoes played an important role in the decoration of the
church. Perhaps the best known and best researched are those removed by the Polish
expedition from Faras cathedral, where careful peeling away of plaster and advanced
conservation techniques allowed at least nine separate phases of motif development
to be defined. Wall paintings were mainly a northern Nubian phenomenon and really began to be painted on a large scale from the eighth to fourteenth centuries. A
number of themes predominate. The life of Christ is an obvious motif and depictions of Christ alongside the Virgin Mary are largely found within the apse of the
church, flanked by apostles, saints and angels. Another religious motif that is fairly
widespread depicts three young men who are about to fall into a fire being saved by
the Archangel Michael (cf. north Africa and Egypt). It is clear that the positioning
and content of these narrative scenes, as well as individual elements, had a degree of
symbolic value in the perception of holy space; it is not surprising that Christ should
be the central image, but secular motifs are also important. Depictions of kings and
bishops, some identified by name, have been noted within the religious iconograph-
ic realm, linking the political patronage and wealth to the sacred sphere.

Away from the most obvious architectural elements and use of space, there is
plentiful evidence for Christian burial. It has been mooted that Nobatia had a small
Christian community during the fifth century, before the historical sources suggest

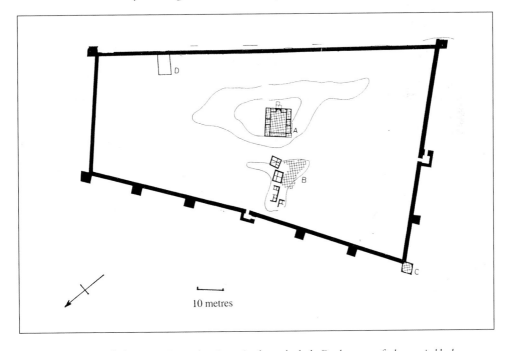

38 *Plan of the walled area at Faras showing: A. the cathedral; B. the area of pharaonic blocks;
C. the south-western bastion; D. the Rivergate Church*

that the conversion to Christianity had taken place; this appears to be witnessed by small church structures as well as Christian-pattern graves with crosses as grave goods, although these graves may represent a small, possibly mercantile Egyptian Coptic presence rather than any local converts. By and large, Nubian Christian graves are markedly different from Coptic types, and if anything seem to borrow from Byzantine sources – does this provide evidence perhaps for a greater dyophysite, Melkite influence than would be suggested by John of Ephesus' traditional account?

The usual tomb consists of a distinctive cruciform grave with a barrel vault, or a simple box grave with a *mastaba* or brick superstructure on top. Crosses are often carved upon the *mastaba*, and not infrequently an amulet – a pentacle or Solomon's seal – is carved above the door as a charm, perhaps against evil spirits. The cross is obviously an important motif; graves at Old Dongola have terracotta crosses on top of the grave, and in many cases small crosses are buried within the grave, again probably acting as charms. It should be noted that the burial evidence alone does not provide a neat, clear picture; recently the British archaeologist David Edwards has noted that in many places 'pagan' forms of burial survive until very late, indicating an extremely patchy uptake of Christianity, or unusual syncretic practices at work.

Nobatia

Having outlined the key features of Nubian Christianity within the archaeological record, let us stay on the thread of church development and consider the best-known and certainly most extensively investigated Christian site in Nubia, the capital of Nobatia: Faras. The city of Faras was initially investigated by the English archaeologist G. Mileham in the 1900s and subsequently by an Oxford University expedition under F. Griffiths in the 1920s, but it was not until the Polish expedition of K. Michalowski between 1961-4, which concentrated on the central mound – or Kom – that a clearer picture emerged of the workings of Faras; firstly as a capital city in its own right, and then latterly as the major ecclesiastical centre of the united Nobatian and Makurian states after the seventh century. The Polish excavations in particular sought to throw new light on the possibility of an earlier Byzantine/Melkite-influenced Christian community as witnessed by the earliest so-called mud-brick church and associated burials; this incipient Christian community was thought to have been strangled at the time of the Sassanian incursions from Egypt during the seventh century.

A number of major Christian monuments in Faras marked it out as an important ecclesiastical and political centre; already the Rivergate Church, the Great Church, the North and South Churches, the Nabindiffi Church, an anchorite grotto and the monastery of Qasr el Wizz to the north had begun to yield important clues, but Polish interest was keenest in the Kom, and the archaeological sequence beneath the five-aisled cathedral of Bishop Paulos. Many of these buildings had a number of architectural traits in common, showing a mélange of traditional Nubian traits – which themselves may have recalled earlier Meroitic motifs – as well as obviously

northern, Mediterranean traits. Where earlier churches utilised stone as a substructure – perhaps up to six courses – with mud brick on top, the Great Cathedral was
completely stone-built, with horizontal rectangular blocks and a smooth surface for
subsequent rendering and painting; much of this stone was re-used from the nearby
pharaonic fort at Buhen.

Aside from the obvious archaeological evidence, textual sources confirmed the
status of Faras as an ecclesiastical centre, and an extensive list of bishops ending with
Yesu in 1169 attests to the continuing importance of the town, although the power
of the see itself declined by 1372, and the town subsequently became an Arab citadel.
Important textual clues also show how the Nubian church swung uneasily between
the monophysite and dyophysite worlds; bishops were more often referred to as an
Orthodoxos rather than Metropolitan, the latter being a Coptic – and hence monophysite – term.

One of the first churches to be investigated at Faras, the Rivergate Church, stands
(as its name would suggest) upon the Nile itself, and was probably converted into a
church from a palace or large guest house. Of a square stone and mud brick con-

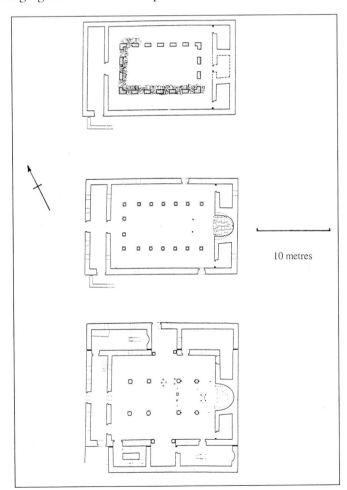

10 metres

39 *Successive building
phases on the site of the
cathedral at Faras: top:
the palace structure; middle:
the first cathedral; bottom:
Paulos' Great Cathedral*

103

struction, it has been suggested by the Italian scholar Giovanni Vantini that the Rivergate Church may represent one of the earliest Christian meeting places in Faras, and that the Christians who used the church may have been of a dyophysite outlook. On a lintel above a doorway is an inscription of an important liturgical formula adopted as early as the Council of Ephesus in 431 as a purely Melkite, dyophysiteite confession. The so-called South Church near the western palace is another note-worthy structure; rhomboid in plan, it lies near to a hypothesised small monastic complex to the north. Particular attention, however, attaches to the mound or Kom and it is here that we shall turn now.

The lower levels of the Kom excavations yielded evidence of a small (15m by 10m; 49ft by 33ft) structure, with an oval apse constructed of mud-brick covered with white plaster. This building, referred to as the mud-brick church, was seem-ingly dated to the fifth century, far earlier than historical sources suggest Christianity to have been present. Atop this structure was a secular building referred to as the palace, which the excavators surmised was destroyed at the same time as the Rivergate church by marauding Sassanians.

At around 625, a three-aisled basilica structure, with an apse and flanking rooms, was built directly upon the palace foundations; this may have been a purely economic choice, but the orientations did not conform to the idealised east-west axis plan. From the few remaining architectural embellishments found here – which include

40 *Reconstruction of architectural detail around a door at the cathedral at Faras*

sandstone carved capitals, fragments of a frieze showing doves and an exterior baptistery with a whitewashed tank some 0.5m (1ft 8in) square – it is clear that we are
dealing with a church of some importance, certainly large enough to be considered
a cathedral. At around 652, it is surmised that this structure was destroyed by the
Dongola incursion of Ibn Saad, and a subsequent re-building took place on the flood
plain to the south of the Kom by Paulos, the fifth bishop of Faras, but this church
was probably flooded at around 700, and the need to build again on higher ground
was then appreciated.

In 707, Paulos and the then king Merkurios renewed the Kom structure when a
five-aisled edifice was constructed. The foundation stones contain Coptic and Greek
inscriptions, indicating a degree of international interest in the renewed building. This
building in turn was destroyed by a fire in 926, and at around the same time a basilica
on the south slope of the Kom was founded, next to a re-used pillar topped by a cross
to provide an instantly identifiable Christian focal point, while the five-aisled cathedral
was rebuilt to incorporate the earlier three-aisled cathedral's baptistery within its southern aisle, and its frescoes were entirely renewed. The roof of this cathedral was then
refurbished in the traditional Nubian brick barrel vault rather than wooden roof, and
brick piers replaced the damaged granite columns. During the eleventh century it is
possible that the roof collapsed, and not being rebuilt, the cathedral filled with sand that
preserved the secrets of the cathedral until excavation in the 1960s.

The frescoes are perhaps the best known of the architectural elements at Faras. As
noted already, a number were removed to Warsaw where they have undergone
extensive conservation and study. The frescoes show a clear stylistic Byzantine influence in choice of motif and execution. Within the cathedral, there is evidence of
extensive re-plastering, whitewashing and re-painting of the pillars, but the paintings
within the apse itself appear not to have been extensively re-worked. The apse group
has the most important and striking scenes; a depiction of the Virgin Mary flanked
by apostles and bounded by a purple stripe and a frieze of doves. Secular figures are
represented by pictures of bishops and of King George I – a tenth-century monarch
of a decidedly international outlook who once visited the caliph of Baghdad – symbolically beneath the protection of a Madonna and child. There is also evidence that
some of these frescoes were altered after the cathedral fell into disuse; some eyes are
scratched out, reflecting perhaps a later Muslim belief in the depiction of eyes linked
to the curse of the evil eye.

One of the best sources of information concerning the Christian settlement at
Faras remains the extensive burial evidence. Some ten tombs of bishops are grouped
around the cathedral, and these have been extensively investigated by the Polish
archaeologist Bogdan Zurawski. Most of the tombs are of a familiar Nubian pattern,
with a flat floor, a vaulted chamber with plaster/whitewash finish all accessed by an
external shaft, which frequently has a cross, or Star of David carved over the
entrance. After about 920 – the time of the major fire – the form of the tomb
changes; now mud-brick structures topped by removable slabs predominate. All
burials tend to be extended, and most have lamps placed to the right side of the skull.
By the beginning of the eleventh century, more grave goods appear within the

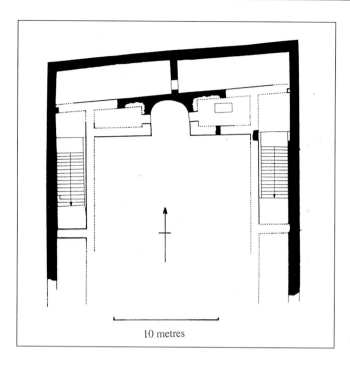

10 metres

41 *Detail of the layout of the church at Qasr Ibrim*

tombs, systematically deposited in certain significant zones. Often at the head and feet a water jar is placed, and in the north-west corner of the tomb is nearly always found a lamp. The elaboration of burial and increase in grave goods is evidence, according to Zurawski, of a gradual re-establishment of Melkite burial practice, which was always more elaborate than Coptic funerary rites. The presence of water jars is also intriguing, perhaps recalling – as Zurawski suggests – the Graeco-Roman practice of water offerings to the dead, a contention that may be strengthened by the presence of small tubes within the mastaba which lead almost directly down to the mouth of the corpse, perhaps another syncretic link to the practice of water offering so prevalent in other non-Christian societies.

There is another fascinating syncretic motif; the head of the bishop Stephanos who died in 926, is flanked by two stone slabs, as if to protect the face. This idea of protecting the head of the corpse is related to the concept of the *caput sacrum*, the holy nature of the head as a spiritual repository, linked as Zurawski suggests far back in time to the pharaonic death masks. The skeletons can also tell us more about the secular life of Faras; a recent pathological study by E. Prominska has identified an average age of death among the corpus of bishops' remains as seventy-one years – quite an advanced age for this region at this time – and apart from the obvious age-related cancer, bone disease and dental problems, all seemed to be rather well looked after, as one would expect from people who resided within the upper stratum of this Nobatia.

The site of Qasr Ibrim also held an important place in the ecclesiastical history of Nobatia. Although threatened by the rising waters of Lake Nasser, this former hilltop fortress some 220km (137 miles) south of Aswan and with remains indicating an occupation history of some three thousand years, now is an island, and is accessible only by boat. The Qasr Ibrim parchment manuscripts are an important source for understanding Nubian Christianity in the formative years; written in Greek, Nubian, Arabic and Coptic they provide an unparalleled source of information regarding the daily workings of the religious and secular communities, and their dating suggests an earlier phase of evangelisation among the Nobatians than is reflected in the traditional church histories. The first Christians here created their place of worship by the simple expedient of converting the Meroitic King Taharqa's seventh-century BC temple into a church with the addition of a mud-brick apse to the rectangular building at some point during the fifth century AD.

Of late, another Meroitic temple has been uncovered at Qasr Ibrim that unusually shows signs of desecration by the new Christian communities; at some point in the sixth century; the interior was defaced and the surrounds were levelled to provide a landscaped area adjacent to the cathedral. We can only assume this temple was unfit for use as a church because unlike the Taharqa temple it did not fit the prescribed east–west alignments. The main cathedral was later built with sandstone from nearby pharaonic buildings, and is probably an enlargement of an earlier building. Beneath the entrance to the northern crypt in this cathedral, the body of bishop Timotheos – who died at around 1372 – was found alongside two parchment scrolls which were subsequently identified as his 'commissary letters' from the Patriarch at Alexandria approving his ordination as bishop of Qasr Ibrim.

Faras has provided a wealth of information about the development of Christianity in Nubia, but as an important political and ecclesiastical centre alongside Qasr Ibrim, it must be regarded as something of a special case. To get an idea of what was happening in the countryside, we must turn to the site of Debeira West excavated by Peter and Margaret Shinnie in the 1960s. These excavations have yielded the clearest picture yet of the day-to-day life of a small medieval village in Nubia; the settlement possessed an exceptionally reliable agricultural base, and supported a sizeable population. The demands of salvage archaeology meant that only a small percentage of the site could be investigated, but some light has been cast on rural Christianity in Nubia. Within the area designated R-44, we have a small church complex, built of mud-brick and dating to the seventh century. The basic outline would conform to an early Nubian plan, but significantly later alterations placed a screen in front of the sanctu-

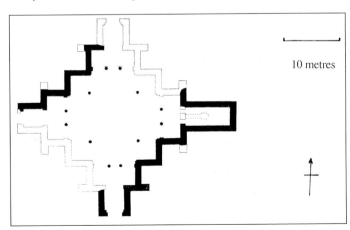

10 metres

42 *Plan of the Cruciform Church, Old Dongola*

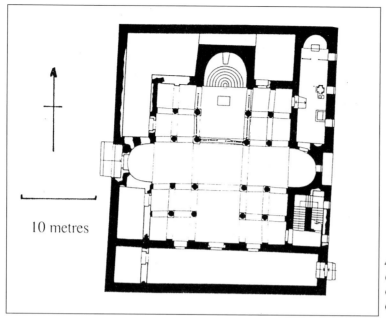

43 *Plan of the Church of the Granite Columns, Old Dongola*

10 metres

ary mirroring patterns found elsewhere. No altar has survived – it may have been of perishable wood – but the outline of the apse is clear, and on each side are the familiar north-south flanking rooms – respectively *prothesis* and *diakonikon* – which probably served as sacristies. Four mud-brick piers divide the nave, while at the north side of the nave a pulpit is located, and behind this, at the eastern end of the aisle, is a screening wall, which formed a small vestibule in front of the *prothesis*. Within the area R-2 is a church with the grave of a certain Peter the Deacon beneath the sanctuary, and a hermit's burial in the south-west of the aisle; it must be emphasised that only the wealthy or holy would find such resting places; for the other inhabitants, the usual long, narrow graves were used, whilst infants were buried in large jars.

Makuria

Having considered the picture of Christian settlement in Nobatia, we now move south to Old Dongola, the capital of Makuria and subsequently of the unified kingdom of Makuria-Nobatia, where Polish archaeologists have been active since the 1960s (**colour plate 7**). One of the most distinctive structures is the massive Cruciform Church, a building quite unlike anything seen in earlier church architecture, and a design that may indicate more of shift towards the eastern Byzantine architectural tradition, away from the monophysite roots of the Nubian church in far-off Alexandria. The walls stand to a height of 4m (13ft), and although only partially preserved, the edifice still presents a striking aspect. Established, it is estimated, at some point in the ninth century, it has seen extensive re-buildings over the 500 years it was in use. The southern arm was clearly altered, and a vestibule added, and after Mamluk raids at the beginning of the fourteenth century it was rebuilt again before its final abandonment at the end of that century. The central bay probably stood some 14m (36ft) high, and the roof was supported by large granite columns topped with decorative capitals. The eastern arm was clearly demarcated by some form of wall, and underneath it two crypts were found, which probably incorporated parts of the earlier (seventh-century) so-called Church of the Stone Pavement. This earlier church was a five-aisled basilica with sandstone flooring – although the *heikal* floor was lined by pebbles – and had a baptistery tank decorated with wave-motifs to give the effect of marbling, which was latterly reconstructed as an oval tank with a Maltese cross motif at its centre.

By far the most striking ecclesiastical building in Old Dongola, its sheer scale (45m by 40m; 148ft by 131ft) makes it clear that the Cruciform Church was at the hub of the religious sphere of the united kingdoms of Makuria and Nobatia, and its erection may have been undertaken to celebrate the safe return of King George from his meeting with the Muslim caliphs of Baghdad. A number of other ecclesiastical buildings at Old Dongola also require brief examination. The sixth-century Old Church is a 30m-long (98ft) tripartite building showing general Greek and Byzantine architectural influence. The associated baptistery is fairly large and contains an oval basin, and a line of sockets, which would probably have supported a dividing screen, demarcates the front of the *heikal*. This building was pulled down in the later seventh century, and a new church, the so-called Church of the Granite Columns, was built (**colour plates 8 & 9**). Measuring 30m by 25m (98ft by 82ft), this edifice was constructed from red (fired) brick, but its outstanding architectural feature was the presence of sixteen monolithic granite columns hewn from rock brought from quarries of the third cataract region.

The North Church, which stands now to a height of 4m (13ft), is of cross-in-square form, and measures 11.5m (38ft) square orientated on an east–west axis. The main structure was built of mud-brick – attaining a maximum thickness of 1.3m (4ft) – finished with a layer of lime gravel plaster upon which fragmentary twelfth-century murals were noted, and floored with tiles. Small finds within the sacristies at the apsidal end included a pottery chalice and lamps – both clear evidence of liturgical functions. Some 240m to the west of this building stands the north-west church, again of mud-brick construction on very shallow foundations, and of similar spatial configuration to the North Church, which would possibly suggest a twelfth-century date for this building. On site D, there is evidence of two superimposed churches of stone and brick construction surrounded by a wall; the latest version unusually has an apse projecting beyond the main body of the church, whereas in normal Nubian practice the apse is usually flanked and largely concealed by the adjoining sacristies/storerooms.

Burial evidence at Old Dongola is plentiful and provides some parallels with Nobatian Christian burial rites. A dedicated cemetery area stands to the north-east of the town; here simple rectangular tombs with vaulted burial chambers and square shaft entrances from the western side predominate, although there is also evidence of some rock-cut tombs. The tombs at site D command special attention; the familiar red-brick vaulted structures are associated with shafts that really serve little practical purpose as they are too small to admit a corpse – perhaps here we are seeing a reflection of the practice at Faras, which Zurawski suggests might be a throwback from earlier pre-Christian burial rites.

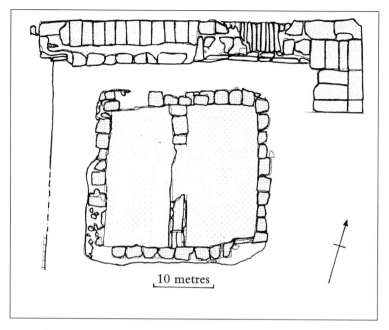

44 *Soba: building Z may be a baptistery structure*

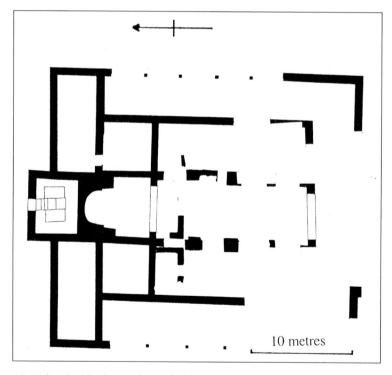

45 *Soba: the Northern Church (building A); phase 2*

Alwa

We now move further southwards to the mysterious state of Alwa and its capital of Soba, which recently has been under investigation by a British team led by Derek Welsby of the British Museum following on from earlier work by Peter Shinnie in the 1950s. The city flourished from the sixth century AD until its capture by Muslim armies in 1504, and the material culture of the Alwan state should present an intriguing contrast with the more Egyptian-influenced states of Lower and Middle Nubia. Little is known historically about the Alwan state, but one of the few relevant historical sources from the Armenian writer Abu Salih suggested that there were some 400 churches in Alwa; recent archaeological work at Soba, however, has yielded few structures that could be solidly defined as churches, and although future work will elucidate the wider picture, it may be that Abu Salih had exaggerated the scale of church building in Alwa.

In other areas of the former Alwan sphere of influence the archaeological picture is similarly patchy; there are possible church remains at Defeia to the north of modern Khartoum, and some graves excavated at Wad el Haddad contained pottery vessels with the *Ichthys* motif and Chi-Ro monogram carved upon them, but few indications of nearby church buildings. Sometimes – as will be recalled from Egypt and Qasr Ibrim – there was no need to build a new church; the Meroitic temple IIIa at Mussawarat es Safra, for instance, was converted to use for Christian worship. Such is the state of our knowledge of the Christian archaeology of the Alwan state; the following discussion concentrates on the data from Soba, a settlement of major socio-economic importance to a medieval Nubian state situated in an area of dependable rainfall, and far enough from the Egyptian sphere of influence to be economically and culturally self-sufficient. How is this potential cultural difference reflected in the nature of Alwan Christianity as revealed by archaeology?

46 *A selection of cross motifs from Soba Ware ceramics*

Initial trial trenching by Daniels' and Welsby's Soba expedition revealed recognisably Christian graves; long cuts with rounded ends and occasionally with three bricks surrounding the skull. It will be recalled that this practice of head protection, perhaps symbolically loaded, was also recognised at Faras in the north as well as Old Dongola, so it is probable that a broadly similar funerary rite was in use in Alwa at the time. On mound B, building A was defined as the northern church; in its second phase of re-building it took on a basilica plan, but unusually possessed wide entrances, a motif that Welsby sees in common with contemporary Armenian churches. Armenia was also of the monophysite persuasion, and it is clear as a whole within Nubian church building that later architectural elements look more towards the east than towards the Mediterranean and Egyptian worlds. In common with later Nubian churches, the *heikal* in building A was delimited by a screen – or *higab* – of red-brick/timber construction, and the screening-off of the area at the eastern end of the north aisle recalls the habit in later times of providing a walkway or closed access for the clergy. The nearby building Z may have served as a baptistery; the tank is rather unusual insofar as it is divided in two by a low wall, and in the excavator's opinion the structure could even be a tomb. Otherwise there is no evidence of a baptistery within the building; this is fairly unusual for a Nubian church.

The earliest complete church plan available from Soba is from phase one of the so-called central church, or building B, located some 4m south of building A. Again this is fundamentally a basilica structure, measuring 24m by 22.5m (79ft by 74ft) square. A monumental western entrance is an unusual feature, and in common with building A may point to architectural influences from elsewhere. Both structures are set on the eastern end of mound B, and are associated with a main burial area; in a sense, then, this is the ecclesiastical zone, and the presence of two adjacent churches – or double churches – is not in itself unusual; both probably served differing roles, catering perhaps to different classes of people.

On mound MN 12, building E was recognised as being a three-aisled mud-brick church, orientated on an east-west axis and measuring 16.5m by 10.5m (54ft by 34ft). The excavators have suggested that the aisle was screened off at the east end in a manner typical of Adams's classical Nubian-type church. On mound Z, building F – a sandstone structure measuring 22.5m by 13.5m (74ft by 44ft) – is suggested to be a church dating from as early as the fifth century. The nearby building G is clearly a secular building that has probably been latterly converted into a church. The basic stone structure measures about 5m square, and was probably an earlier Meroitic temple subsequently reused; to the east is a small cemetery area characterised by tombs with a stone superstructure atop an oval pit containing extended burials. Pathological analysis of the bones indicates a high instance of bone disease, cancer and tooth problems. Small finds from Soba include a variety of iron crosses, alongside cross designs on mud flask stoppers, stamps and pottery clearly indicating a variety of depictions of the most basic Christian symbol.

Apart from the main urban centre of Soba, little is known about rural settlement in Alwa, although of late intensive archaeological ground surveys around the margins of the capital and along the Nile have sought to rectify this problem. Of special interest is

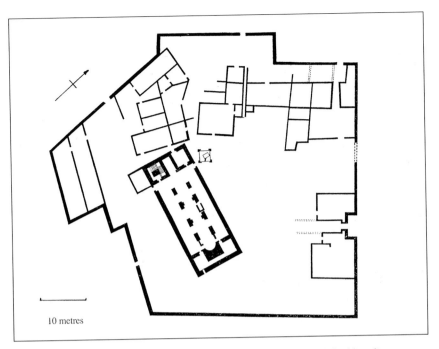

47 *Plan of the monastic settlement at Ghazali. The major church building lies on an east-west axis, with a small baptistery building to the north end*

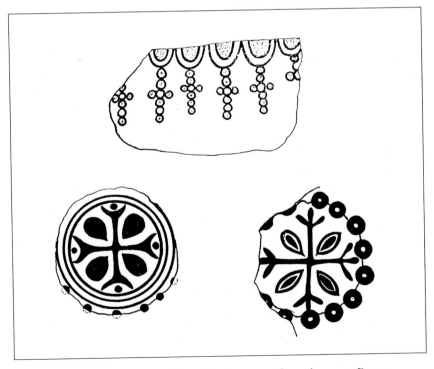

48 *Ghazali monastery pottery. Top: painted cross motif on a large pot. Bottom: impressed medallions from the centres of bowl bases. Approximately half size*

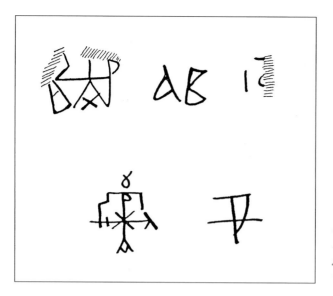

49 *Ghazali monastery: a selection of stylised cruciform graffiti on pottery, approximately half size*

recent salvage work carried out in the environs of Soba east in response to threatened destruction by road building. Here, a cemetery has been uncovered that may yield more clues about the nature of the transitional funerary practice between Meroitic and Christian times. Obvious Christian indicators – such as a vaulted tomb and seven extended burials orientated in the familiar east-west configuration are present – alongside two semi-contracted burials, one of which contained copper alloy earrings *in situ*, perhaps indicative of grave goods. A single burial was totally contracted, showing recognisable pre-Christian body layout practice, but it lacked any form of grave goods, and the excavators suggest this burial may be of a transitional nature.

The monasteries of medieval Nubia

Peter Shinnie and Neville Chittick of the Sudanese Antiquities Service excavated the tenth-century Nobatian monastery of Ghazali in the late 1950s. As with any monastic settlement, the church is of commanding importance. Here it is a dressed stone foundation and mud-brick superstructure construction measuring 28m by 14m (92ft by 46ft), with an interior plaster covering which has been covered by graffiti. The basic outline is basilican in plan; the nave is divided from the aisles by arcades, and there is a bench running the length of the north aisle. A tribune of seven steps approaches the *heikal* or sanctuary, and jars inserted into the floor at this point may have served to support a screen next to the remains of a pulpit. Beneath the tiled floor is a drain system that may have connected with the baptistery area; in the diakonikon, or sacristy to the south of the apse is a large pottery dish set into the floor – which may have been used for foot washing – and the overall layout of the sacristy complex, according to the excavators, would appear to be of a Greek rather than Coptic style, indicating again the probability of a heavy dyophysite liturgical emphasis. The baptistery itself – which con-

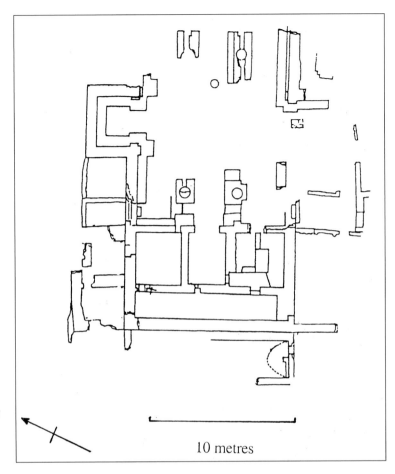

50 *Hambukol: plan of the North Kom church. This monastic church has only been barely excavated*

10 metres

tains a small plaster-lined tank – is of special note as it is located at the northern entrance to the church rather than within the south-eastern corner of the nave.

The associated monastic buildings are set in three groups; all are built roughly of schist and mortar, and most contain large amounts of occupational debris and water pots. Building K is suggested to be a refectory, and the presence of circular benches recalls similar Egyptian structures. A wall encloses the whole monastic complex, and a latrine area is situated beyond. The cemetery is characterised by box graves with frag-mentary crosses, bearing both Greek and Coptic inscriptions, and as Coptic inscrip-tions are clearly in the majority, it may be hypothesised that a large number of Egyptian monks resided here, possibly having escaped persecution in their homeland.

To the south at Old Dongola, the seventh-century monastic complexes of Kom H and DM are fairly well known, but recent work at Hambukol to the north of the town by a Canadian team seems to have recovered what would appear to be a monastic set-tlement. The three-aisled red-brick church measuring some 25m by 35m (82ft by 115ft) is of a basic basilican plan, with four interior pillars, pulpit and square baptistery tank in the usual configuration. Associated ceramic finds – which include a chalice – would seem to place the occupation of the building during the eighth century AD.

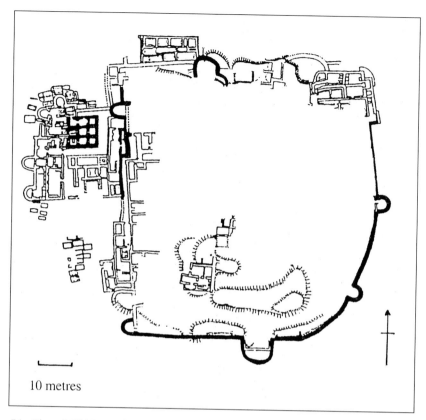

51 *Plan of Old Dongola Kom H monastery. Note the number and size of the cell groups, and the well-defined wall*

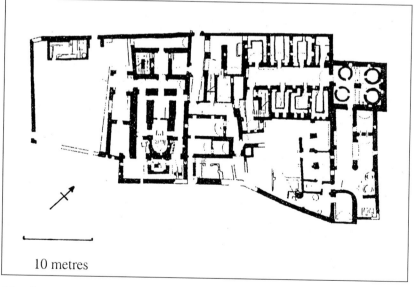

52 *Plan of the monastery at Qasr el Wizz. Compared to Old Dongola Kom H monastery, this is a very compact settlement*

The associated monastic structures were enclosed by a wall, which may have been fortified around the fifteenth century by the addition of bastions – a picture noted at the Old Dongola Kom H monastery. The fortification and strengthening of walls, which previously served the purpose of merely delimiting the settlement, would have been a necessity as Nubian Christian society crumbled in the face of Muslim incursions at the time. The kitchen zone is clearly recognised by the presence of grain storage silos; the refectory exhibits a similar configuration to that at Ghazali with circular benches, and the cells within the compound are – as at Qasr el Wizz – of variable size reflecting a possible hierarchical organisation among the monks within the monastery.

The end of Nubian Christianity

By the fourteenth century, the southerly parts of Nubia had begun to succumb to Muslim incursions, although a small Christian statelet of Do-Tawo was established after the Muslim destruction of Old Dongola at Gebel Adda, and Qasr Ibrim still remained an important bishopric. During these later periods, this sense of unrest is reflected in the secular architecture; now more fortifications are noted, as witnessed especially by the castle structure at Kulubnarti, and individual tower houses. These external pressures increased, and by the beginning of the sixteenth century the king of the Muslim Fung – a northern Nubian kingdom centred on Sennar and Umara Dunqas – destroyed Soba, and with it came the decline of Alwa.

Although some textual records do suggest that in rural areas Christianity still precariously survived, Nubia was effectively now cut off from the centres of Christendom, and these small communities died out gradually to leave Nubian Christianity, once so vital and dynamic, a mere memory – but perhaps its ghost survives? Vantini has suggested that some archaic folk customs among the now Muslim Sudanese peasantry may recall long-forgotten Christian tradition: the Mariya custom of washing a new-born baby can be linked to the rite of baptism, and in the Nuba Mountains until recently, crosses were used as amulets to ward off sickness.

Unlike northern Africa or Egypt, Christianity in Nubia developed outside the Roman cultural milieu; there does seem to be a very distinct and sudden socio-cultural change at the time of the emergence of Christianity in Nubia, although some indigenous elements were retained in terms of architectural style. This stark cultural dichotomy is perhaps clearer here than elsewhere: new building forms and new modes of burial all appear on the Nubian archaeological stage within a very short time. Insofar as proving or disproving the historical data, it does seem from the archaeological evidence that small Christian communities were present in lower Nubia far earlier than the traditional accounts would suggest.

The resolution of the archaeological material, however, is not fine-grained enough to be able to support the historical contentions surrounding the processes of conversion and the dichotomy between the Melkite and monophysite missions. There are few cultural features within church architecture or burial practice that would support a firm diagnosis of, say, monophysite liturgy at work as opposed to a Melkite rite, although it has been noted that some inscriptions and titles may provide limited evidence. In truth, this picture is far too complex, and simplistic assertions of liturgical choice are simply untenable; choices of 'Christian brands' may have been dictated purely by political circumstance rather than primacy of missionary contact. It is entirely probable that the Lower Nubian cultural sphere saw an uneasy alliance of the two opposing streams of Christianity.

So, in summary, the archaeology of Nubian Christianity is remarkably homogenous within certain areas; there is little north-south dichotomy in terms of religious culture, although in the secular sphere it is clear that Egyptian influence was more marked in the north. As Egypt came under Muslim sway this influence declined as a whole, and Nubian Christians, in their final few hundred years, sought influences from elsewhere. The Nubians, unlike the Copts, were unable to resist the Muslim tide, and in a sense lost their struggle for survival, but away from these wide desert expanses, our attention now turns to the south-east towards the massifs of the Ethiopian highlands, the stronghold of Ethiopian Christianity. As much as the Copts of Egypt, the Ethiopian Orthodox Church is a fellow custodian of the flame of African Christianity in antiquity.

Further reading

Nubia has received comparatively little archaeological attention in comparison with Egypt, and as such perhaps has tended to be regarded as an offshoot of Egyptology rather than as a discipline in its own right. Nevertheless, three important texts are essential for understanding the broad archaeological background: W.Y. Adams (1977) *Nubia: Corridor to Africa* (Princeton: Princeton University Press) which, although now somewhat dated is still invaluable, P. Shinnie (1996) *Ancient Nubia* (London: Routledge Kegan and Paul), see especially chapter 9 for Christian Nubia, and the most recent and thorough survey by Derek Welsby (2002) *The Medieval Kingdoms of Nubia: Pagans, Christians and Muslims along the Middle Nile* (London: British Museum Press). A useful and very up-to-date article considering the archaeological evidence for Christianity in the Sudan is D. Edwards (2001) 'The Christianisation of Nubia: some pointers' in *Sudan and Nubia* 5, pp. 89-96.

A good overview of the historical evidence for Christianity in the Sudan is G. Vantini (1981) *Christianity in the Sudan* (Bologna: Emi), and the same author has written a fairly accessible book on the summary of the Faras excavations: (1970) *Excavations at Faras: a Contribution to the History of Christian Nubia* (Bologna: Nigrizia). Key site reports for Faras are scattered among a number of conference proceedings, but perhaps the most informative and accessible are the papers in M. Krause (ed.) (1986) *Nubische Studien; Proceedings of the Fifth International Conference for Nubian Studies* (Mainz: Von Zabern). The Debeira West site is published by P. and M. Shinnie (1978) as: *Debeira West: a Medieval Nubian Town* (Warminster: Aris and Phillips). G. Vantini (1976) *Oriental Sources concerning Nubia* (Warsaw/Heidelberg:

Polish Academy of Sciences/Heidelberger Akademie der Wissenschaften) is an invaluable collection of Byzantine and Arabic documents translated into English.

Moving southwards, the Old Dongola reports mainly make their appearance in the journal *Polish Archaeological Missions*, and interim reports can be found in the journal *Archéologie du Nil Moyen*. The Soba excavations are published in: D. Welsby and C. Daniels (1991) *Soba: Archaeological research at a Medieval Capital on the Blue Nile* (London: British Institute in Eastern Africa) and D. Welsby (1998) *Soba II; Renewed Excavations within the Metropolis of the Kingdom of Alwa in Central Sudan* (London: British Institute in Eastern Africa/British Museum).

Two key works are of importance in understanding Nubian monasticism: P. Shinnie and N. Chittick (1961) *Ghazali: a Monastery in the Northern Sudan* (Khartoum: Sudan Antiquities Service Occasional Paper 5), and for a more up-to-date synthesis J. Anderson (1999) 'Monastic lifestyles of the Nubian desert: seeking the mysterious monks of Makuria' in *Sudan and Nubia* 3 pp. 71-83. *Sudan and Nubia*, the Bulletin of the Sudanese Archaeological Research Society, is an invaluable source of recent discoveries in Nubia, and another journal (once defunct but now back in circulation) which contains detailed reports of the 1960s salvage operation is *Kush* – for an understanding of the archaeology of Lower Nubia this journal is of the utmost value.

5 In the lands of Prester John: the archaeology of Ethiopian Orthodox Christianity

Encompassed on all sides by the enemies of their religion the Aethiopians slept near a thousand years, forgetful of the world by whom they were forgotten.

(Edward Gibbon: *The Decline and Fall of the Roman Empire*)

The overnight air-traveller flying into Ethiopia from the north awakens over the Red Sea to an unforgiving sunlight and a desolate landscape below. To the right is the Sudanese coastline around Port Sudan and the ancient city of Suakin; to the left, into the rising sun, are the arid coastal fringes of Saudi Arabia. Soon, ahead, the Eritrean coast is crossed. This coastline was Ethiopian up until the early 1990s, but when the old Italian colony of Eritrea broke away to declare its independence after a lengthy and bitterly contested internecine war, Ethiopia became, as it had usually historically been, a landlocked and seemingly physically isolated entity.

Other factors have contributed to this physical isolation. Soon the desolate coastal strip gives way to a high escarpment, the ragged mountainous strip seems from the air to reach upwards to meet the traveller. It is a dramatic and unforgettable sight; stark evidence of the dichotomy between the arid lowlands and the lush plateau. The scale of these mountains is almost supernatural; it is this plateau, crossed by deep river gorges, that has enhanced the sense of physical isolation from the rest of tropical Africa; it is a physical entity that has burned a sense of spiritual and intellectual isolation into the Ethiopians – formerly known as Abyssinians – down the millennia.

The geographical nature of Ethiopia has clearly influenced the cultural and social development of its inhabitants. Historically, the Christian Abyssinian homeland was centred on these highlands; to the north, on the Red Sea fringes, to the west on the Sudanic steppes, to the east in the arid deserts of the Ogaden, the peoples were either Muslim or pagan pastoral nomads, whose raids threatened the borders of the kingdom. The isolation of Ethiopia, this highland kingdom, guaranteed the survival of its own form of monophysite Christianity against Muslim incursions, and has bred in its inhabitants a degree of idiosyncrasy and cultural conservatism – an aloofness almost – that can still be felt today. Ethiopians do not regard themselves as being African; their light skin, their sense of deep-rooted history, a historiography of considerable antiquity, all conspire to emphasise their sense of difference. They are, so they believe, the heirs of the Queen of Sheba, the guardians of Christian tradition in Africa.

Another important factor explains this sense of socio-cultural conservatism: Ethiopia was only briefly colonised by European powers. For many years in the nineteenth century, rival European powers assiduously courted the Abyssinian emperor, mindful of the country's strategic position. Although in no sense could Abyssinia be regarded as having had a unified history, the perceived threat of outside interference was always enough to draw rival warlords together in a common struggle. The Italians certainly underestimated the force of national feeling in 1896 when, having long cast covetous eyes at the highland riches of Abyssinia, they invaded from their Red Sea colony of Eritrea and were promptly massacred at the battle of Adwa. Mussolini, his eyes on a greater Italian eastern African colonial sphere – and mindful of avenging the Adwa defeat – invaded in 1935, and in the face of international criticism and the amount of inaction, was able to keep a hold in Ethiopia for only three years.

Ethiopia Today

It would be reasonable to begin this chapter with a brief consideration of modern Ethiopia, its land and peoples, for perhaps nowhere else in the history of African Christianity are the fortunes of the Church, the inhabitants and the landscape so

53 *A map of medieval Ethiopia showing principal areas and sites discussed in this chapter: 1. Aksum, 2. Debra Damo, 3. Lalibela, 4. Lake Hayq, 5. Debra Libanos, 6. Adulis*

visibly intertwined. The modern state of Ethiopia, which has largely retained its historical boundaries, contains one of the largest mountainous areas in Africa, which reaches its maximum height of some 4600m (15,000ft) at Ras Dashen in the Simien Mountains. Large areas of the high plateau lie above 2000m (6500ft), and the plateau is crossed by numerous rivers and deep gorges. The Blue Nile drains from Lake Tana in the north-west of the plateau at the beginning of its long journey to Egypt. The rainfall patterns on this plateau, which are largely predictable and fall in two seasons, have for millennia provided the lifeblood for Egypt, carrying down the river massive quantities of life-giving rich riverine silt to the arid desert areas to the north.

Ethiopia is still a predominantly agrarian society, home to an idiosyncratic and conservative farming complex. The rich volcanic soils and predictable rains allow a range of crops to be grown, often with two harvests a year. Sorghum, millet and barley are the main cereals grown, but perhaps the most widespread, and a traditionally uniquely Ethiopian crop, is the fine grass *tef*, the base of the ubiquitous local sour bread *enjera*. Livestock are important too; cattle have traditionally been seen as an important source of wealth, sheep and goat also play a part in the day to day economy, and chicken are also important. Ethiopian Orthodox Christians, however, like their Muslim neighbours, are forbidden to eat pork or shellfish. This is a unique custom of these Christian peoples, and one which may hint at a degree of past contact with the Jewish faith. We will consider this idea later in this chapter.

A wide variety of languages are spoken in Ethiopia; the *lingua franca* is Amharic, spoken by the central highland peoples, but understood by the majority of Ethiopians. Amharic belongs to the Afro-Asiatic language family, and is a Semitic language similar to Arabic and Hebrew in terms of basic vocabulary and grammatical structure, but is perhaps more closely related to the now dead South Arabian languages. It is certainly clear that the Ethiopic alphabet owes its origins to the Southern Arabian alphabet. Closely related are the languages of Tigrinya, spoken in the north, and Tigre, spoken in the west of Eritrea. The three languages are descended from the extinct original Ethiopian language Ge'ez, which, it is assumed, had already developed in written and spoken form by around 1500 years ago. Ge'ez survives as the liturgical language of the Church, and bears witness to the rich history and antiquity of Ethiopian historiography. Although a range of other languages are spoken in and around the plateau, we will be concerning ourselves here with the cultural history of the Semitic-speaking peoples, who are at the core of the history and development of the Ethiopian Orthodox Church.

The Ethiopian Orthodox Church in Outline

The roots and antiquity of Christianity in Ethiopia have already been considered in chapter 1; Ethiopian Christianity maintains – along with the Coptic, Armenian and Syrian Churches – a monophysite theological outlook, yet the Church also retains certain elements of a possibly earlier, pre-Christian contact with Judaism. Although

Christianity is not an official state religion – this position was eroded when the Marxist *Dergue* (Junta) came to power in 1974 when the massive ecclesiastical land holdings were nationalised – it remains the major religion in terms of numbers of adherents. There are large Muslim communities – perhaps almost as numerous as Christians – who are mainly concentrated in the east and north. There are small numbers of followers of other Christian sects, mainly the result of fairly recent missionary activity, as well as a sizeable number of adherents of traditional, animist religions on the fringes of the plateau.

Since 1959 the Ethiopian Church has been autocephalous, or self-governing. Before this time, the Patriarch of the Coptic Church in Alexandria would nominate a bishop to head the Ethiopian church; frequently the *Abuna* – or Patriarch – had never even set foot in Ethiopia, and the position was viewed as something of a backwater. The seat of the Church in Ethiopia has historically been centred on Aksum, in the northern province of Tigray. Here, emperors were crowned, and where Ethiopian legend has it that the son of King Solomon and the Queen of Sheba, Menelik, took the Ark of the Covenant, where it is believed to remain to this day. Aksum is where the next important figure in the church, the *Nebura-ed*, resides; he is in charge of the ecclesiastical complex at Aksum. Beneath the top levels of clergy are a number of distinctive clerical grades. The *kes*, or priest, may be married, officiates at the local church, and maintains a total social involvement with his community. Deacons and sacristans fulfil similar roles, while *dabtaras* – or scribes – form an educated core of theological scholars. The monastic system has also developed in Ethiopia, both coenobitic (communal) communities of monks and nuns – who are frequently elderly widows – as well as the eremitic, solitary lifestyle, which is rather more rare today.

Ethiopian churches vary in degree of decoration and building style. The two large cathedrals at Aksum are obvious contrasts, as we shall later see. One, is a castle-like long and low building of a seventeenth-century date, the other was built in 1966. Generally speaking, the earliest church forms are rectangular, and as one moves progressively southwards from Tigray, the traditional circular house plan is adopted for the church. Most small village churches are simply furnished, rounded buildings often roofed with corrugated iron, and all are sited on places linked in some way to their founding saint – a prayer grotto for instance. The exceptional rock-hewn churches of Lalibela, of which more later, bear witness to the centrality and wealth of the Church in secular life – until 1974 the Church was the wealthiest landholder and administered a complex system of tithes and rents.

Whatever their plans, churches all contain a holy of holies area – *maqdas* – to the rear, where the sacred *tabots* are kept. *Tabots* represent the Ark of the Covenant, but do not bear any resemblance to the biblical descriptions; the *tabot*, which is taken to mean a chest, is in effect a portable altar, and it contains a tablet called a *sella*, which are long, flat tablets of wood or stone with a Ge'ez inscription of dedication to the church's saint. All churches have a *tabot*, which plays a special part in the yearly ritual cycle. It is a strange sight to see the wild chants and dancing of the priests before the *tabot*, an echo of King David's dance before the Ark of the Covenant.

Ethiopian Orthodox Christians celebrate the Sabbath on the Saturday *and* Sunday. Children are circumcised on the eighth day after birth – Copts will generally wait until the sixth year of the male child's life. Unusually, there is equal authority of the Old and New Testaments in the liturgical canon, and the Levirate form of marriage – where a man may wed his widowed sister-in-law – is widely followed. There are other aspects, not Judaic, that also set this brand of Christianity apart. The celebration of *Timkat*, for instance, is a form of ceremonial re-baptism, the liturgical calendar is different too and possibly shows some degree of Coptic influence: Ethiopians divide their year into 12 months of 30 days and one month of five days. Similar Coptic influences may be recognised in the writing of Ethiopic holy texts; words in red are for important holy titles or religious utterances, other more secular words are in black. The Syriac Orthodox background is also manifested in certain liturgical elements. Another unusual trait is the survival – within the religious sphere – of folk magic; Christians believe in demons such the feared *zar*, the evil eye (*buda*) and the power of amulets and charms. Ethiopian Orthodoxy, more than any other manifestation of indigenous early African Christianity, exhibits a clear syncretic streak. But it is this archaic Judaic element that needs to be followed closely.

We have already noted the unique dietary aspects of Ethiopian Orthodox Christianity. The general influence of Judaism is subtle, yet instantly noticeable, no more so than in the dietary restrictions. The Church maintains the common Semitic taboo of the prohibition of certain types of food: pork, meat from animals with the cloven hoof, and shellfish. Fasting is another important element; two days in the week, Wednesday and Friday, are set aside as days when no meat may be taken. On these days, simple vegetable stews will be eaten. When the other fasting days of the liturgical calendar are taken into account, it is clear that the day-to-day diet of the country dweller may be almost entirely vegetarian. To gain an understanding of this Judaic thread in the Christian milieu, it is necessary to look briefly at the so-called Black Jews of Ethiopia: the Falashas.

Until recently small communities of Falashas existed in the central highlands; these peoples regarded themselves as black Jews. Outwardly, little distinguished them from traditional Ethiopians. They dressed the same, lived in the same types of houses and farmed the same crops. Perhaps the most noticeable facet of the Falasha community was the lack of a church; instead a small, square building was at the centre of the villagers' lives, and if one looked closely, one could make out not a cross on the roof, but a Star of David. These peoples did indeed follow an exceptionally archaic form of Judaism, but they were considered Jewish enough for the Law of Return to apply to them. At the height of the civil war of 1974-1991, the Israeli government airlifted the Falasha peoples from refugee camps in the Sudan home to Israel in the very aptly titled Operation Moses – named, of course, after another fabled exodus.

Controversy rages about the nature of Falasha Jewishness or indeed their history in Ethiopia. Traditional Ethiopian belief has it that the Queen of Sheba – claimed as their own by Ethiopians – went off to Jerusalem to visit King Solomon. In a charming tale, King Solomon impregnated her, and the result of the union was a son Menelik. Menelik quarrelled with his father and left, taking with him the Ark of the Covenant and a retinue of Jewish advisers. He founded, according to legend, the Solomonic dynasty, which, apart from a hiatus around the thirteenth century AD – when the Zagwe dynasty briefly asserted itself – ruled unbroken until 1974 when the self-styled Lion of Judah Haile Selassie was driven from power by the Marxist *Dergue*. Sadly, as with any romantic story, there is little grain of truth in the legend of Menelik. Other authorities have argued for Jewish contact via the Nile valley, or South Arabia, while it may be suggested that the Falasha are remnants of the pre-Christian Semitic ideology. It is certainly unusual that the Falashas follow an arcane form of Judaism; they adhere to pre-Talmudic, Pentateuchal precepts which mainstream Judaism adopted in the fifth century BC. They also have an element of monasticism, and share a number of traits with their Orthodox neighbours.

The Falashas are not alone in combining a mélange of shared religious traits. In the western central highlands, the Qemant peoples combine an odd amalgam of distinctive Hebraic ritual with a local animist belief. The Qemant peoples – who have now largely disappeared – hold groves of trees as being sacred and make offerings to them, yet also follow Judaic dietary laws. In the course of this chapter we will run into this syncretic motif again. There is a patchwork of beliefs and ritual systems within the Christian Church, culled from a variety of areas.

Ethiopia in travellers' tales

A consideration of the wealth of historical sources concerning Ethiopia is a vital adjunct to the study of the archaeology. Perhaps the earliest references to the region are found in early Egyptian texts; the reliefs of the Temple of Hatshepsut at Deir el Bahri in Egypt (*c.*1473-1458 BC) make mention of the wealth of the Land of Punt far to the south. The polity of Punt has never been satisfactorily located, although archaeologists are in broad agreement that it centred on and around the coastline of modern Eritrea. References in classical works to the area are rather more plentiful, although it should be borne in mind that the term 'Ethiopian' was applied to any number of peoples south of the Egyptian border. By the time of the rise of the Aksumite kingdom, during the first century AD, sources such as the *Periplus of the Erythraean Sea* – essentially a trader's guide to the Red Sea written by an anonymous Alexandrian in the first century – give ample evidence of the riches of Ethiopia. With the conversion to Christianity of King Ezana of Aksum, the region became rather more integrated into the sphere of the Roman world; now writers such as Cosmas Indicopleustses and Nonnosus tell us more of the strange world that existed in the highlands far to the south of Egypt's borders.

With the rise of Islam in the seventh century, Ethiopia came rather more to prominence as a bulwark of Christianity. As Arab conquests in Egypt and later Nubia took hold, Ethiopia suddenly acquired a strategic importance to the western Christians. In later centuries, European powers actively sought Ethiopian assistance

54 *The title page of Alvares' 1540 Portuguese edition of* The Prester John of the Indies *showing a very European view of the mythical monarch, his soldiers and military architecture*

55 *Engraving of the Aksumite church at Agula excavated in the 1860s by members of Napier's military expedition, from R. Acton's* The Abyssinian Expedition and the Life and Reign of King Theodore. Illustrated London News, London, 1868

against the Muslims. The Ethiopians, however, already enjoyed moderate relations with Muslims, they had a foothold in Jerusalem, and were certainly inclined towards a policy of live and let live.

In Europe, however, stories of a fabled eastern Christian Kingdom under the command of a warrior priest king circulated; here, in the lands of Prester John, it was credibly reported, the most fantastic sights of nature could be seen. Here was a man who should be a trustworthy ally in the struggle against Islam. In the sixteenth and seventeenth centuries it was the Portuguese who led the race to contact and gain the favour of the Ethiopian Christians for a putative military alliance against the Turks. Nothing concrete came to pass politically, but from the writings of a number of the Portuguese travellers and priests, we are left with vivid pictures of daily life in this ancient Christian Kingdom.

Writers such as Francisco Alvares, De Almeida and Jeronimo Lobo paint an odd picture of Ethiopia. In a very detached way these writers took great pains to record meticulously the land and its peoples. Alvares' accounts are especially valuable in that he provides an eyewitness description of the cathedral at Aksum before its destruction by the Harari Muslim warlord Ahmed Gragn during his *jihad* of 1535. While obviously impressed by the piety of the people, their godliness and religious heritage, these writers regarded them as savages waiting for the benefit of Portuguese civilisation. Indeed Portuguese military intervention saved the country from the depredations of Gragn in

1543, and as an indirect result, the then Emperor Suseynos converted to Roman Catholicism, although this did not prove popular and the formal Portuguese links with Ethiopia largely ceased upon their expulsion by King Fasilidas in 1632.

In the following centuries, the idiosyncrasies of this strange highland kingdom still attracted European attentions. The Scottish traveller James Bruce stayed for three years in Ethiopia from 1769, where his travels convinced him that he had discovered the source of the Blue Nile. Sadly his impressions of the country seem to be rather coloured, and inaccuracies abound in his work *Travels to Discover the Source of the Nile*. To many scholars, Bruce remains something of an enigma, certainly something of an egotist. Of more value, from the archaeological perspective, was the work of another Briton, Henry Salt, who arrived in Ethiopia in 1802. Salt produced a detailed description of the monuments at Aksum, as well as a number of evocative lithographs of the antiquities of the town.

The first scientific archaeological excavations in Ethiopia were conducted by General Napier's Indian Army during the 1860s at the site of the Aksumite-period Red Sea port of Adulis. During the nineteenth century, as more became known about Ethiopia, more travellers arrived, and the perceived riches of the country caught the eye of Italian colonialists – with ultimately tragic results. Finally, in 1906, the foundations of modern archaeological scholarship in Ethiopia were laid by the Deutsche Aksum Expedition, who stayed in Aksum for three months and in 1913 published a lavish and highly detailed excavation report showing the potential for scientific investigation in the holy city of the Ethiopians. No longer would Aksum be a backwater.

Into the twentieth century, Aksum held the attentions of Italian, French and British archaeologists. Of late, the British Institute in Eastern Africa has completed an extensive research project in Aksum essentially building on the 1972-4 work of Neville Chittick. A joint American/Italian team is also at work near the town at the time of writing, and Aksum is slowly beginning to yield its secrets, as its former excavator Neville Chittick so famously suggested, as the last great civilisation to be revealed to modern knowledge.

The archaeology of highland Ethiopia, however, remains imperfectly understood; recent political events have made scientific work in the country difficult, if not impossible. Research priorities, perhaps, have not helped matters. Aksum remains the archaeological jewel in the crown, and the Aksumite period is comparatively well known. There remain large gaps in our archaeological knowledge, and this is true of recent historical periods. For the purposes of this study, we will focus on the Aksum region and neighbouring areas of Tigray, for it is here, more than anywhere else in Ethiopia, that we have the clearest picture of the emergence and subsequent development of Ethiopian Orthodox Christianity.

Hunters to herders to empires

The antecedents of the Aksumite polity are obscure. The highland zone of northern Ethiopia, the Aksumite homeland, shows evidence of a long period of human settlement. It is probable that the local hunting peoples began to adopt a semi-sedentary lifestyle with crop cultivation and animal husbandry at some point during the second millennium BC, although future archaeological work may push these boundaries back further. The worldview of these early farmers would have been geared directly to their perceptions of their wealth, which in the cases of these early pastoral peoples would have been invested in cattle ownership. All over the northern highlands of Ethiopia and Eritrea, rock paintings of cattle reflect this concern.

These depictions cannot be directly dated, but academic consensus places them in the third to second millennia BC. The earliest paintings would seem to be naturalistic, and the subject matter, although illustrating cattle, are also concerned with other animals, sheep, goat, dog and rarely show humans. Wild animals are also depicted in 'hunting' scenes, but a few paintings show evidence of agricultural activities. Later paintings are much more abstract; this group of pictures, which are picked out of the rock, indicate a clear trend towards stylisation. Cattle are not faithfully depicted, what one is seeing is an attempt to present an idealised depiction of a cow. The horns in most cases are grossly exaggerated, and the body is small in overall proportion. In this idealised sense, then, these drawings are icons. They represent an idea rather than a faithful depiction. The widespread distribution of very similar depictions in the northern highlands would suggest that for a large number of people these cattle were of more than purely economic importance. For the first herders and farmers cattle had a truly ideological role to play in their day-to-day lives.

During the first millennium BC we see in these highlands the emergence of a new cultural phenomenon, the so-called pre-Aksumite phase. During this period there are the beginnings of a more nucleated pattern of settlement and the first signs of a definite cultural influence from across the Red Sea. The origins of the pre-Aksumite culture remain debatable; many cultural facets are recognisably local, but some influence is clear from the South Arabian Sabaean sphere. The most obvious indicator is the adoption of the South Arabian Himyaritic alphabet for the writing of inscriptions. On the ideological level, evidence points to the adoption of the South Arabian Semitic pantheon of gods headed by *Almakh*, the sun god.

Yeha, some 40km (25 miles) to the northwest of Aksum, was the centre of this mysterious polity, which is known from (unvocalised) South Arabian inscriptions as DMT. Although little is known about the pre-Aksumite ideological outlook, it is clear that Yeha represented an important place in the cultic sphere. The so-called temple built of large stone blocks and measuring approximately 18m by 15m (59ft by 49ft), is quite unlike anything hitherto seen in the area. Friezes of ibex, preserved in the modern church and once belonging to the temple, clearly show a degree of South Arabian influence. The nearby structure known as Grat Beal Gebri possesses large dressed monolithic pillars similar in style to the so-called moon temple at Marib in South Arabia. Similar ibex friezes, statuary and pillars were noted at the nearby site of Hawelti-Melazzo along with possible ex-voto offerings of models of phalli, animals, remains of incense altars and burnt animal bone in building foundation deposits.

The pre-Aksumite polity seems to have disappeared during the first century, and its decline has not been satisfactorily explained. From our perspective a key point may be noted about the ideological outlook of the pre-Aksumites. Although there are clear parallels with contemporary South Arabian cultic behaviour, there remains an essential local element; the image of the cow survives as a cultic object – alongside that of the ibex – as witnessed by a number of cattle models and depictions that have been found in pre-Aksumite contexts.

The rise of the Aksumite Empire and the coming of Christianity

During the first seven centuries AD the northern Ethiopian highlands were witness to one of the most powerful manifestations of an indigenous African empire. Aksum minted its own tri-metallic coinage and engaged in widespread trade with the Roman world (and, indeed beyond) through the vital Red Sea routes. At the time of its conversion to Christianity in the mid-fourth century by the Syrian Frumentius, Aksum could project considerable power on the regional stage, casting its eyes towards Nubia and acting for the protection of Christians in southern Arabia.

The origins of the town and polity are obscure. Legend has it that it was sited near a sacred spring, and it is also suggested that the later cathedral was located on the floor of a lakebed which was miraculously drained by God. This thread of water is an important motif in the use of sacred space in Ethiopia. Aksum was ruled by a semi-divine king known as the *Negusa Negast* or *Basileus Basilion* – King of Kings – although there is evidence to show that on occasions there were co-regents. Essentially he ruled over a powerful city-state with extensive trade interests. There was a definite elite sector that lived in large 'palace' complexes such as Dungur or Ta'akha Maryam. A distinctive Aksumite architectural style also emerged, using recessed buttressing and alternate wood and stone coursing. These wooden ties are known as monkey heads, and this type of building style survives in ecclesiastical architecture today.

Essentially the religious thread discussed above, continued into Aksumite times. Tradition has it that before the coming of Christianity three forms of religion were dominant in the northern region: Mosaic law (hinting at an early Jewish presence), worshippers of the serpent god *Arwe* and worshippers of a solar deity. The latter clearly match what is known, from contemporary inscriptions, about the pre-Christian religions of northern Ethiopia; the South Arabian pantheon contained the Gods *Almakh*, *Ashtar*, and *Dhat Himam* (or *Ares*), the chief deity of the sun, who was represented by a crescent/disc motif and was identified with the divine kingship and war.

The process of conversion to Christianity was, it is suggested, initially piecemeal. We have noted in chapter 1 that unlike the Roman Empire, in Aksum the leader was the first adherent of this new faith. The slow nature of the conversion process may have meant that large areas of the Aksumite polity remained loyal to the old gods, but at the very top the situation was different. The new faith began to filter down to the masses from a strongly Christianised top layer. Indeed the Christian kings carried a great deal of weight on the international stage. In 356 King Ezana felt confident enough in his new faith and position to resist calls by the Roman Emperor that

Frumentius be examined for grave doctrinal errors. The historical background is clear, but what of the cultural record?

Perhaps the most obvious place to start is with burial tradition. The most distinctive features of Aksum are the freestanding monolithic stelae. Within Africa, there is evidence of a long tradition of using monoliths set upright as grave markers; this may be true to some extent of Egyptian obelisks. Over 140 stelae are known at Aksum and of these six are finely carved. These stelae are located in spatially distinct zones, and it is generally held that they were erected during the third and fourth centuries, i.e. before the coming of Christianity. Perhaps the most striking, and certainly most visible of these monoliths is stela three. Standing some 20m (65ft) high, the stela is finely carved on two sides in a series of multi-storied registers and stone-rendered monkey-head bosses. At the base, by the securing plate, is a carved representation of a door, while at the top is a curved, almost crescent-like finial. To the west is the site of stela two. This finely carved monolith was removed to Rome on the orders of Mussolini in 1937 where it stands to this day,

56 *Aksum: the Tomb of the False Door. Scaffold supports a tin roof protecting the site*

its future in doubt. Perhaps the apogee in every sense of stelae building is embodied in stela one.

Stela one lies smashed and recumbent at the western end of the Stelae Park, its top resting on the capstone of the megalithic tomb known as Nefas Mawcha. Stela one would have been some 30m (100ft) in height and would have weighed in (at a conservative estimate) at about 517 tons; this would put it high on the list of the largest monolithic objects that humanity has attempted to raise. The stela is carved in the representation of a 13-storey building, again with a door representation on each face. The monolith was clearly associated with a large subterranean tomb complex – the mausoleum and east tomb – which was extensively robbed out in antiquity. This is clearly a very large construction undertaking; the stelae would have been quarried some 4km (2.5 miles) to the west at Gobedra Hill and manhandled all the way. The effort in excavating the tombs and raising the stelae would have been immense. These were clear symbols for a wealthy elite. But something went badly wrong.

The Aksumite engineers may have overreached themselves with stela one; the carved section itself is some 30m (100ft) long, but the stub of the stela, designed to sit in a socket, is just over 2.5 m (8ft) long. It is highly probable that at some point in the late fourth century when the stela was due to be raised, it fell in the process, smashing itself to bits on the ground, a symbolic neutering of the power of the semi-divine king. The stela was never upright. It fell during erection at a time when the conversion to Christianity was just under way. Was this an omen? This theory has been recently advanced by David Phillipson; what clearer sign could there be of a change in the cosmological order than the failure of a *grand projet* designed to appeal to the old gods? Certainly, after the adoption of Christianity as the official state religion, monumental stelae erection ceased, yet the pattern of burial, which would have been regarded as a key motif for religious change, did not fundamentally change.

The Tomb of the False Door, which came into use during the early fifth century, retains some clear architectural features, especially the false door motif, but, as with other tombs in the vicinity, past robbing has reduced our information on burial practices severely. On a hilltop to the north of Aksum we find the sixth-century tombs of Kaleb and Gebre Meskal; the former is an underground ashlar construction comprising a large chamber with three rooms to the east. The latter tomb is similar in construction, but has crosses carved on the walls, although these could be later additions. Essentially continuity is the order of the day, and the question of the continuation of grave good usage is not clear. Christian-period shaft tombs in the Central Stelae Park do contain ornaments, but it is only in seventeenth-century burials around Nefas Mawcha that we see the classic Christian burial alignment with the heads to the west and hands crossed over the body.

It is clear that stela erection died out, but it is also probable that the false door motif died out too. What does the door mean? Is it a symbolic entry portal to the afterlife, or more prosaically a continuation of architectural representation? On Stela one, the handle of the false door is still visible on the underside, but the open surface it has been chipped away carefully. Is this mindless ancient vandalism or some-

57 *Aksum. Gold coins produced during the reign of the Aksumite King Ezana during the fourth century. Top: note the crescent pagan motif. Bottom; a Christian issue with a cross taking the place of the crescent symbol. Scale is twice actual size*

thing of deeper significance? Did the removal of the handle signify that the gate to that afterlife, as represented by the pagan cosmology, was no longer valid in the Christian Aksumite world? There are other cultural clues to be found.

The Aksumite tri-metallic coinage of gold, silver and bronze came into operation around 270 and persisted until at least the seventh century, and was clearly designed with Roman trade in mind following as it did the Roman Imperial coinage standards. Early coin issues show the king –frequently crowned– surrounded by ears of corn with the typical pagan motif of a crescent and disc at the top. After the adoption of Christianity, this motif was replaced with the cross; in some early pre-Christian issues the king holds a flywhisk, and this too was replaced by a hand-cross. Inscriptions on the coinage change too; King Mehadeyis used Constantine's motto *in hoc signo vinces* – by this sign you will conquer – rendered into Ge'ez. Ezana's coins have mottoes such as 'By the grace of God' and 'Christ is with us'. Extant inscriptions record this change in outlook; 'Son of Mahrem' is replaced by 'Servant of Christ', but some inscriptions may be more ambiguous; 'Lord of Heaven' could refer to any deity, Christian or pagan.

Apart from the coinage, other domestic items mirror the shift in state ideology. During the fifth century, clay crosses and cones appear in large numbers, while the cross becomes the dominant motif on Red Aksumite pottery. By the sixth century the Brown Aksumite wares have crosses on the rims and ledges, in a variety of shapes and forms, and almost a half of the motif types on Brown Aksumite burnished wares are of crosses – either the flared-top Aksumite cross or the bifurcate plain cross. So much for the domestic-level signifiers; the slow adoption of these key motifs hints at a gradual acceptance of Christianity over the longer term from the top downwards. But what of the ideological focus of the new faith, the place of worship?

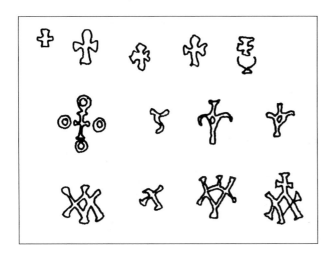

58 *A selection of cross motifs found on Brown Aksumite ceramics. Approximately full size*

It would appear that the area around the stelae maintained, for the new religion, a cultic significance. Tradition has it that the church at Aksum was built on miraculously reclaimed land, although current geomorphological evidence does not support the contention that a large body of water ever existed here. We are dealing with folk tradition, and a pre-Christian association of water and ritual. The Mai Shum reservoir to the north of the town combines the secular and the ideological; the water of the king, the water of baptism, the water for day-to-day drinking and washing. To

59 *Aksum. An eighteenth-century print of the cathedral of Maryam Zion upon a much larger, probably Aksumite-era, podium*

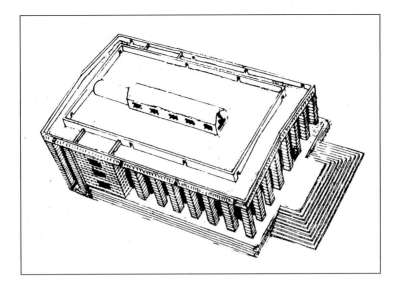

60 *Buxton and Matthews' conjectural reconstruction of the cathedral of Maryam Zion, Aksum as it may have looked before it was destroyed by Gragn in the sixteenth century*

the east of the town, the dramatic monastery of Abba Pantaleon (**colour plate 12**), founded, according to tradition, by one of the Syrian missionary nine saints, sits atop a site of pre-Aksumite cultic significance. Further to the east, at Yeha, the old pagan temple was converted for use to a church. It is clear that certain situations, such as hilltops and proximity to sacred wells were favoured by pagan and Christian alike, and some evidence of site continuity is clear.

There is little direct evidence to enable us to reconstruct the appearance of the Aksumite church. The Old Cathedral sits on an Aksumite-period podium measuring 65m by 40m (213ft by 131ft), some 3.5m (11ft) off the ground surface. This podium is clearly Aksumite in architectural appearance, but whether it represents the remains of the first church foundation or a re-use of an earlier pagan temple is open to debate. We do know that this cathedral was dedicated to Mary of Zion (Maryam Tsion), and must have undergone extensive rebuilding after the sacking of Aksum by Queen Gudit in the eleventh century. Alvares, the sixteenth-century Portuguese traveller, has left us with a description of the church as it would have been before the destruction of Aksum by Gragn in 1535; he describes a building '200 spans long by 100 spans wide' situated in a courtyard. The building was essentially basilican in shape, with five aisles and seven chapels.

The British architect Derek Matthews and Ethiopianist scholar David Buxton have attempted to reconstruct the features of the early building; utilising the dimensions given in the seventeenth-century Book of Aksum. They have matched the traditional system of measurement of one *ell* with a measurement of 1.5m (5ft) dimensions, which accords well with Alvares' description and the surviving podium. They have suggested that the Lalibela rock-cut church of Medhane Alem was a direct copy of the original Maryam Zion, and as such it may have had a large number of inter-

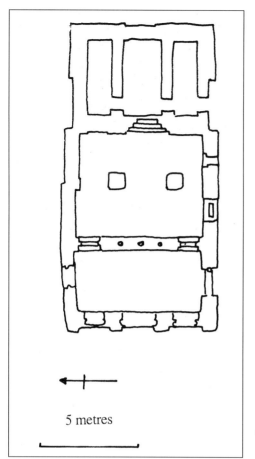

5 metres

61 *Ground plan of the small, old church at Yeha, Tigray*

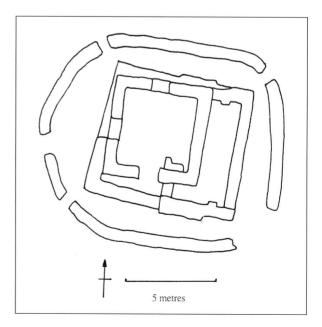

5 metres

62 *Plan of the square Aksumite church (two phases) at Enda Cherqos, Tigray. The building is surrounded by a low wall*

nal supporting columns as well as a façade of similar square-cut pillars. The building that we see today was largely constructed by King Fasilidas (1632-67) in the style then in vogue at his capital Gonder. The building is rectangular, with a series of crenellations which bring to mind Fasilidas' Gonderine castles, although recent research has suggested that this building re-incorporated features from the cathedral destroyed by Gragn.

Within the immediate area of Aksum, Aksumite-period churches are few. A basilica on the summit of Beta Giorgis was excavated by an Italian team in the 1970s. The building was a typical apsidal basilica, with side wings flanking the north-south walls at the eastern end. A later structure took the form of a rectangular room with four supporting columns that may have been re-used stelae from the nearby pre-Christian Aksumite-period graves. Associated with this basilica a number of small pottery crosses were found, as well as Aksumite pottery with cross-motif decorations. As the prime city of the Aksumite polity, and the seat of the king, it might be expected that the church at Aksum would have been a striking building in relation to its central position at the heart of the empire. But in the satellite settlements of the polity, we have evidence of the centralised direction of state Christianity at the time.

There are remains of Aksumite churches at the sites of Kohaito, Tekondo, Quiha and at Enda Cherqos. At Matara, a key Aksumite-period urban settlement, there is a group of three churches – one a three-aisled apsidal basilica – and to the east of the compound is a baptistery with a piping system constructed from broken amphorae to supply the water to a free-standing cistern. The church at Agula is sited atop a probable pagan-period plinth, as is the basilica at Wuchate Golo, where we see a baptistery area with a circular cistern lined by a large, round stone surrounded by benches.

Certain Aksumite-period elements may have survived at the impressive church complex at Degum – some 100km (62 miles) to the south-east of Aksum – although the main complex probably dates from the tenth century. Here, four key architectural elements are present in the complex. Building A is described as a church orientated east-west, with a typical Aksumite-style façade, building B is largely incorporated into the modern church, and would appear to be the remains of an older rock-cut church. Building C is described as being a funerary chapel and crypt complex, but particular interest attaches to the baptistery – building D – which is especially unusual. Here, to the south-east of building A, instead of a pool built up from masonry, we have a basin carved out of the rock with internal steps and benches.

At Adulis, the key Aksumite port on the Red Sea coast, Napier's British Army engineers uncovered a so-called 'Byzantine basilica' in 1869. The building had an apsidal annex to the eastern end, was divided internally by lines of square columns, and large pieces of carved marble were recovered in and around the building. Later work by the Italian Paribeni uncovered more marble fragments from the church; Paribeni claimed, with some justification, that the marble was sourced from Asia Minor, and was used in the on-site construction of liturgical furniture (screen supports, benches), that showed clear affinities to contemporary eastern Mediterranean material; the Greek cross is a dominant motif on the marble carvings.

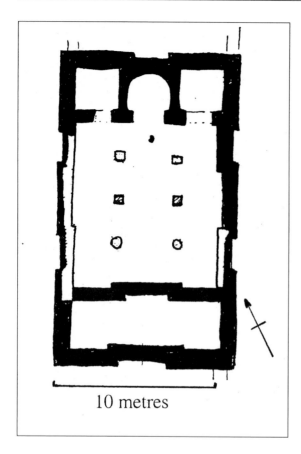

10 metres

63 *Plan of the church at Adulis (modern Eritrea). The church is of a typical basilican plan, with rooms flanking the apse. A narthex is also present*

After Aksum: rock-cut churches

Perhaps the most compelling and unusual features of Ethiopian church design are embodied in the fabulous rock-cut churches of the Lalibela region. This advanced and time-consuming technique of building has few parallels elsewhere in Africa. Although drawing on Aksumite-style building features, the Lalibela churches belong to a distinct southern Agau cultural sphere. The Agau were converted to Christianity during the eleventh and twelfth centuries, and at the time of the building of the churches had attained dominance of the Ethiopian political scene. They were the so-called Zagwe dynasty, and it is suggested that the building of underground churches followed earlier pagan practice of worshipping underground in caves. In practice, however, there is a clear link to be found in Tigray where a number of earlier rock-cut churches exist.

The Tigray churches are clearly an intermediate form between the rectangular Aksumite church and the rock-hewn churches of Lalibela and Lasta. These forms – of which David Buxton recognised five broad types – are not wholly rock-hewn. Frequently a natural grotto, cave or cleft in the rock has been enlarged over the years

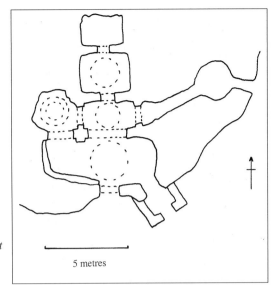

64 *Plan of the non-basilican rock-hewn church of Tamba Maryam, Tembien, Tigray. The body of the church consists of four rock-hewn and linked chambers. Archways connect the portions, and a small wall/entrance has been built up at the front*

5 metres

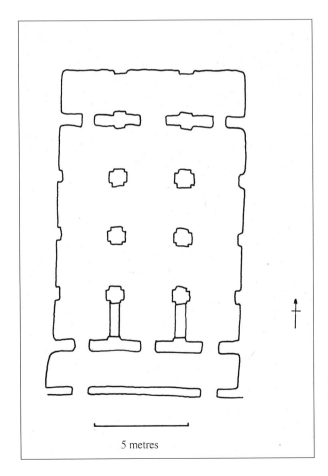

5 metres

65 *Plan of the basilican rock-hewn church at Debra Maryam Korkor, Gheralta, Tigray. This is a much more standardised plan than that of Tamba Maryam (above, fig. 64)*

66 *The rock-hewn monastic church of Ganneta Maryam, Lalibela. The scaffold supports a tin roof designed to keep the elements out and to provide some form of basic building conservation*

and the front has been screened with a stone-built façade that often echoes the Aksumite feature of alternate wood and stone coursing. The interiors are painted with biblical scenes, and the churches are typically sited on a spot sacred to the founder. These churches generally date from around the eleventh century onwards, and later versions become more elaborate and recognisably basilican in floor plan.

To the south, King Lalibela of the Zagwe dynasty founded his eponymous capital in the thirteenth century. According to tradition, God appeared to him in a dream and commanded him to build a replica of Jerusalem; the sacred geography of the old settlement mirrors his conception. A small watercourse that runs through the site is called the Jordan, there is also a Mount of Olives and a Golgotha – even a Bethlehem. The two major concentrations of rock-cut churches are perhaps the best known images of Ethiopia, and although the site has been justifiably designated a UNESCO World Heritage Site like Aksum, it is clear that the churches are deteriorating at an alarming rate, and international action is urgently required to remedy the situation. The latest solution involves the erection of sheet-metal roofing supported by eucalyptus scaffold over the church building; as a short-term measure this seems to work well, but does little to enhance the impact of the church within the landscape.

The church of Medhane Alem is one of the most elegant of the rock-hewn churches. This church is held to have been a copy of the old cathedral of Maryam Zion at Aksum, although it would appear to be slightly smaller than the original.

The façade of pillars is one of the more unusual architectural features. The church of St George is perhaps the best known of the rock-cut churches and certainly one of the more unusual. The church itself is cruciform in shape and sits in a rock-cut pit. Measuring 33.5m by 23.5m and 11m high (109ft by 76ft by 36ft) this church is testimony to the skill of the masons. Firstly, it would appear that a square trench was cut in the rock leaving a freestanding portion in the middle. Here the church would be gradually formed; an interior was excavated and the outside of the block was roughly formed into the shape of a cross. Two carved Greek crosses top the flat roof.

There is a degree of divergence in the design of the Lalibela rock-cut churches; some follow the intermediate Tigray style with a façade fronting a natural cave which has then been enlarged. Others are excavated from the rock in varying degrees of completeness and finished with freestanding masonry. What is noticeable is the survival of the Aksumite-style building technique – wooden monkey heads and horizontal coursing – albeit executed entirely in carved stone. The interiors of the church largely conform to typical church plans and are decorated to varying degrees. The ostrich egg is a dominant motif (as in the Egyptian Coptic church), and may sym-

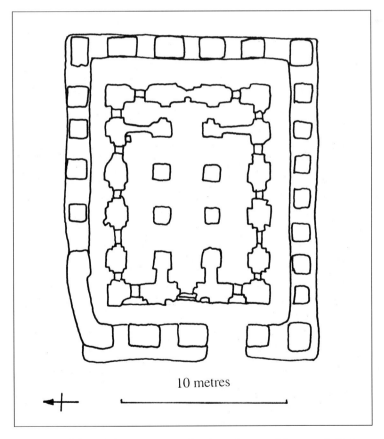

10 metres

67 *Plan of the rock-hewn monastic church at Ganneta Maryam, Lalibela. An ambulatory encompasses a basilica-plan church building*

bolise the concept of birth and resurrection; it is also important to note that the familiar pre-Christian symbol of the crescent and disc is seen too at the churches of Bilbala Cherqos and Ganneta Maryam. Was this motif borrowed from the Aksum region, or was it too an important pre-Christian symbol for the Agau peoples subsequently appropriated by the Christian Church?

The development of monastic communities

According to legend, monasticism entered Ethiopia through the efforts of the Syrian missionaries (the nine saints), although it is clear, from the evidence of the two preceding chapters, that the monastic concept may have also been introduced via the Nile Valley route from Egypt and Christian Nubia. Ethiopian monasteries are often situated on high *ambas*, or flat-topped hills – ideal defensive positions. During the crises with Queen Gudit in the eleventh century and Gragn in the sixteenth century, these settlements served to preserve the Christian ideal. The initial focus of Ethiopian monasticism was in the north; the antiquity of this system is unclear, but it is held that the fifth-century AD King Kaleb of Aksum retired to the monastery of Abba Pantaleon after his abdication. By the fourteenth century, largely through the efforts of the southern Shoan missionary Tekla Haymanot, monasticism became established in the central highlands (e.g. Debra Libanos) and on islands in Lake Tana. One of the finest examples of a traditional Ethiopian monastic settlement is to be found at Debra Damo, some 100km (62 miles) east of Aksum, and it is here that we can gain the best picture of the archaeology of an Ethiopian monastery.

The monastery itself is situated on the top of a flat-topped mountain (*amba*) measuring some 600m by 250m at an altitude of 2225m (7300ft). The only way in

68 *The monastery of Debra Damo is situated upon a steep* amba *or flat-topped mountain*

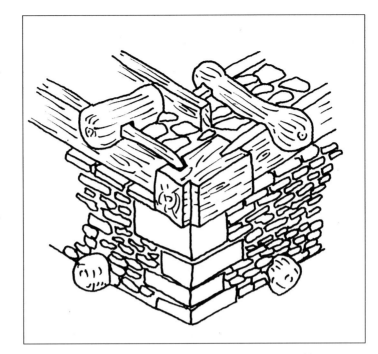

69 *The survival of Aksumite-era building techniques at the monastery of Debra Damo, Tigray. Wooden beams and cylindrical ties ('monkey heads') interlaced with rubble and stone walling. This type of architecture is skeuomorphically represented on the Aksumite stelae*

is via a 50-ft climb up a rope; no females, either human or animal, may enter the compound. In essence, the monastic settlement differs little from traditional villages, but cannot be entirely self-sufficient. Small groves of eucalyptus and olive dot the summit, and here and there humped cattle – male of course – graze. In this regard, the monastery is not a physically isolated entity; to provide for itself some form of economic symbiotic relationship is required with its neighbouring farming settlements.

The monastery was visited by the German Aksum expedition in the 1900s, but the bulk of our archaeological knowledge comes from restoration works carried out by the British architect Derek Matthews in the 1940s. The monastery is suggested to have been a sixth-century AD foundation; legend has it that the founder, one of the nine saints by the name of Abuna Aragawi, was dropped on top of the *amba* by a serpent. It has also been suggested that the monastery occupies a site of earlier pagan importance; legend has it that the large water cisterns were formerly used in pagan times to venerate water spirits – a familiar theme.

The modern monastery preserves an amalgam of architectural features. The community is centred around the two churches which embody Aksumite architectural attributes such as horizontal coursing, buttressing and recessing and wooden monkey heads. The larger church is entered via a traditional two-storied gateway that contains a bell and provides for storage of drums. The rectangular church building is entered from the west and is sectioned by six main carved monolithic columns. The domed sanctuary is a later addition to the original foundation. There is also a smaller rectangular church located adjacent to a series of grottoes; these caves have been used for burial, but would probably have served as hermits' cells in the past. Both churches are sited – according to legend – where the founding saint first set foot on the *amba* and where he finally reached the summit.

Houses for the monks are grouped irregularly; each house represents a self-suffi-cient social and economic unit within the wider community. Each house has a gar-den and water provisioning, and the upper stories are used as contemplation and prayer rooms. Livestock enclosures are also present. Because of its special place in the history of the Ethiopian Church, it is considered a great honour to be buried at Debra Damo; bodies are often brought in and set aside in a protected and highly sacred burial area to which admittance is strictly controlled. Social roles within this special community have developed along rigid lines. Two 'orders' or social group-ings are recognised: one group, locals, are given economic priority with emphasis on leading a more individualistic lifestyle. The second group come from outside the dis-trict and are expected to live communally and share their wealth.

The sheer inaccessibility of Debra Damo meant that it was able to withstand the unrest that took hold of the Christian state at the time of Gudit and Gragn; it became a refuge, a place where the survival of the Church could be guaranteed against all odds. Sadly, however, the famous library, with its priceless collection of manuscripts, was totally destroyed by fire in 1996; the loss of this heritage to the Ethiopian Church has been immeasurable. Initially monasticism was confined to the north of the highlands, but as Christianity spread southwards to the Amhara after around 1000, monasticism became the main means for conversion of the pagan peo-ples. This campaign was led by a man called Tekla Haymanot, who pioneered the development of monasteries in the south during the fifteenth century. A large group of monastic settlements can be found on the islands of Lake Tana; their isolation over centuries has contributed to their preservation. Again, the settlements cannot be entirely self-sufficient; the traditional means of servicing their needs was by the papyrus *tankwa* boats, which can still be seen on the lake today, and which recall similar types used by the ancient Egyptians. Here, in the south, rectangular stone church buildings are not the norm; there are circular, wooden-built churches with the *maqdas* in the centre.

Debra Libanos, near Addis Ababa, is the most important and powerful monastery in the contemporary church. Founded by Tekla Haymanot in the fifteenth century, it is allegedly sited on a place of earlier pagan importance. Monasticism was an impor-tant catalyst in the incorporation of newly-conquered territories into the existing Christian state; the conquests of the southern and central plateau areas of Gojjam and Shoa were accompanied by the founding of new monasteries in an effort to rapidly Christianise the new subject peoples. Debra Libanos was such a frontier community.

Originally founded as Debra Atsbo, the initial community consisted of a few monks living in a small cave. The cave itself was simply divided into a church area and living quarters. Initially, when arriving in a new area, the monks would keep to a rigid ascetic life, but make themselves useful to the wider community by offering themselves for agricultural labour. At this stage they subsisted mainly by gathering, and it was only as the community became established that dedicated dwellings and a church would be built. The siting of Debra Atsbo is also significant; the original cave situation was on an ideal defensive position, and in broader terms was located upon a vital strategic area on the borders of a number of different social groups.

Until fairly recently a yearly sacrificial feast was held in the community; this feasting was held to have had its roots in pagan times, and few of the monks understood the significance of this long-lived ritual that owed little to Christian tradition. Today, Tekla Haymanot's prayer grotto has become a centre of veneration, but the monastery has developed of late in terms of wealth and scale. An old peoples' home is located within the complex, but there are other motives to its presence; when they are widowed, the elderly are encouraged to become monks and nuns in the monastery and nearby convent – in this way a steady supply of recruits is guaranteed! There is no better symbol of continuity and tradition than the monastery of Debra Libanos; in the library old manuscripts are available to view with their traditional iconography. Traditional images of saints battling demons and wild animals crowd the crumbling pages, while in the new church stained glass by the famous modern artist Afewerk Tekle shows the same images, albeit from a newer stylised perspective.

Discussion

Ethiopian Christianity has struggled for hundreds of years for its survival; it has successfully resisted Islamic incursions and has developed, through isolation and years of struggle, idiosyncratic cultural facets. Perhaps more than anywhere, this is a fine example of religious syncretism. The initial conversion of the elites of the Aksumite polity was successful, yet Christianity would not become the unchallenged state religion for many more years. Indeed the Christianisation of the southern Agau and Amhara ethnic groups would not be completed for another thousand years. In all cases the process was entirely piecemeal, which would explain the persistence of what might be termed pagan cultural and social elements for a number of years.

These syncretic elements had a vital part to play in the development of the new religion, or they would have died out fairly quickly. In the first place the syncretic amalgam was fostered by the ruling Aksumite elite, who sweetened the pill for their people – who by and large remained adherents of the old religion – by appropriating key pre-Christian cultural motifs. The siting of new churches on older sacred sites facilitated the acceptance process, and is a motif that is constantly recognised. The architecture of the new places of worship clearly mirrored the architecture of the older order, but the style did not die out, quite the opposite. A thousand years later it would still be seen in the Lalibela monolithic churches, yet these would be idealised skeuomorphic (copied in a different medium) representations of the Aksumite architectural order. The Zagwe builders of these churches obviously needed to legitimise their claims to the ancient and venerable Solomonic throne. What better way of recalling the glories of Aksum – and unintentionally its pre-Christian roots – than by utilising these architectural motifs? By using the past, they were legitimising and consolidating their present.

This thread of continuity and syncretism runs through to modern times. The new cathedral at Aksum has a bell tower which is an architectural interpretation of the pre-Christian stelae, and those stelae participate in the holy festivals at Aksum. Every November, at the feast of Maryam Zion, the Patriarch is solemnly enthroned before stela three. Around him is a cacophony of noise, with wild dancing and shaking of sistra (rattles), which themselves are so similar to ancient Egyptian rattles. It is this sense of cultural isolation and the remembrance of the struggles against invaders that has fostered this idiosyncratic yet vital self-identity. For the Ethiopian Christian, a great survivor, the meaning of the present is informed by the past.

Further reading

A good general introduction to the way of life of the Ethiopians remains David Buxton (1970) *The Abyssinians* (London: Thames and Hudson), although for a fuller, but arguably rather dated account see Edward Ullendorff (1960) *The Ethiopians* (London: Oxford University Press). An excellent and thorough more recent introduction to Ethiopia is Richard Pankhurst (1997) *The Ethiopians* (Oxford: Blackwell).

For an up-to-date introduction to the Ethiopian Orthodox Church, its historical development and its art, the richly illustrated *African Zion: The Sacred Art of Ethiopia* (edited by R. Grierson, 1993: New Haven: Yale University Press) is a key text. In a similar vein, also see E. Hein and B. Kleidt (1999), *Ethiopia- Christian Africa: Art Churches and Culture* (Ratingen: Melina Verlag), which is again a beautifully illustrated book.

For anyone seeking to understand the archaeology of ancient Ethiopia, the best and most accessible starting point is David Phillipson's *Ancient Ethiopia* (1998, London: British Museum Press); this book contains new information from the author's recent excavations at Aksum. For a more historically orientated overview, see Stuart Munro-Hay's 1991 book *Aksum: an African Civilisation of Late Antiquity* (Edinburgh: Edinburgh University Press), which gives a detailed overview of aspects of material culture, including coinage and belief systems. The excellent bibliographies of both books provide ample scope for following up more detailed aspects of Aksumite culture and history. For a theory on the erection and significance of the Aksumite stelae see David Phillipson's 1994 article 'The Significance and Symbolism of the Aksumite Stelae' in the *Cambridge Archaeological Journal* 4/2 pages 189-210.

Elements of medieval church architecture are well covered in Ruth Plant's 1985 book *The Architecture of the Tigre, Ethiopia* (Worcester: Raven's International), and David Buxton's 1971 article 'The Rock-Hewn and Other Medieval Churches of Tigre Province, Ethiopia' in *Archaeologia* 103, pages 33-100. For a well-illustrated description of the monolithic churches of Lalibela see either Georg Gerster's 1970 book *Churches in Rock and Early Christian Art in Ethiopia* (London: Phaidon) or Irmgard Bidder's *Lalibela: The Monolithic Churches of Ethiopia* (London: Thames and

Hudson). For a thorough description of the monastery at Debra Damo –and its ren–
ovation– see Derek Matthews and Antonio Mordini (1959) 'The Monastery of
Debra Damo, Ethiopia' in *Archaeologia* 97, pages 1-58.

One of the key foreign sources for understanding medieval Ethiopia is Alvares'
account, and this has been translated and edited by C. Beckingham and G.
Huntingford (1961), *The Prester John of the Indies* (Cambridge: Hakluyt Society).
Finally, for an intriguing – although somewhat archaeologically and historically fan–
ciful theory on Ethiopia's claims to the Ark of the Covenant – see Graham Hancock's
1992 work *The Sign and the Seal* (London: Heinemann); a controversial book, but a
good travelogue, which fills in some of the more 'legendary' aspects of Ethiopian
civilisation.

6 African Christianity and European Colonialism

> At that great time
> With great slashes of civilisation
> Spitting holy water on domesticated brows,
> Vultures in the shadow of their claws
> Built the bloody monument of a tutelary era.

(From *Vultures*, by David Diop)

In 1884, representatives of the major European powers sat down in Berlin and carved up Africa into arbitrary spheres of influence; the scramble for Africa was now over, there was enough for everybody to be satisfied. These boundaries cut through established African socio-political/ethnic groups, and made little geographical sense. In essence the Berlin Congress represented the final stage of a process that had been going on for hundreds of years, it codified merely, on a formal basis, actions that had been part of Europe's avaricious goals since the first Europeans set foot on the continent. It will be recalled from chapter 1 that the Portuguese made the first concerted efforts to exploit the economic fruits of a hitherto untapped continent; engaging in prospection for new gold sources to exploit luxury items and indeed slaves, the Portuguese also began to spread the message of Christianity. They were soon followed by other European powers, anxious not to lose out on the economic potential offered by Africa. By the end of the nineteenth century, European imperialists were firmly entrenched in Africa, and alongside the national politics and scope for economic development, came the first truly structured and concerted attempts at conversion of the locals to Christianity; to the eyes of the colonialists, the benefits of 'western' civilisation went hand in hand with the acceptance of western religious values.

At the outset here, we should be clear that the archaeology of African-European contact has been relatively neglected and it is really only in the last few years that we have seen a much stronger, active research profile in the area. Rigid terminological definitions here are difficult. We are dealing with what would be termed elsewhere 'historical archaeology', where the interpretation of the cultural material may be assisted by the use of documentary sources, and indeed vice versa. Within the Africanist context, this is not a satisfactory label to apply. Christopher De Corse, an American archaeologist who has worked widely on European settlement in west Africa, prefers the term 'historical sites archaeology', whilst the British Africanist

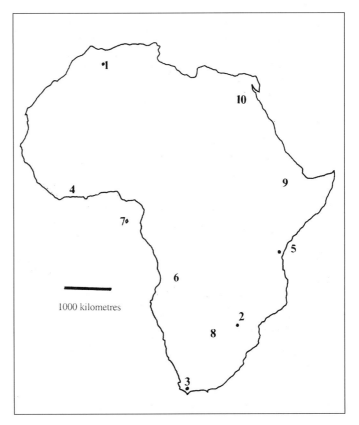

70 *Some of the key sites discussed in this chapter:*
1. Qsar es Seghir,
2. Dambarare, 3. Cape Town, 4. Area of the Gold Coast forts, 5. Mombasa and Fort Jesus, 6. Area of the Kongo Kingdom,
7. São Tomé, 8. Sphere of the nineteenth-century Tswana kingdoms, 9. Area of the Abyssinian Empire,
10. Mamluk and Ottoman Egypt

archaeologist Paul Lane seeks to remove the term 'historical archaeology' from a problematic European/American terminological context. The new emphasis, he suggests, should be put squarely upon the study of the African/European interaction, especially in regard to the indigenous African cultural responses to European acculturation and economic exploitation. Potentially this is a fascinating, yet very understudied area of research, for one of the key questions we need to pose, especially within the context of this present work, is the study of how the culture of Christianity impacted upon traditional social fabrics, belief systems and the material cultures of the newly converted African societies. Interaction is a two-way dynamic; it should not be thought of purely in terms of European acting upon African; both sides clearly act upon each other.

The archaeological data discussed in this chapter range over some five hundred years and across the whole continent. In effect, it is a fairly sparse database, a factor which bears witness to the relative paucity of research on the archaeology of Africa during the late second millennium AD. Here we will consider the nature of Christian archaeological material from the earliest Portuguese occupations of the fifteenth century up to the archaeology of mission stations of the nineteenth century, and the advent of large-scale European colonial church building. Let us begin with the picture of the first tentative Portuguese steps in Africa, and consider the nature of Christianity's impact on the indigenous belief systems of Africa.

71 *Luanda, Angola. The Portuguese fort of San Miguel built in 1641. This fort is in south-western Africa, but does not differ markedly from contemporary Gold Coast forts*

Forts and traders on the Gold Coast

The area known as the Gold Coast (roughly the coastline of modern Ghana) would not have seemed inviting to the first Portuguese adventurers who set foot there in the late fifteenth century. Within the hinterland were numbers of different social groups who might not be relied upon to give a warm welcome; for European bodies, the heat and dangers of disease were also ever present, and mortality rates among the traders spiralled. But the obvious riches of the region were too good to overlook. Here supplies of gold, luxury items and above all slaves could be found; the trade in human commodities was driven by the need to sustain the markets of the Portuguese colonies in the New World with free labour. The exploitation of human slaves was not merely a one-sided European affair; local rulers and chiefs also played their part, both as middlemen within the trade system, as well as owners of slaves themselves. It is against this background of uneasy treaties with local polities that the first permanent trade stations were to be established, and these trade stations subsequently became large fortified castles, small European communities planted upon this lucrative coast – in time attracting large numbers of African subjects, drawn by the possibilities of wealth acquisition. These Africans also provided a pool of potential converts to Christianity, a process initially only reluctantly undertaken by the Portuguese, for above all, theirs was a primarily economic mission.

After the first Portuguese contacts with western Africa in 1482, some 50 key trading posts were established along over a thousand miles of coast. At the northernmost extremity, some 320km (200 miles) north of the Senegal River, was the fort of

Arguin, founded by the Spanish in the sixteenth century, and latterly occupied in the seventeenth century by Brandenburg merchants from what is now Germany. The southernmost extent of this chain of multi-national, self-sufficient trading centres is found at Whydah, a fort which had a chequered ownership pattern: successively during the seventeenth century Whydah was occupied by the English, the French, the Dutch, the Brandenburgers and finally by the Portuguese. The Portuguese concerns tended to be directly owned by the Crown, whilst those of the other nations were run by autonomous, private chartered companies who enjoyed a nominal degree of independence from governmental control. The forts had to be essentially self-sufficient concerns; within the community were store-rooms, factories and often a chapel. The need for labour to maintain the self-sufficiency of the fort often resulted in the presence of a large, subordinated African community around the settlement augmenting the relatively small European population. Within this new developing economic 'Atlantic zone', each country's traders jealously guarded their trade monopolies. The key to wealth was largely the control of the slave trade, but other nationalistic concerns also held sway; one of the main factors was the attempt to isolate Muslim expansion into western Africa, and here Christianity would prove to be a powerful tool.

Initially the Portuguese employed chaplains to cater for the spiritual well-being of the Europeans within the fort; but life in the community could often be tedious, and tensions would inevitably build. To this end, the job of the chaplain was not particularly attractive, but did often mean a position of relative authority within the hierarchy of the community. During 1566, the King's Chaplain of the Portuguese fort of Elmina was paid quite a healthy sum of 40 reals (gold coins) a year with the proviso that he said a mass a day for the soul of King Henry the Navigator. Under this chaplain, was a senior priest – paid 50 reals a year, a sum reflecting a greater degree of practical responsibility. There were also two other minor chaplains. The Portuguese pay scales were generally comparable to those elsewhere; in the seventeenth century the Dutch lay preacher at Elmina – latterly captured from the Portuguese – was paid 36 florins a year, and his colleague at the fort of Axim received 28 florins a year. The Danish chaplain at the fort of Christiansborg at the same time received 1,488 kroner a year, whilst a subordinate catechist received 928 kroner. These were fairly good pay rates, but they could not camouflage the relative tedium and indeed danger of a career in western Africa. For many years forts often did without chaplain and chapel. During the Dutch period at Elmina, the old Portuguese church was converted into a store and services were held in the Governor's dining hall before a new Dutch chapel could be built. Religious improvement did not rate as a high priority in many minds. The Dutch at Elmina provided a large library filled with improving religious books, but the Governor was often forced to rely on unordained priests or lay preachers. The Danes did not provide chapels until relatively late in their occupation, and the major function of the preacher here was to provide a broad education for the community.

Inevitably some Africans began to be attracted towards the spiritual side of the fort's life. The Portuguese ran a concerted missionary effort dedicated to the mem-

72 *A print of Elmina Castle, Gold Coast (Ghana) probably around the eighteenth century*

ory of St Francis of Assisi; legend has it that a white lead statue of the saint turned black in the west African environment, thus producing a miraculous omen. As early as 1491, the Portuguese had succeeded in converting the King of Benin to Christianity, and soon Africans were flocking to the faith, some even becoming ordained priests. In 1766, the English had the part-time services of the African minister Philip Quaque, who had been sent by the London-based Society for the Propagation of the Gospel. During the eighteenth century a Dutch captain's slave 'Kaptein' had been trained up to serve as a minister in the Dutch Reformed Church. Kaptein was latterly appointed to the important position of chaplain at Fort St George, Elmina, and his lasting legacy was to translate into the Fanti language the twelve articles of the Apostles' Creed around 1744. The Danes too accepted African ministers into their forts, one of the most famous and effective being Christian Protten, a half-African appointed as a minister by the African Moravian Mission.

Having considered the social impact of these forts on the indigenous peoples of the Gold Coast, let us turn now to the archaeological evidence for this dynamic interaction. The European trading settlements were in no way physically standardised. All provided large-scale defensive works and extensive storage rooms. Three rough categories – based on size – may be recognised. The smallest, and possibly most archaeologically nebulous entity, would have been the semi-permanent 'lodge' settlement. Moving up the scale would be the fort, and largest, and most socially complex, would be the Castle, of which the massive constructions at Elmina and Christiansborg are representative. It is important to recognise that the available building materials were not suited to construction on a grand scale; rough masonry initially predominated, and bricks had to be imported from Europe as ships' ballast. Lime for the fabrication of mortar could similarly not be had locally in sufficient quantities, and this material too had to be imported. These construction problems are reflected in the few extant remains of churches and chapels associated with these trading settlements. In many cases secular buildings were used for divine service, and in only very rare cases can we recognise separate buildings dedicated solely to ecclesiastical usage.

A small, stone Portuguese fort begun in 1661 became Danish in the eighteenth century, and as Christiansborg Castle, became the focus for Danish trading activities on the Gold Coast. The original Portuguese church of 1679-83 had fallen into ruin by 1735. The Danish evidently felt, perhaps for compelling religious reasons, that a Roman Catholic place of worship would be unsuitable, or perhaps more prosaically they saw no need to provide for a dedicated religious building, as indeed was the norm in many Danish trade settlements on the Gold Coast. During the mid-eighteenth century, a small chapel was constructed, but for some reason it was used as a powder magazine and services continued to be conducted in a room under the dining hall. The chapel formally became the sole place of worship in around 1790. The building itself measures some 25m by 12m (80ft by 40ft), and has a rather charming painted porch at the gabled southern end. The date of 1791 is inscribed over the

73 *Elmina Castle, Ghana. Interior of the fort*

doorway; this probably refers to the consecration of the chapel rather than a date of construction. The recessed gable top for hanging a ring of bells is now missing. In essence, the building presents a neat, compact and economic appearance with little room for overly ornate decoration. The pragmatic needs of the community took precedence, and there was minimal financial investment in religious buildings.

Perhaps the best known fort on the coast is that of Elmina, a Portuguese/Dutch castle, founded in 1482 by Don Diogo D'Azambuja, a Portuguese, near the settlement of Dondou. The castle was subsequently seized by the Dutch in 1637, and was finally ceded to the British in 1872. The modern face of Elmina castle bears witness to a number of periods of rebuilding episodes, and after an effective programme of restoration little evidence of the earliest castle remains. The early building of the Church of St George was demolished around 1598; a later (1668) engraving shows a rather ornate and over-stylised building quite out of character with contemporary architectural tastes and building techniques. In around 1598, a church was built in the middle of the castle's courtyard, and this was latterly altered by the Dutch. The biggest architectural change involved the addition of four upright bands of brick along the gable end, and whilst the earliest Dutch surveys indicate the presence of a side chapel, this does not remain today. It is important again to note that the Dutch did not use the Portuguese church for services, these tended to be conducted in secular areas of the castle. In 1645, the courtyard was paved and architectural embellishments were removed from the Portuguese church for use elsewhere. Evidently, the Dutch had no symbolic attachment to what was a Roman Catholic place of worship. By 1660, however, the Dutch had built their own chapel, a building that would perhaps not have looked out of place in a seventeenth-century Dutch village. This building, described by an observer in 1682 as 'a pretty, neat building' makes no concessions to grand architectural statements. The plaster front shows some elements of embellishment, with plaster fronting decorated with circles and triangles in projecting brick courses. The tall, round-arched windows are an obvious Dutch motif, and above the doorway is a Dutch carving of Psalm 132. There is no attempt at embellishment or of being over-ornate; the chapel is just a pragmatic and obviously Protestant place of worship.

For Christian burial, a separate area was set aside outside the walls. A seventeenth-century engraving shows this cemetery area associated with a small chapel with gabled roof. Bodies were buried within brick-lined tombs in coffins, in a definite Christian tradition. Nearby burials of Africans (and we may assume that they were not converts) were buried in the traditional manner beneath the floors of their huts, wrapped in cloth and associated with grave goods. Other burial data were recovered from the site of Bantama, a site that was traditionally considered as being a very early French settlement. Of the eighteen skeletons recovered, eight had their heads to the east, but four were associated with grave goods. The general consensus is that this site was not an early French settlement, but was more likely a much later settlement of mixed European/African population. In summary, then, the extant documentary sources and the very obvious architectural nature and design of the ecclesiastical buildings all point to a strong Christian element within the forts, and funerary evi-

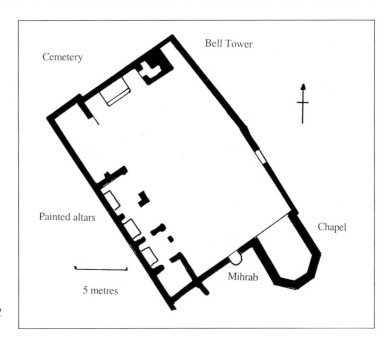

74 *Plan of the main church at Qsar es Seghir, the Santa Maria Misericordia showing a number of key features, including the mosque's mihrab*

dence suggests a broad pagan versus Christian cultural dichotomy. Of the African cultural reaction to the limited missionary process, we have very little data.

Portuguese expansion into Africa

Portuguese settlement in Africa was not confined to the Gold Coast. Geographically, the coasts of northern Africa offered a logical springboard into the interior of the continent from the homeland. In 1415, the Portuguese had entered Ceuta, just on the northern tip of Morocco – today a Spanish enclave on the Straits of Gibraltar. After a number of campaigns, Ceuta finally fell to King Alphonso the Fifth's army, and it rapidly became integrated into the Portuguese economic and political frame-

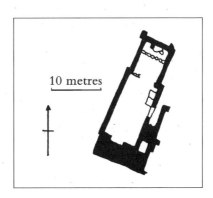

75 *Plan of the church of San Sebastian, Qsar es Seghir: a much simpler building than the main church*

155

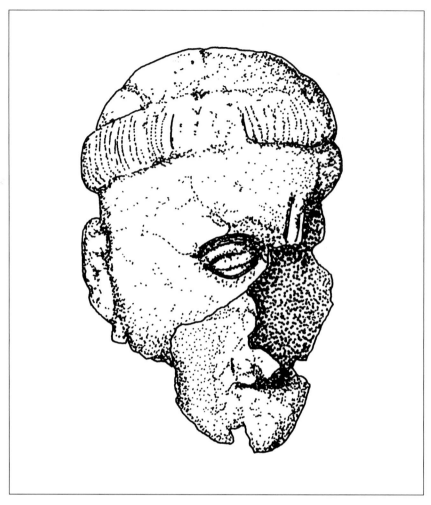

76 *A life-sized terracotta head found in the main church of San Sebastian, Qsar es Seghir. The hairstyle resembles a monk's tonsure*

work. One of the first steps in this process was the appropriation of the town's mosque and its conversion into the church of Santa Maria Misericordia. Some 30km (19 miles) to the east of modern Tangier is the archaeological site of Qsar es Seghir; this important medieval town was investigated by the American archaeologist Charles Redman, and excavations here have yielded a fascinating picture of the role of Christianity in these formative Portuguese colonial settlements. This town is especially important as it was located on the frontier zone of Portuguese influence, the point of contact between cultures. Redman recognises the strange position of the frontier town; these settlements are often subject to rapid change owing to external pressures, and demographically they do not mirror more centralised settlements. There is usually a higher proportion of younger males – traders, soldiers, adventurers – in these towns, and the archaeological record often mirrors this disparity.

Within Qsar es Seghir, no expense was spared in providing an ornate and striking place of worship. In a process that by now will sound familiar, the town's mosque was razed, and its site was used for the subsequent building. The main chamber is 20m long and 12m wide (66ft by 39ft), and is entered by a flight of descending steps from the main plaza. The floor is set with paving stones; some of these are memorial stones indicating sub-floor burials of important secular and ecclesiastical figures. The motifs are immediately recognisable from a European medieval context; two bear a symbol of a down-turned waning moon, and one has the familiar *memento mori* of a bas-relief death's head in the form of a skull. Within the corner of the building are the remains of a bell tower and its internal staircase. Special attention attaches to four separate chapels adjacent to the main chamber, each being furnished with its own altar. One of these shrines, or chapels, is a five-sided structure opening off the south-eastern wall of the church next to where the *mihrab* (prayer niche) of the mosque was located. The walls and floors were decorated with lustrous glazed polychrome tiles.

The rough stone walls of this imposing building were covered with lime plaster. The altars were made from rough drystone walls, filled with rubble, faced with plaster and then painted with religious figures such as angels and fishermen. Small finds within the building included an iron crucifix as well as a 40cm (1ft 4in) high terracotta figurine of what would appear to be an unidentified saint. A second church, possibly dedicated to San Sebastian, is of a similar construction. The solitary altar is another rubble-filled construction and is bordered by a single step. Within the floor of the south-eastern corner of the main chamber a nearly full-sized terracotta head was discovered, the significance of which is not immediately clear; it may belong to a statue of a saint. Also within the chamber are a number of sub-floor burials, indicative no doubt of high-status individuals. Socially, Qsar es Seghir contrasts sharply with the fort settlements of west Africa. The town is on a much larger scale, and the

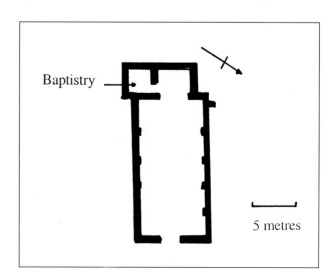

Baptistry

5 metres

77 *Plan of the simple church at Fort Jesus during the seventeenth century*

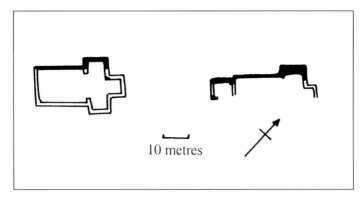

78 *Gereza, Zanzibar. Left: the cruciform Portuguese church of 1560 and (right) incorporated into a portion of the Omani fortifications of 1710*

major Portuguese cultural elements are more highly integrated. This is clearly a Portuguese town transplanted into a new cultural setting, and the scale of church building bears witness to the social and financial power wielded by the clergy here. There are also clear indicators of differing economic priorities; the forts, as market centres geared towards African exploitation, did not need the scale of church building as was required at the town of Qsar es Seghir, with its more socially mixed population and differing spiritual needs.

Inevitably the Portuguese began to range further afield. On 7 April 1498, the noted explorer Vasco de Gama made landfall on the eastern African Indian Ocean coast near what is now modern Malindi (Kenya), and initial Portuguese interest centred on the large Swahili coastal settlement of Kilwa during the early sixteenth century. The first Portuguese traders encountered here a society which was markedly cosmopolitan in outlook. For hundreds of years, the Swahili coast, an area roughly covering the coastlines of southern Somalia, Kenya and Tanzania and the island of Zanzibar, had been at the centre of trans-Indian ocean trade. Settlements such as Shanga, Kilwa and Manda displayed an amalgam of local African Bantu and Arab cultures. Islam held sway on this coast, and the Swahili economies were based on the transfer of luxury items and slaves from the interior and the importation of Arab, Persian, Indian and even Chinese luxury items. The Portuguese therefore had a ready economic system to exploit for their own purposes, but an ideological battle would also be taking shape, the Muslims of the coast against the high-minded Roman Catholic interlopers.

After a number of years of feuding and stress, the Portuguese finally captured the key settlement of Mombasa in 1593, and set about a vigorous programme of consolidation. The massive castle of Fort Jesus was constructed by the noted Italian military architect Cairato between 1593-6; it soon became the focus for Portuguese activity on the Indian Ocean coast. With massive ramparts of rubble and coral block – 4m (13ft) thick in places – Fort Jesus stood as an example of Portuguese military might, and it was not captured by Arab armies until 1698. As with the forts of the Gold Coast, the Portuguese made clear provision for the spiritual well-being of the inhabitants, although at first there was little regard for missionary work outside its walls. The chapel within Fort Jesus is located at the western end of the main court-yard. The building exudes a functional air; a flat-roofed building, the nave measures 17m by 14m (56ft by 46ft) with an altar at the western end. The sanctuary measures 4m long by 5m wide (13ft by 16ft), and the walls within the sanctuary were proba-bly painted with red ochre. In the late seventeenth century the western end was rebuilt, and an arch was placed over the altar. Some burials have been found beneath the floor of the nave, although a separate cemetery was provided in later times on what is now Thika Street.

As the settlement grew, provisions were made for the spiritual needs of those who lived outside the fort and those indigenous inhabitants who had been attracted to Christianity, although it should be noted that the Portuguese missionaries had scant suc-cess with the conversion of the Muslims of the coast. Most of the new adherents came from the hinterland – where traditional animist religions still prevailed – and sections of the population excluded from urban Muslim Swahili society. The church of the Misericordia was established in around 1590; the exact location of the building has not been satisfactorily established, but would appear to be at the junction of the Ndia Kuu and Old Kilindi Roads. An eighteenth-century map shows an Arab fortress at this loca-tion, and it is probable that this was the converted church. The *Igreja Matriz* or Mother Church is similarly difficult to locate. Probably located at the southern end of Ndia Kuu, the building appears to have been intact around 1728, but was a ruin at the end of the eighteenth century and by 1840 the remains of the building were used as a cow stall. A convent of Augustinian friars was established around 1597 off the Rapozerra towards the shore. Dedicated to St Anthony of Padua, this building was latterly used as a military base by the Arabs, and its remains were noted in 1846 by a French traveller. Linked to the convent was a small Augustinian hermitage of the late seventeenth century; named *Nossa Señora da Esperança* (Our Lady of Hope), this building was sited atop a Shirazi fort. Nearby was a pillar with a cross erected in 1505 and destroyed in the 1870s. The chapel of *Nossa Señora das Merces* (Our Lady of Mercies) overlooked the harbour, roughly on the site of the modern golf course. Of two isolated churches shown on Rezende's 1643 map on the shore at Kilendini, no trace remains.

Recent survey work by the British archaeologist Mark Horton in Tanzania and the strategically important island of Zanzibar has uncovered a few traces of Christian archaeology in a predominantly Muslim context. The fort of Gereza was built by the Portuguese between 1590 and 1610, and contained an Augustinian mission. The fort was seized by Omani Arabs in 1710, but enough remains to elucidate the archaeo-logical development of the church within the fort. The earliest religious building was a chapel in the western part of the fort, the remains of which are still visible in the northern wall. The church would appear to be roughly cruciform in plan, but the transept was subsequently filled in, and the rectangular nave windows were bricked up. The second phase of development made provision for cannon ports on top of the roof, and a square tower at the west end of the church.

79 *The Portuguese cathedral at Luanda, Angola dating from 1628*

As at Qsar es Seghir, the Portuguese Christians encountered an established and integrated Muslim society. Mission effectiveness was negligible amongst the coastal Muslims, and there was often outright hostility. The Mombasa settlement had indeed begun with the closed fort-like mentality, but the gradual development of Portuguese power allowed for a planned settlement along the lines of Qsar es Seghir, and a relatively large number of churches built on such a scale so as to leave the local Muslims in no doubt as to who was firmly in charge.

The coasts of south-eastern Africa, centred on modern Mozambique, attracted the Portuguese because of the promise of gold in the interior. Around 1505, the Portuguese had established a base at Sofala, and they soon began to establish tentative contacts with the peoples of the hinterland. The initial penetration took the form of 'trade fairs', opportunities to meet at fixed points for trade and exchange. The sites of these fairs soon became important settlements in their own right, particularly the three key sites of Massapa, Luanze and, in what is now Zimbabwe, the site of Dambarare, excavated in the 1960s by Peter Garlake. Historical sources from the 1630s refer to Dambarare as being a fort with a church serviced by a Dominican friar. The archaeological site of Dambarare was readily identified from aerial photographs; a number of mounds and earthworks could be clearly seen, and Garlake concentrated on one of the largest mounds, an earthwork some 55m (180ft) in length.

Excavation yielded a church building, and two building episodes could be recognised, each phase utilising a different type of brick. The second-phase church reconstruction followed the plan of the earliest church, but it became apparent that real interest would attach to the burials found in and around the church. The excavated burials totalled 31 graves, but more remained unexcavated; from these data a rough spatial chronology emerged. Three corpses were interred either before the occupation or very early in the history of the first church. A number were subsequently interred beneath floors D and E of the first church, and then after the demolition, in an occupation hiatus, a number of other burials were found. Two burials lie in the occupation levels of the final church building. The burial tradition closely followed standard European Christian practice; the skeleton was laid out full length, with the arms crossed at the chest, clasped at the waist or as in two occasions, clasped firmly to the head. The orientations of the body were all standard east–west configurations, and the majority of the burials (21) had their heads to the west. The grave cut size was broadly consistent, being 1m (3ft 3in) deep. Most of the interments were individual, but the burials AA6 and 7, between the walls of the first church, were of a European male and African female. Occasionally a few grave goods were recovered, a practice that curiously runs counter to the standard Christian tradition. A rectangular clay tablet was found against the right thigh bone of the European male burial C5; the tablet bore a depiction of a virgin and child as well as an armorial device. The copper ornaments associated with the C4 burial probably helped preserve the remains of the shroud, and jewellery and assorted pieces of metalwork were often noted within the grave cuts.

A certain pattern begins to emerge from the burial evidence at Dambarare. Predominantly European males were buried within the church, often with quality adornments and mostly with their arms crossed. Outside the church, probable lower status burials were located; women, children and men mostly with arms uncrossed. The attribution of racial characteristics in human skeletal material is often problematic, but it would appear that there may be a dichotomy between European and African burial locations. The crossing of the arms could indicate that the person was a full communicant of the Church, whilst the uncrossing of the arms may suggest that the deceased was not a full member of the Church, and had somehow existed on the periphery of the Christian locus. Dambarare has yielded fascinating evidence concerning the interaction of the indigenous and Portuguese cultural spheres. Here we can discern a greater African participation in the dynamics of the settlement. It appears that socially the native Africans were not marginalised as perhaps happened elsewhere, but played a seemingly full role in the Christian community.

In chapter 1, during the discussion of the expansion of Europeans into Africa in the sixteenth century, mention was made of the kingdom of the Kongo, and the conversion of the African king Mbemba Nzinga Nkuwu who became the Christianised King John the First. The earliest church built here was that of San Salvador in 1490, around which gathered a concerted missionary effort in south-western-central Africa. Until now we have largely considered the salient European and African manifestations of the conversion process from a broadly European cultural perspective, but it may be possible that the missionary efforts of the Portuguese along the Congo impacted on traditional cultural *mores* in other ways. At the 1962 Pan African

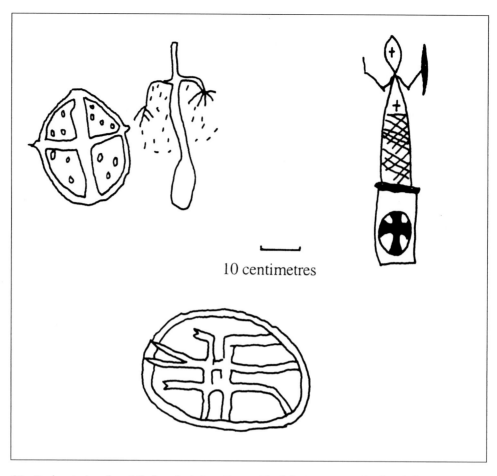

10 centimetres

80 *Rock paintings from Mbafu rock-shelter, Congo. Top left: 'group F' stylised medallion and possible crucified figure. Top right: 'group F', representation of a priest? Bottom: 'group B' a stylised Portuguese cross*

Congress of Archaeology, the archaeologists G. Mortelmans and R. Monteyn reported a potentially fascinating discovery that they had made at the rock-shelter of Mbafo in 1954.

The rock-shelter of Mbafo is a 14m-deep (46ft) fissure which appears to have been artificially modified and remodelled to some extent. Of special interest were the paintings on the wall – executed largely in manganese – which showed, it was suggested, a strange assimilation of African and European motifs. Stylistically, the mode of depiction was of a recognisably central African motif, but some of the subject matter was unusual. The pictures could be grouped together according to their positions on the walls. The A groups were largely geometric designs, box designs, zig-zags and stick figures, as indeed were those of the C and E groupings; these motifs are usual for rock art in the area. The B group began to pose some questions in regard to subject matter; here, it was suggested, was a depiction of a Portuguese cross. The D group composition showed a hunter with bow and arrow, as well as a serpent and woman with child; the last two images, although a widespread theme in rock art the world over, also have overt biblical connotations. The F groupings, however, were claimed as being the most significant in terms of putative Christian imagery. The figures have their arms outstretched – claimed as depictions of Christ on the cross – but perhaps most important is what is described as a 'priest figure', an outline human with a cross upon the body located centrally in the frieze.

Interpretations of the Mbafo paintings should obviously invite caution. It is very difficult to date rock art, and although seventeenth-century ceramics were found in the cave, they cannot in any way provide a satisfactory chronological indication for these paintings. Some of the interpretations of the motifs may be overly speculative; by and large the motifs are consistent with similar schema in African rock art, and the use of a figure with arms outstretched need not betoken an identification with Jesus Christ. The so-called priest figure is admittedly harder to explain away, but the interpretation of these paintings may remain contentious. This does not devalue the worth of such data; the study of the rich wealth of recent rock art in Africa may yet yield up clues as to how indigenous artists negotiated their ideological relationships with their new colonial overlords.

The archaeology of the missionary process

So far we have discussed mostly the earlier, somewhat grander manifestations of the archaeological record for Christianity in Africa, and have rather ignored one of the key elements of the development of the religion within its new surroundings. We need to concentrate now on how the process of conversion, this subtle interaction between two conflicting ideological schemes, occurred. We now jump a few centuries, after the Portuguese interest in Africa has waned, and other interested European parties step onto the scene. Before going on to consider the cultural responses inherent in the process of mission and mass conversion, we need to sketch in the broad socio-historical context of the development of the missionary ideal.

During the 1850s the pioneering British missionary explorer David Livingstone had come to the conclusion that the vast swathes of the interior of sub-Saharan Africa were ripe for colonial exploitation. There would necessarily be economic benefits; slavery was now formally outlawed (although in practice it still carried on), but the commodities that could be provided here would greatly assist the burgeoning industrial markets of Europe. In short, Livingstone was convinced that the best way to help alleviate poverty was capitalism backed up by a strong central church. But it could not be a basic, one-sided relationship of raw exploitation. Europe now needed, he felt, to pick up the reins of the Portuguese centuries earlier. With the exception of the Portuguese enclaves in Angola and Mozambique, there was little to show for the fruits of their earlier missionary strategy. Now the time was right, it was held, for a concerted effort to bring civilisation to the African, and part of the process of civilisation involved the mass adoption of Christianity. The knock-on effects would not be merely spiritual – altruism was not wholly the order of the day here; in effect the 'westernisation' of African societies in the interior would also create healthy new markets for mass-produced European goods. Consumers were being sought, both of religion and European goods. During the last decades of the nineteenth century, European adventurers were setting forth across the continent armed with treaties to gain access to vital raw materials. By the time of the conference of Berlin this had become a nationalist campaign, and hand-in-hand with the political and economic influence came the work of Christian missionaries.

To vigorous colonialists such as Cecil Rhodes, the idea of the 'white man's burden' appealed. Conversion to Christianity was a short step away from overt political control, although this was perhaps not uppermost in the minds of the earliest missionary groups as they set out on their spiritual crusade. As a rule, different denominations carved out their own spheres of influence across the continent. In eastern Africa, for instance, the Church of England and the Church of Scotland took the lead. Early efforts on the coast had been made by the German missionary Krapf, but it took the spectacular success of the colonial politician Sir Henry Bartle Frere in outlawing slavery on the coast to begin to make a clear difference. In 1875, the Church Missionary Society established a planned settlement outside Mombasa – named Freretown in honour of the liberator of the slaves – for those now free. Stretching over some 404ha (1,000 acres), Freretown contained some 450 inhabitants at its apogee. Here was a true, planned Christian community, essentially self-sufficient, offering new opportunities to those who had suffered the depredations of slavery. The success of the Freretown model encouraged the C.M.S.; between 1875 and 1914 they penetrated ever further into the hinterland. Their emphasis was on the use of small, lightly staffed mission stations to allow for maximum spread of resources and speed of conversion. It was almost conveyor-belt conversion, systematic, quick and largely effective.

Beyond Lake Victoria, around what is now Uganda, the C.M.S. had already penetrated by 1870, and by 1890 had over twenty stations in the kingdom of Buganda, although tensions were already being felt with Roman Catholic French missionary counterparts. In this interlacustrine region, the missionaries set out to conserve traditional African customs where appropriate and moreover where they might be useful for mediating the peace. The blessing of produce, for instance, was not too far away from the traditional European Christian conception of the harvest festival. In the Toro kingdom, one of the benefits of becoming Christian was access to a degree of solid education, and the local flavour of Christianity there soon began to resemble something of a literacy movement: it was known as Kusoma Christianity, kusoma being the verb to read. Amongst the Ufipa of the southern interlacustrine region, missionaries developed a special tolerance of traditional belief. It paid not to act too piously, especially if the traditional customs could be translated into the Christian milieu. Parents would freely have their children baptised, but would forego the process themselves. There were clear convergences of belief that could be exploited; after all, the Ufipa notion of veneration of ancestral spirits had some propinquity to asking for the intercession of Christian saints. These were almost universal concepts that could be clearly understood by one and all.

81 *The Blantyre Mission Church, Malawi; Victorian neo-Gothic in an African setting. A print taken around 1876*

In southern Africa, the mission process had been established somewhat longer, but there are points of similarity with the east African experience. A large Dutch Calvinist community had been gathered at the Cape since the mid-seventeenth century, and the overriding social influence was the Dutch Reformed Church. Initially only a few indigenous Cape inhabitants – the Khoisan – showed much interest in Christian belief. In the interior of the Cape, the San (formerly known as Bushmen) hunter-gatherers maintained a cosmological scheme with significant shamanic additions, whilst the Khoe pastoralists soon began to forge links with Dutch farmers. As a means of social control, African slaves were often bribed with brandy and tobacco to become baptised, but the Calvinist Synod of Dort in 1618-19 had ruled that baptised slaves should be freed, a conclusion generally disregarded by most Cape Dutch. The eighteenth century saw the establishment of German Moravian missions and the London Missionary Society in the Cape, but progress was at best erratic, and it is only really in the mid- to late nineteenth century that mass missionary efforts began to prosper.

At the cutting edge of the conversion process during the nineteenth century were the frontier missions. These establishments attracted a wide range of people; lower-middle class missionaries predominated, and frequently little interest was shown in formal education. This concept was taken to its ultimate conclusion by the Wesleyan missionary James Allison – who operated out of Edendale in 1851 – when it was discovered that he had been embezzling mission funds. What appear to be un-Christian practices flourished widely in the mission stations. The place of the mission within the wider economic system cannot be underestimated. Although the mission area in effect became a ritual space, it was equally the imported, day-to-day artefacts such as clothes, jewellery, food which all became associated with the Christian world view. For the African, the mission meant not just a new ideological beginning, but the chance for education, wealth and indeed the ability to participate in the colonial consumption dynamic. For the colonial authorities the success of the missions hinged upon the creation of a broadly obedient, fairly well-educated and largely contented peasant class untainted by tribalism. Again, Christianity appealed to the world view of traditional African religion. In southern Africa, this was mediated by the participation of Christian and animist alike in the rainmaking ceremony, a cherished rite, and the proof of chiefly magical power. A degree of crossover had to be accepted; even Bishop Colenso of Natal generally turned a blind eye to the still prevalent practice of polygamy amongst the new African converts.

Elsewhere in Africa, other European countries were assiduously at work. The French style of colonial rule emphasised the concept of assimilation; unlike the British who took an essentially hands-off attitude to colonial administration, the French sought to integrate their colonies fully into the French socio-cultural system; adherence to the Roman Catholic Church was very much a part of the process. The foundation of the Society of Missionaries of Africa by Cardinal Charles Lavigerie put in place the machinery for a concerted missionary effort in French spheres of influence. The Belgians tended to allow a number of disparate missionary groups of all nationalities to work within their vast territory of the Congo Free State, whilst German missionaries had been active in eastern Africa since the 1840s, and were now at work in the new German spheres of influence in South West Africa amongst the Herero and Nama peoples.

On the Gold Coast, German missionaries had been working amongst the Ewe peoples since 1847. A missionary by the name of Lorenz Wolf settled in the region and built a house of African materials in a square, European style, more healthy, he decided, given the nature of the climate. Subtly, Wolf was beginning to change African cultural perceptions through his choice of design of domestic space. The mission church, for instance, would also be square, not round in the African vernacular tradition. This theme of the reaction of domestic architecture styles to colonial contact is one that we shall pick up later in the context of missions amongst the Tswana peoples of southern Africa in the nineteenth century. Essentially, Wolf created a transplanted southern German peasant farm in the tropical rain forest. The mission post was the first point of contact between the missionary and the potential pool of recruits to Christianity, but again we need here to emphasise the question of economics and consumerism. The lay-out of mission posts rarely varied, and in this region they were generally fairly homogenous in appearance. The central residence, school house, and chapel were located at a distance from the main village, perhaps uphill and for good measure directly upon a sacred site as if to emphasise a new spiritual superiority. Social roles changed too. As converts became more European and Christian in outlook, the emphasis was placed squarely upon the idea of manual work as being a vehicle for salvation in the eyes of God. Work was good. To this end, mission posts often featured workshop areas for craft production as well as agricultural installations to keep the community as self-sufficient as possible. The good works had, of course, another more pragmatic motivation: a pool of cheap labourers, producing goods for sale elsewhere, and earning just enough money to join the ranks of consumers. The central mission house, often a two-storied affair with surrounding verandah, became the heart of the settlement, and all the new converts could aspire to building such a style of house. The use of domestic space had now altered too; the emphasis of the house was now on the nuclear rather than traditional extended family. As there were now no more menstruation taboos, discrete huts for females were not needed.

The idea of the mission as a Christian village had also taken hold in southern Africa. The earliest Moravian missionary post at Genadendal (Cape Province, then known as Baviaanskloof) was founded in 1737 as an idealised village; thatched cottages crowded around a spacious green area giving the local target group, the Khoe pastoralists, a vision of how comfortable and homely the Christian way of life could be. The village of Mamre in the Cape was founded in 1808 as Groene Kloof by the Moravians, and was designed to encourage manual work; the village is still preserved much as it would have been during the nineteenth century, and we can still see the steam mill, areas for market gardens, tanners, smiths, carpenters and bricklayers. In Natal, the mission village of Campbell was established in 1820 to spread Christianity among the local peoples. Here the focus of the settlement was the combined church/school building, a simple, thick-walled construction of stone and clay and thatched roof, almost a European interpretation of Griqua architecture but with a different spatial emphasis.

Life at the mission was hard and regimented, but the Christian ethos followed in death too. The question of funerary ritual in Mission settlements is fascinating, and has yet to be satisfactorily addressed by archaeologists working on African historical-period sites. The graves excavated at Bonda Mission, Zimbabwe by M. Bordini, are those of European inhabitants who had died during an influenza epidemic at the beginning of the twentieth century. Of the nineteen graves, ten have headstones. Grave fifteen had an inscribed rectangular stone lying atop the grave cut; this slab measures approximately 2m by 1m (6ft 6in by 3ft 3in) and carried an incomplete inscription 1.7. ? 7. The burial was of a child, and contained no coffin. The graves were arranged in four rows, and to all intents could have been a small British family grave plot transplanted into an African landscape. In Nigeria, the site of Zungeru (located 400km (248 miles) north-east of Ibadan) has been recently investigated by A. Ogedengbe. This site was occupied from 1911, and was an important missionary centre: a ruined church and 38 graves survive at Zungeru. The funerary data here, in contrast to Bonda, points to a clear hierarchical pattern. A cemetery is located on a large hill outside the village; an iron fence delimits one area, and here are found graves marked by polished tiles and iron and concrete crosses. Europeans were buried in this portion of the graveyard, whilst high-ranking Africans were laid to rest in the north-western part. Other, presumably low-ranking Africans, were buried outside the cemetery fence on the southern side by the gate.

One of the most intriguing archaeological studies of the experience of mission contact in Africa has been recently conducted by a team from the archaeology unit at Gaborone University in Botswana, and this project clearly highlights the wealth of potential data for African mission archaeology. During the nineteenth century, Bantu-speaking Tswana peoples moved into the area and soon found a role as economic middle-men between the Kalahari hunter-gatherer groups and Europeans. The settlement pattern essentially consisted of dispersed large towns, or *metse*, at the centre of the *merafe* polities. The clash of ideologies between the *dikgosi*, or rulers, and incoming missionaries is one of the most intriguing stories in African mission history. Essentially, the rulers needed Christianity, but only under certain conditions and only under certain controls. Kings would occasionally allow themselves to be baptised in public, but their commitments to their new faith varied according to how they viewed their relationships with the mission groups.

The settlement of Ntsweng was the capital of the Bakwena polity or *merafe* between 1863 and the 1930s. In the 1860s the then ruler Sechele the First had a rather ambiguous relationship with the Mission. The church servicing Ntsweng, for instance, when opened in 1867, was situated some 2.5km (1.5 miles) away from the town; in Sechele's eyes, perhaps, a healthy enough social distance. Sechele maintained his own unique view of Christianity; he did not, for instance, forego polygamy or rainmaking ceremonies, but did attempt to have the LMS church rebuilt in his compound. Sechele had also followed the missionaries' example of building domestic architecture in the rectangular form rather than the traditional Tswana circular form. Ntsweng's architecture was becoming noticeably more linear in appearance, far removed from the normal Bantu conception of domestic space.

Other rulers amongst the Tswana took on a different relationship with the Christian missions. In 1889 the ruler of the Bangwato, Khama the Third, moved his capital from Shoshong to the site of Old Palapye/Phalatswe where it remained until 1902. For Khama Christianity was a sign of elite status, and the London Mission Society church occupied a central place in the town both physically and politically. Khama decided he needed Christianity, and he too began to adopt the rectangular architectural plans in the European style (**colour plate 14**). The Church of 1891 could almost have been transplanted from Britain: a rectangular nave flanked by two aisles and built throughout of clay brick on stone foundations. An enclosed cemetery area has a mix of traditional grave types as well as two with marble headstones.

More than anywhere else, the examples of the Tswana response to the Christian missionary effort show just how complex the relationship between converter and converted could be. Incoming Christian missions had to adapt socially and culturally to the climate within which they operated. Missions also served a more secular, economic purpose. The emphasis on work and education shows that what the Europeans perceived as becoming Christian meant a lot more than undergoing a baptismal rite. It meant adopting the habits of the Europeans' world.

Colonial consolidation

With the scramble for Africa over, the colonial powers now began to stamp a cultural authority upon their new territories. In southern Africa, this process had been
going on for almost 300 years; in other areas, for instance, the newcomers to the
scramble – such as the Germans – began to shape their new acquisitions in
Tanganyika, Togo, Kamerun, South West Africa and in Ruanda/Urundi. With the
colonisers' self-confidence – if not arrogance – the new colonies were transformed
into mirror images of the mother countries. The churches of the period of colonial
consolidation have largely survived well, and often still serve as important places of
worship. In this section we will look at the historical, colonial-era church buildings
of Africa, a discussion that moves somewhat away from archaeology of sites towards
the archaeology of buildings. It is in the archaeology of these buildings that we can
perhaps gain the greatest sense of the varieties of the colonial experience in terms of
styles of architecture and the cultural imprint of the colonisers upon the colonised.
More than anywhere else in Africa, it is the Republic of South Africa that perhaps
displays the greatest variety of colonial-era church architecture, and it is here where
our survey can conveniently begin.

It has been recently estimated that there are some 4000 Christian denominations
represented in modern South Africa; this makes for a bewildering mix of styles of
ecclesiastical architecture and places of worship. Of this figure, the predominantly
Afrikaans-speakers of the Dutch Reformed Church make up about sixteen per cent
of the total; other English/Xhosa-speaking Protestant churches make up about
twenty-three per cent, the Methodists being the largest grouping. About ten per
cent are Roman Catholics, and the rest so-called independent African churches.
Each of these denominations has left its unique cultural imprint on the church
buildings of South Africa. Ever since the Portuguese explorer Diaz erected a limestone pillar – or *padrão* – at the eastern Cape in 1488, Christianity has had a foothold
in southern Africa. The Dutch arrived in 1652, and after the establishment of the
Groote Kerk in Cape Town in 1666, there were some five Dutch Reformed church
buildings in the region by 1792. In 1824, the Dutch Reformed Church broke away
from the Netherlands-based synod, and became independent, although from an
architectural point of view it maintained a marked Dutch influence in terms of
church building.

The first Sunday service to be held by the Dutch at the Cape was observed upon
the ship Dromedarius on 14 April 1652. After making landfall, few thoughts were
given to providing a permanent church, and initially temporary shelters were used.
A timber shed within the Cape Castle inner court (itself completed in 1679) was
converted into a church with the addition of a stone floor and simple gable and a
smaller church was built adjacent to the walls of the castle in 1665. Burials initially
took place within the courtyard, but subsequently a nearby abandoned garden was
used as a cemetery. It was on this site that a simple cruciform church was erected in
1702, and a spire was added the following year. This church – the first dedicated
place of worship at the Cape – was designed according to the idealised *preekkerke*

plan, which emphasised the involvement of the congregation in the service rather than isolating them physically. The church was finally opened in 1704 with room for 180 burial vaults (some of which received the remains of the Governors of the Cape). The vaults were filled in during renovation work in the 1840s, but the Groote Kerk retains an air of seventeenth-century Calvinist simplicity.

During the eighteenth century, as Cape Town grew, so did the number of adherents of other religions and Christian denominations. The Lutherans, for example, were forbidden freedom of worship by the Dutch Reformed Church, so in 1774 a Lutheran by the name of Martin Melck surreptitiously built a 'warehouse' which in fact turned out to be a rather opulent building measuring 28m by 19m (92ft by 62ft) with a domed ceiling and columns. The building of this Lutheran place of worship was studiously ignored by the then Governor Ryk Tulbagh, and the Lutheran congregation, soon free to worship, carried on improving the church, which was re-inaugurated in 1820 along with an associated parsonage and sexton's house (**colour plate 17**). The front gateway of the compound is decorated with a swan-topped lantern, a Lutheran motif. Other denominations have shared in shaping the historic ecclesiastical architecture of Cape Town; St Mary's Cathedral on Stal Plein was completed in 1851 to a Cape Gothic style, whilst St George's Cathedral on Wale Street is based upon the neo-classical lines of St Pancras' Church in London with some neo-Gothic additions.

Cape Province is especially rich in old churches, many showing a wide variety of colonial-period architectural influences. At Claremont, St Saviour's (1850) was built to a stock design of the English Victorian architect William Butterfield, who designed Keble College Oxford and Adelaide Cathedral in Australia in similar mid-Victorian, high Gothic style. By way of contrast, the small Rhenish mission church at Braak, Stellenbosch (1824), shows a clear Germanic influence in the use and design of roof gables. The Settlers' Church at Port Alfred (1823) was of a simple stone, clay and thatch construction. Destroyed in 1846, the building was sympathetically restored in 1938. Contrasts exist elsewhere too. In the Karoo, the Dutch Reformed Church at Graaf-Reinet (1821, and the sixth-oldest church in the Republic) displays especially fine Dutch gables. In common with most of the early church buildings, the roof was originally thatched and then latterly covered with iron sheeting. The Gereformeerde Kerk on Church St West in Pretoria was originally founded as the Paul Kruger Church in 1896, and has a particularly fine Dutch-style spire. The spire of the nearby Grootkerk Bosman on Vermeulen Street presents a different picture; the spire here is a wild confusion of Russian Orthodox, Venetian and Dutch elements. The Nederduits Hervormde Kerk on Church Square, Potchefstroom, was the first church to be built by the Voortrekkers in the Transvaal in 1866. Again, originally thatched, the church was extensively renovated in 1859 with the addition of plastered brick walls, a corrugated iron roof and spire. This wide variety of ecclesiastical architecture is testimony to the multifarious religious groupings in South Africa's history. The overwhelming European architectural influence also emphasises the rejection of the vernacular, African values. Given the racial tensions inherent in South Africa this is not surprising. These churches then represented grand, almost nationalistic statements.

82 *German ecclesiastical colonial architecture: a Lutheran church in Cameroon, with a hint of southern German influence*

In eastern Africa, the British influence in ecclesiastical architecture is stronger, but here more concessions are made to an acceptance of local stylistic values, especially upon the coast. After the Arabs regained control of Mombasa in 1729, virtually all traces of Christianity were extinguished. With the coming of concerted missionary efforts, and the martyrdom of David Koi, a Christian of the Giriama people murdered by Muslims in 1883, Christianity began to flourish. Under the British administration, church building began in earnest. The Mombasa Memorial Cathedral (1905) is of a compact, cruciform shape incorporating certain Moorish elements such as the dome, although the British influence is present in the addition of Gothic stained glass. The Romanesque-style towers set off a very cosmopolitan-looking structure. The Moorish elements in the cathedral at Mombasa were a tribute to the character of the town, but local building techniques could give other advantages. The Anglican cathedral on Zanzibar (1873-9) has a roof of cement and local coral, allowing for a large load-bearing capability and an unusually wide nave span. In the interior of Kenya, a more traditional British ecclesiastical architectural style predominated. The new European suburbs of Nairobi – which developed from the 1920s onwards – were once memorably referred to by the journalist James Cameron as being 'equatorial Ealing'; quintessential English commuter-belt architecture in the highlands of east Africa. It was no different with church building, where most examples in the towns and cities of the interior would not have looked out of place in south-eastern England.

By way of a comparison, the Germans provided their own distinct architectural contribution to late nineteenth/early twentieth-century colonial-era church buildings. In Cameroon – occupied by Germany between 1884 and 1914 – we find churches with a definite southern German (Bavarian) architectural flavour. The spires are perhaps the most noticeable feature, and the church at Yaonde (1906) has an especially fine spire in the Swabian/Alsatian style, unsurprisingly so given that the majority of missionaries hailed from that area. In Namibia (formerly German South West Africa), there is a fine range of German colonial buildings. At Lüderitz the Evangelical Lutheran Church (1909) tends towards a variant of the Cape Gothic style rather than a pure German style as the builders came from South Africa; the stained glass was donated by Kaiser Wilhelm the Second. The church at Swakopmund (1912) is more neo-baroque in design, a very southern German theme, whilst the Windhoek Christuskirche (1910) is more of a neo-Gothic composition, albeit with heavy Germanic overtones.

Similar architectural statements were made by the French, Portuguese, Belgians and the Spanish within their African territories. The cultural stamp of the mother country was applied firmly to its colonies, both in the realms of secular, administrative architecture and church design; there was little consideration for the traditional vernacular forms. The very nature of this church architecture made a statement of economic and political power over and above its religious aspect.

Discussion

In the course of this chapter, we have covered a vast geographical and temporal range seeking out the experience of European colonisation and the missionary effort. The questions raised here are potentially fascinating, but the archaeological record itself is sparse, and it will only be with more intensive research that we can finally begin to find some answers. The archaeological indicators of the Christian faith in the formative years of concerted colonial contact are obviously amorphous. These indicators – the church building and burial rites – were associated with a very small-scale, economically-orientated settlements. The initial wave of mission effort, then, has left us with few traces. It is only with the development of Portuguese-style town settlements (such as Qsar es Seghir and Mombasa) that Christian remains become more visible. Dambarare, a settlement on a smaller scale, shows evidence of perhaps a greater degree of European/African interaction, whilst the problematic rock paintings of Mbafo provide us with a tantalising hint of how the new indigenous converts may have mediated their new faith with traditional artistic practices.

The economic (rather than spiritual) motives behind the missionary efforts of the nineteenth century are witnessed by the structure of the surviving mission posts; the church at the centre, but also provision for crafts and industries. Apart from providing converts, missionaries also provided a new source of consumers. The African reactions to this process varied; when conversion came from the top down, European cultural traits would be relatively rapidly accepted, although the chief or king would interpret Christianity according to his social and economic needs. The missionaries were wise to this too, and in many cases an uneasy syncretic mélange of Christianity and traditional values emerged. Having now considered this background, we come to the present day, and a discussion of how modern African Christian art and artefact – the archaeology of tomorrow – has been shaped by the experience of the past.

Further reading

There are no major syntheses of the wider, continental aspect of historical-period African archaeology. Most of the key sources will however be found in fairly accessible journals or collected papers, and the historical background is largely very well catered for. Two authoritative works deal with the historical context of European (specifically Portuguese) expansion into west Africa: J. Thornton (1998, 2 ed.) *Africa and Africans in the Making of the Atlantic World, 1400-1800* (Cambridge: Cambridge University Press), and A. Hilton (1985) *The Kingdom of Kongo* (Oxford: Clarendon).

The classic work on the European forts of the Gold Coast remains A. W. Lawrence (1963) *Trade Castles and Forts of West Africa* (London: Cape), whilst more recent archaeological research is presented in the following: C. De Corse (2001) *An Archaeology of Elmina: Africans and Europeans on the Gold Coast 1400-1900* (Washington: Smithsonian), C. De Corse (1992) 'Culture contact, continuity and change on the Gold Coast AD 1400-1900' *African Archaeological Review* 10: pp. 163-96, and (1993) 'The Danes on the Gold Coast: culture change and the European Presence' *African Archaeological Review* 11: pp. 149-73. For other areas of Portuguese/African contact see: C. Redman (1986) *Qsar es Seghir: An Archaeological View of Medieval Life* (New York: Academic Press). J. Kirkman (1974) *Fort Jesus: A Portuguese Fortress on the East African Coast* (Oxford: Clarendon).

The process of missionary work in southern Africa, and the social dynamics and responses to it are dealt with in two key texts: P. Landau (1995) *The Realm of the Word: Language, Gender and Christianity in a Southern African Kingdom* (London: J. Currey/ Portsmouth N.H.: Heinemann), and D. Chidester (1992) *Religions of*

Southern Africa (London: Routledge). The Tswana case study material may be found in: P. Lane (1999) 'Archaeology, Nonconformist missions and the 'colonisation of consciousness' in southern Africa *c.*1820-1900' in T. Insoll (ed.) *Case Studies in Archaeology and World Religion* (BAR S755. Oxford: Archaeopress) pp. 153-65 – a number of the sites mentioned in connection with Mission archaeology in southern Africa are noted in the very thorough bibliography – and A. Reid *et al.* (1997) 'Tswana architecture and responses to colonialism' *World Archaeology* 28/3: pp. 370-92. Two other papers deal with the western African perspective: B. Meyer (1997) 'Christian mind and worldly matters. religion and materiality in the nineteenth-century Gold Coast' *Journal of Material Culture* 2/3: pp. 311-37 and A. Ogedengbe (1998) 'An historical archaeology of Zunguru colonial settlement' in K. Wesler (ed.) *Historical Archaeology in Nigeria* (Trenton NJ: Africa World Press Inc.).

D. Picton-Seymour (1989) *Historical Buildings in South Africa* (Cape Town: Struikhof) presents a comprehensive and well-illustrated coverage of the rich building heritage of South Africa, and Nnamdi Elleh's (1997) *African Architecture: Evolution and Transformation* (New York: McGraw-Hill) is a broad survey of all aspects of African architecture, colonial and vernacular. A number of guide books have also been consulted in the writing of this chapter, especially town guides of Namibia, Kenya and Ghana.

7 Towards a cultural history of African Christianity

Having considered the rich experience of the archaeology of the Christian faith in Africa, we now need to draw the threads together and seek common patterns of development. However, before looking at the broader temporal and spatial picture, a consideration of the contemporary aspects of African culture history in relation to Christian art and architecture is needed. We cannot just stop at the nineteenth century; African Christian art is a dynamic force in many contemporary societies, it embodies a number of meanings, and to truly set out – as was stated in the introduction – to frame a cultural history of Christianity in Africa, we need to understand just what Christian art means to the African of the recent past and the present. These are archaeologies of the future.

The sheer breadth of geographical, ethnic, linguistic and cultural variety represented in Africa means we can only make generalisations about the study of African art in the modern and historical context. The study of African art, as a subject in its own right, is only a recent innovation, triggered largely by the impact of the European colonial experience in the nineteenth century, when it could be regarded with a detached and intrigued curiosity as being somehow 'primitive' in nature. We have come a long way from such simplistic statements, African artistic traditions have informed the work of a number of important western artists including, for example, Gaugin and Picasso, and has provided a means for artists of the African diaspora to identify with their roots in a western context.

In terms of Christian art, we have a wide variety of traditions and media to study. This is an important and intriguing research question, seeing how effectively a new, transplanted ideological scheme changed the artistic outlook of rooted traditions many hundreds of years old. How did these traditions meet the challenges and demands of this new symbolic framework? How did new meanings become imbued in older schemes of representation? In truth (and in common with a similar lament running through this book) this is a virtually unstudied topic. African Christian artistic representations are often overlooked by collectors, scholars and the public in general. Let us consider a recent example that illustrates this point. The *Africa: Art of a Continent* exhibition that attracted large numbers of visitors to London's Royal Academy in 1995 effectively covered the scope of the human cultural experience in Africa, from early eastern African Olduwan hand axes, to north African Islamic material and the treasures of ancient Egypt. African Christian art, however, was signally unrepresented in the final catalogue. To be sure, the salient material was there:

Coptic Egyptian Christian pieces, the odd medieval Nubian piece and a corpus of Ethiopian crosses and manuscripts. All very visually satisfying, but hardly representative of a rich seam of material. Apart from a few artefacts from the Kongo kingdom, there was little to tell of the vibrancy of modern and recent historical Christian art in Africa. This is a pity, because as we will briefly consider here, there is a wide and dynamic tradition of Christian representation from across the continent, firmly rooted within the African artistic milieu.

African art and artists

Coming back to generalisations, we may make a number of broad observations about the qualities and meanings behind African art. African art is often innovative; artists constantly recreate and create new interpretations of traditional themes. It is usually visually abstract; in this sense 'true to form' and naturalistic interpretations are rare. In terms of form, sculpture often is the primary means of representation, although of late – and outside mainly northern Africa – painting has become a powerful medium. Sculpture is often used, both in traditional and Christian ideological frameworks as part of a ritual performance cycle – one need only think of the rich traditions of African masquerade. Anthropomorphic qualities are also important in sculpture and in painting; it is the human form that predominates – although these forms incorporate an assemblage of meanings rather than a simple single interpretation.

The people who make this art are also important, often having special status within their societies. In many cases these artisans are people wholly dedicated to the production of art in traditional societies, and may be regarded as a separate caste apart. Sometimes the distrust of separate castes spills over into outright fear because it is often believed that the artist possesses some sort of supernaturally-inspired creative skill. In many areas of Africa the process of iron-making, for instance, is regarded as almost an alchemical exercise, and the production and symbolism associated with the creation of iron is bound up with all manner of taboos, both sexual and mystical, which show parallels, for example, with the western hermetical magic tradition. Artists and artisans, because of their exclusivity and their creativity, live as a class apart, even in what may be termed highly christianised societies.

The notion of a separation of an artisan from the social context within which he or she works is not an exclusively African trait; one need only consider the institution of craft guilds in medieval London, almost early trade unions in a sense, that safeguarded the interests of their members but which in certain cases, rather like the Freemasons, became something more than a loose agglomeration of craftsmen of similar ilk.

Within the African context, even the negotiation of domestic space is often tied directly to the nature of the inhabitants' work. Amongst the Senufo of the northern Ivory Coast, southern Mali and fringes of Burkina Faso, for instance, villages are strictly segregated into wards. Farmers predominate; one ward is reserved for female

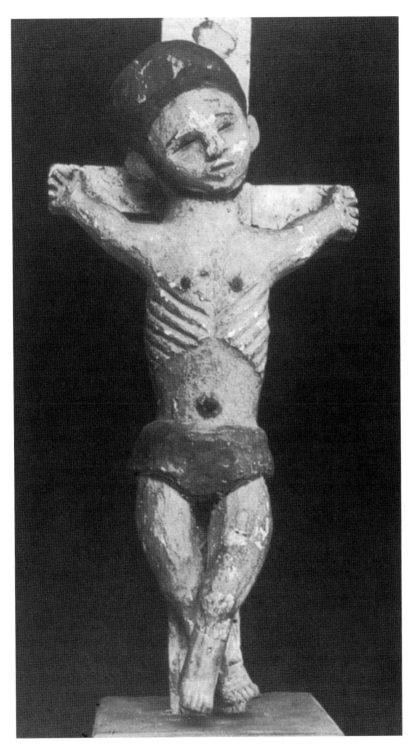

83 *A stone crucifix from the Congo region*

potters and one for male blacksmiths. A separate ward is set aside for the *Jula* weavers who are exclusively Muslim, and indeed speak a separate language (Mande). We need to be aware that the artist is often physically and socially isolated from the very society that provides the economic and ideological market for his work. In the case of the Senufo, rigid gender-based criteria also come into play, and it is possible that certain artist groups do not speak the same language, or share the same religion, as their hosts.

Primarily, then, the major concern of African art is the body and human representation. In areas where Islam became the dominant force in sub-Saharan Africa, the depiction of human forms was soon proscribed, but in terms of the acceptance of the Christian faith, with a heavy emphasis on the depiction of Christ, Mary and the saints, a rich seam of artistic licence could be mined. These depictions, as was the case with the early church elsewhere, were essentially of a didactic nature; they helped a largely non-literate and newly converted congregation understand the bible better through visual language.

African Christian art: some themes from around the continent

In the Kongo kingdom of south-central Africa the initial influence from an artistic point of view came from contact with the Portuguese from 1491 and received further impetus with the conversion of the king some ten years later. Such was the quality of these local Christian-orientated carvings, that they were soon in demand by the Portuguese themselves, and may represent an early form of wholly 'tourist' art. Likewise, when Portuguese newcomers encountered the Sapi peoples of Guinea, such was the beauty of the Sapi ivory carving tradition that it came into demand in fashionable circles in Lisbon, and these carvings – often specially commissioned – mainly dealt with Christian themes. Crucifixes were particularly popular in the early Christian Kongo kingdom of south-west/central Africa from the sixteenth century onwards.

Kongo crucifixes were mainly manufactured from copper alloy, although some later wooden examples survive. In terms of overall physical proportion the crucifix is largely based on the European model, but the Christ figure often displays recognisable African features, and unusually small mourner figurines, again of a highly abstracted African figurative style, are also to be found upon the cross. Although the Christian kingdom of Kongo was destroyed in 1665, the cross remained an important motif. Symbolically the cross was identified with the crossroads, the meeting place of the living world (*nza yayi*) and the dead world (*nsi a bafwa*). This is a concept to be found in the western European tradition, where crossroads took on a special, mystical significance of liminality, the meeting point between worlds and a place favoured for the burials of suicides. Also of importance, within the post-Christian context, are the Santus, cross-shaped fetishes used still even in non-Christian areas to guarantee hunting success.

In terms of statuary, a number of themes recur in Kongo-kingdom Christian art of the early seventeenth century. St Anthony of Padua was a favourite subject; usually depicted as a European figure complete with robe and tonsure, he carries, however, a recognisably African Christ child figure in his left arm, and as if to emphasise

84 *The thatched, circular Namirembe cathedral, Kampala, Uganda c.1890*

the African nature of the Christ, the baby usually carries a fly whisk in his left hand. *Pfemba* images depict a mother and child, and it may be that this image owes its origins to Christian-period Madonna and child motifs, although this type of image is very widespread in Africa as a whole. This depiction still survives in the *toni malau* figurines, where in areas of Christian revival such figurines are used in healing cults. *Nzambi* figurines display a series of Christian-influenced traits and perhaps are an extension of the basic crucifixion motif; made from wood, these figurines have outstretched arms set within a wooden frame.

The stone figurines of this region called *mintadi* (singular: *ntadi*) may in pre-Christian times have served a devotional purpose, but now, even in Christian societies, retain a degree of symbolism as grave markers. Not all traditional artistic traditions survived the christianising process, especially if they were too ideologically bound to the old ways. The *minkisi* were reliquary statues used for magical purposes by diviners or *nganga*; in most cases these were defaced or destroyed when the owner converted to Christianity. In terms of modern Christian art, statuary is still a dominant mode of expression in the general area today, although the Zairean painter Nkusu Felelo's work represents a new and very dynamic interpretation of Christian imagery within a central African artistic context.

Let us consider the west African picture. Here there is an uneasy clash of religious experience: the indigenous versus the transplanted Muslim and the Christian worlds. These tensions are reflected to some extent in the art of Nigeria, where the three faith systems predominate. In terms of Christian imagery, nativity scenes are very important, especially among artists grounded in the Yoruba culture of Ife, and are stylistically related to the Nok terracotta representations of the first half of the first millennium BC.

In christianised societies of western Africa, traditional forms of human representation, even if they are from a non-Christian context, are invested with deep symbolic meanings. In Sierra Leone, for instance, Mende farmers still uncover soapstone figures that may date back as far as the tenth century AD. These 'found spirits' (*mali yafeisia*) are deemed to represent the former owners of the field, and are set up on the field boundaries to guarantee the fertility of the land and confer some degree of symbolic protection.

In Ghana, the traditional concept of the second burial has been enthusiastically embraced by Christian communities, and a new and vigorous tradition of human sculpture has emerged. The second burial entails a festival celebrating the life of the dead person held at varied times after the death, and its scale varies according to the prestige and social standing of the deceased. A notable aspect of the second burial festival is the erection of a commemorative statuary group above the grave. Within Christian contexts, this has been reinterpreted to include cement groups of angels and biblical characters and angels alongside highly coloured family figures. A similar motif may be noted amongst the Ibibio peoples of the lower Niger River. Here funerary monuments took the form of *nwomo* or draped cloths above the grave accompanied by cement figures – again usually hung as part of a second burial rite. Interestingly, Christian groups banned the hanging of the cloth but actively encouraged the making and use of the cement figurines. But it would be too broad to suggest that Christians found traditional funerary sculpture to be totally acceptable in their religious framework; the Fang peoples of Gabon made extensive use of reliquary figures, essentially transportable ancestral shrines, a custom reminiscent of the traditional Roman Catholic conception of the relic. These sculptures, however, and very probably for political rather than religious reasons, were banned by the French colonial authorities.

Within the art of eastern Africa, carved human figurines tend to be rare, and the emphasis switches to pottery, textiles and painting. Even in Ethiopia, which has a rather rigid and conservative tradition of ecclesiastical painting, a new wave of artists, predominantly western-trained, are beginning to reassess their traditional styles. Gebre Kristos Desta, for instance, who taught at the Fine Arts School in Addis Ababa, caused some controversy with highly abstracted works of art with underlying Christian themes; one such painting on glass was a simple abstract crucifix rendered in red paint. Afewerk Tekle is a noted technician in stained glass, and his works have been in demand worldwide. The output of both artists is characterised by an underlying and rather uneasy Christian imagery, and shows just how far the tradition of ecclesiastical painting in Ethiopia has broadened. Even traditional forms of church architecture here are now being challenged, with new and imaginative church buildings drawing influences from across the world, situating them within an Ethiopian Orthodox framework.

A switch from colonial-period church architecture towards a new vernacular understanding is now readily apparent to students of modern African architecture. In post-independence Kenya, to take but one example, the emphasis in church building has shifted away from the overwhelming English-orientated, Anglican architectural style, towards a reassessment of vernacular values. Earlier, colonial-period church architecture was influenced to a great extent by missionary motives and perhaps English settler nostalgia – the latter forms seen to great effect in the church at

Subukia with an instantly recognisable square pinnacled tower and massive double roof trusses, and to some extent in the charming little church at Maseno, built in 1905 and complete with a thatched roof upon a stone/mud superstructure. The choice of architectural form was also directly influenced by the High or Low Church nature of the worshippers.

As early as 1940, however, the influential mission church writer Edwin Smith had called for a move back to indigenous forms of architecture in a special effort to appeal to the widening number of African Christian converts. He suggested that the traditional Bantu circular *gwalo* form of building, essentially a secular meeting place, would better emphasise the communal act of Christian worship within a specifically African social framework. Recent church architecture in Kenya reflects this mood. The Krapf-Rebmann memorial church at Kilifi on the coast was designed in the early 1960s by the church architect Richard Hughes. Here curved coral walls pay homage to an earlier Swahili, and overwhelmingly Islamic, architectural tradition. The chapel of the Good Shepherd at Maralal emphasises the need for the sympathetic use of local building material, although the striking cedar walls are hardly set off by a very basic and ugly corrugated iron roof.

In terms of local cultural tradition within Kenya, other elements have taken their place within the paraphernalia of Christian worship. The use of music within the church service is an important part of the communal act, and in many cases traditional musical instruments play a vital role in this respect. Kamba peoples of the Mount Kenya area still use the *kithembe*, a drum of about 60cm (2ft) in height constructed from a sisal trunk and bound with hide. When used in conjunction with smaller *ithembe* drums, the rhythmic effect is immense. The Bajun peoples use the traditional *pembe* horn in Christian marriage ceremonies; the horn is not blown but is beaten with a stick to produce a sharp, almost metallic click. For the Nandi, the use of the *amadinda* (xylophone) in the act of Christian worship is an important element of the liturgical music canon. We have here then another example, away from the architectural and portable art facets of African Christianity, of how the demands of the new faith have been met by traditional socio-cultural ideals and have been reinterpreted within that framework.

Moving southwards, we find at the mission community of Serima, in Mashonaland, Zimbabwe, another very African interpretation of church architecture. The building and its embellishments incorporate many clear elements of local Shona artistic tradition. Founded in the 1940s by a missionary Father Hans Groeber of the Swiss Mission as essentially a training establishment in Christian faith and in traditional crafts, the churches here are a testament to the skill and imagination of the local artists who have been at the forefront of the planning and execution of the church buildings.

The central mission church itself is of an unusual groundplan; the two rectangular naves are set at 45 degrees to each other, and converge on the high altar. There are associated chapels dedicated to the Sacred Heart, and, more importantly for the African tradition, to the Uganda martyrs. Cement castings of angels – rendered in a very African anthropomorphic style – are set around a cylindrical belfry, although

85 *Serima, Zimbabwe. The main door to the church; a carved statue of St Peter stands between the two entrances*

special attention attaches to the rich corpus of wood carvings that adorn the interior of the church and form the doors. The main nave doors, for instance, are separated by a large statue of St Peter, who stylistically is represented in a typical Shona anthropomorphic form. A similar marriage of the teaching of the Christian faith allied to the training of artists and artisans in traditional crafts is also seen in Bulawayo, Matabeleland, Zimbabwe at the church of Cyrene. Here, in the early years of the community and under the tutelage of the missionary Edward Patterson, local trainees worked to build a church within the context of traditional architectural and artistic styles.

We have briefly surveyed the continent and the last hundred or so years and seen how the advent of Christianity impacted upon the traditional artistic and ideological milieu. It is noteworthy to consider the scale of syncretic elements that were able to survive this conversion process, and how dynamic traditional artistic systems were able to reinterpret the Christian faith in the light of their own backgrounds. How, for instance, would this impact compare with the meeting of the African ideological world with another world religion? Apart from the dubious claims for an early Judaic contact in sub-Saharan Africa, we must turn to the advent of Islam and its impact upon the peoples of western Africa for an example.

Some points of contrast and comparison may be noted between the process of christianisation and islamicisation. Let us consider firstly the nature of the place of worship and what if anything it owes to the African world. The early nineteenth-century Friday Mosque at Zaria (in the region of the Hausa peoples of Nigeria) was planned and built by a *malam* (learned man) of local roots by the name of Mika'ilu. In terms of architectural style, this mosque owes little to local tradition; it is representative of a very rigid, broader Muslim framework that owes its origins to the Egyptian way of doing things. Northwards into the Sahel zone – and within the area of the former kingdom known to the Arabs as Ghana and to the local Soninke peoples as Wagadu – the tenth-century mosque in the capital of Kumbi Saleh is a copy of the Great Mosque at Qairouan, Tunisia. In the latter, stone columns were used, but at Kumbi Saleh this feature was locally interpreted by the use of stacked stone discs.

Islamic architectural forms permeated slowly into the traditional African sphere. Asante traditional shrines in Ghana often show a clear Islamic architectural influence, although this is due less to a conscious desire to ape Muslim architecture, than to the fact that most of the builders of these shrines were themselves Muslim. The builder of the Ka'aba in Mecca, however, was an Ethiopian by the name of Habakkuq (or Baquum), probably originally Christian, and this building, one of the most holy in Islam, shares distinct architectural motifs with highland churches of Ethiopia. An intriguing crossover of religious architectural elements may also be noted in Lagos, Nigeria at the Central Mosque (destroyed in 1980). A large number of Yoruba peoples – both Muslim and Orisha worshippers – were taken as slaves to Brazil where many underwent conversion to Christianity. Some of these peoples returned to Nigeria upon emancipation, and it was a converted Roman Catholic architect by the name of João Baptist Da Costa who designed the Central Mosque (1908-1913) in what appears to be a Portuguese Baroque church style.

Across eastern Africa and the Swahili coast of Kenya and Tanzania, it is generally clear that mosque buildings here largely owe their architectural form to Arabian or Yemeni roots rather than adapting to any prevailing indigenous architectural tradition. The arguments surrounding the origins of the Swahili coastal settlements of the ninth-sixteenth centuries AD are not of direct relevance to this question, but it may be briefly stated that there has been a gradual reassessment and strengthening of the African input at the expense of the Arab. In terms of use of space and planning of these towns, it is probable that there is far greater local Bantu input than has previously been given credit for, and initially the actual numbers of Muslim converts on this coast were small (this would seem to be attested to by the relatively small size of the earliest mosques at the town of Shanga). It would appear then that here at least we are dealing with small, relatively isolated Muslim communities probably focused upon the Arab commercial classes, although in time Islam has grown to become the dominant faith upon this coast.

Apart from architecture and the use of space, there are other cultural elements that suggest that Islam never had the same sort of cultural impact upon traditional African artistic traditions as was the case with Christianity. The proscription of the depiction of human forms within Islam, for instance, made the tradition of statuary redundant in those areas where it had previously thrived. In a sense, the lack of associated paraphernalia readily appealed to the new converts to Islam in northern Africa. They were traditionally nomadic herdsmen, and to them the simplicity of Islam meshed well with a very mobile lifestyle. In short, there was possibly more room for cultural syncretism within the Christian artistic tradition, although politics in recent times have played a large part in this picture. In Guinea, for instance, the then Marxist government of the 1960s banned any form of non-Muslim masquerade, notably the *d'mba* masquerade of the Baga peoples, although of late this ban has been relaxed and traditional belief systems are now tolerated. We have now brought the cultural history of African Christianity up to date, and have briefly looked at points of comparison with the other major world religion represented in Africa today: Islam. Now, by way of a conclusion, and in an attempt to draw the threads together, let us see if we can identify and define common themes in the archaeology of Christianity in Africa.

The archaeology of Christianity in Africa: seeking themes

A number of questions have arisen from this book. We have covered a very wide area and a timescale of almost 2000 years. What conclusions and interlinked themes can we draw from this study? I propose that we can address a number of important questions here in terms of a thematic framework. Firstly, what are the geographical and temporal parameters? Secondly, what of the process of conversion itself and the timescale for adopting Christianity? (We could call these first two questions the 'where' and 'when'). What is the nature of the evidence, and how does the concept of syncretism fit in (particularly in terms of re-use of sacred space)? We can also define other sub-themes, such as monasteries, pilgrimage and martyrs and indicators of liturgical conflict (perhaps an archaeology of heresy). These themes may go some way as to answering the elusive 'why'. Let us take the geographical and temporal scales first.

The timescale of the introduction of Christianity into Africa encompasses a period of some two thousand years, right up to the present day as various denominations seek new converts. Christianity found acceptance, in its initial phases at least, among disaffected Jewish populations of Palestine, and it would be expected that the proximity of Egypt to this area, and the cosmopolitan outlook of her capital city Alexandria, facilitated the development of Africa's earliest Christian communities here. In essence, the rest of the story entails a diffusionist explanation. The planting of Roman influence in northern Africa across the Maghreb region again saw a spread of a cosmopolitan mentality across the region. In terms of the process of religious change, this was essentially a 'bottom up' scenario; it was the lower classes initially who embraced the new faith, and it was only after a considerable period of time, and indeed survival through torrid times of persecution, that the faith finally filtered through to the uppermost strata of society. It was a case perhaps of religious change occuring by osmosis.

Within firstly Ethiopia and then the medieval states of Nubia, the story was different, although the mechanisms for delivering the message were the same. Here, with direct links to the eastern Mediterranean economic sphere, it was inevitable that the religious interest would go hand in hand with the economic interests. Significantly, it would appear that the ruling classes underwent conversion first, and the resulting spread of the faith, imbued now in the state machinery, was relatively rapid, although the Nubian picture may be slightly more clouded. In the state of Nobatia, for instance, some piecemeal earlier conversions occurred, resulting in a very uneven cultural record even as late as the tenth century, although in contrast it would appear that the picture in Alwa was probably more clear cut. Hypothetically the differences between a 'top down' and 'bottom up' conversion process would be visible in the archaeological record; in the case of the former, luxury items and large-scale public structures would rapidly and very overtly proclaim the new faith. One might envisage a concerted programme of church building, a shift in elite burial practice, and in the case of Aksum change in coinage motifs, all enforced strictly from above; change would only then be observed in the more domestic-level cultural record. Where the lower classes were the first to embrace the new faith, frequently under the threat of persecution, the cultural record would be sparser, and it would take much longer to recognise the gradual adoption of the Christian faith.

In terms of the colonial experiences of the mid- to late second millennium AD (the second part of the timescale into which we can divide the uptake of Christianity in Africa) we have a very patchy picture. In the earliest phases of Portuguese contact, the desire to make treaties with kings in order to secure lucrative market rights may have resulted in the relatively rapid spread of Christianity among the ruling classes; this certainly happened in the Kongo kingdom, but was less of a success on the

Indian Ocean coast where Islam had largely and effectively taken hold. During the nineteenth century, mission activity was largely directed towards the conversion of some of the poorest and lowliest members of society, and culturally this saw the direct transplantation of European ideas on to (in effect) a new set of consumers.

From an archaeological viewpoint the initial phase of mission activity would have been preceded by an intensive phase of cultural contact as witnessed by the presence of large numbers of imported objects. During the phase of European colonial contact, from the Portuguese right up to the nineteenth century, mission activity was more organised and again linked in some cases to overt political ends. In the case of the Portuguese, this process augmented the economic demands of the slave system; within the context of nineteenth-century imperialism, the mission process was often a useful tool in breaking down tribal divisions and thus making a newly acquired territory easier to govern.

And so what of the cultural indicators and our set of defined sub themes? It is very clear that the 'check-list' approach referred to in chapter 1 has little relevance for investigating the archaeology of Christianity in Africa. Each chapter tells its own stories of syncretism within the Christian cultural record; check lists are too simplistic. The archaeology of African Christianity presents a number of much broader themes. We have seen examples of churches being housed in old pagan temples, of new Christian shrines appropriating pagan sacred space, of martyrs' tombs becoming great commercial and spiritual pilgrimage centres, we can compare the missionary zeal and spatial structure of the monasteries of Egypt, Nubia and Ethiopia with the small, down-at-heel mission stations of colonial Africa. The ethos may be the same even if the buildings are on different scales. And what of the archaeology of heresy? Again, no check lists can help us differentiate adequately the Donatists from the mainstream, nor the monophysite from the Melkite. There are small hints, but no universal equation to explain it away. This is the challenge when dealing with such a complex subject as ours.

It is the 'why' question that is perhaps hardest to tackle. What is it that makes the transition to a completely new faith so attractive? What is the motivation? Why should (in some cases) centuries-old belief systems be abandoned and a new faith enthusiastically embraced? Why did Christianity survive so well in certain areas, yet fade quickly in others?

> At first the people worked for him because he fed and clothed them. Then naturally when all the trees started fruiting, it became a different story....In this way, the old gods appear to have defeated the Christian God, and the ministers fled the island, never to return.

(R. Hardy and A. Schaffer (1978) *The Wicker Man* (London: Pan): p.138)

In the cult British horror film *The Wicker Man* (1973), we are introduced to a small Scottish island that has reverted to a rather manufactured sort of paganism from a previous strict Calvinistic existence. In this case, the transformation back to the 'old gods' was part of a scheme to further the productivity of a previously barren island by giving a new set of nature-based beliefs back to the people. Within Europe and the United States, this perception that Christianity has somehow lost its affinity with nature has led to the rise in popularity of neo-pagan beliefs such as Wicca.

In Africa there are more syncretic elements to the version of Christianity celebrated there; it is still bound up with beliefs in the land and nature and meshes well with traditional belief systems. In the case of traditional concepts of ancestor worship, Roman Catholicism has a parallel in using saints for intercession. Rainmaking beliefs and blessings of fields can also sit easily within the Christian sphere. The very attraction of Christianity – and this is rooted in the world-view of Africa – is its adaptability and ability to absorb elements of traditional belief. This is perhaps the reason why Africa is now a dynamic force in shaping world Christianity.

Christianity replaced – within the continent – a vast range of differing belief systems, monotheistic and polytheistic. The challenge for the missionaries – whatever their motivations – was to make this message attractive to the potential converts. Over the two different time frameworks dealt with here – the Church of antiquity and the Church at the time of European contact – political and economic concerns obviously played a key part in the process. In many cases it was the perception of economic advancement among upper and lower classes that drove the implantation of a new belief system. And what of the greater picture and broader mechanisms?

In north Africa, the process was linked wholly to the same phenomenon then being played out within the whole of the Roman Empire. More than anywhere else in Africa, the case of Roman north Africa is linked solidly to the European scene. Nubian Christianity was a phenomenon driven by outside economic and political concerns, and, unlike Roman north Africa, was initially enforced (although this may not be the case with Nobatia) from the top down. Again, as an inherent part of the state machinery, Christianity was vulnerable when the system broke down, as it did from the eleventh century AD onwards, and the area was susceptible to a relatively rapid spread of Islam, and the 'choice' to swap one belief system for another.

It is only in Egypt and in Ethiopia that the great churches of antiquity in Africa have survived. In Egypt, Coptic culture has adapted to survive alongside Islam, and a dynamic monastic system alongside a geographical proximity to the great ecclesiastical centres of the eastern Mediterranean have both ensured the survival of Christianity. The pattern of conversion in Egypt parallels that of Roman north Africa, but the dynamism of the monastic systems – both coenobitic and eremitic – maintained the impetus of the conversion process. In Ethiopia factors of geography have assisted in the survival of Christianity. The initial conversion here was probably largely driven by a desire for closer links with the worlds of the eastern Mediterranean and the lucrative trade sphere. Enforced from the top down, Christianity rapidly became the state religion of the Aksumite polity. In subsequent years, surviving the predations of enemies on the borders of the high plateau, the core Christian focus expanded southwards and military conquest went hand in hand with religious conversion spearheaded by a vigorous monastic movement.

And what of the rest of Africa? Missionary activity forms the core of the process of conversion, and again political and economic gains on the parts of the converters and converted played a major part in the transplanting of Christianity in new lands. Adaptability here was the key, and the syncretic elements in the cultural record attest to this flexibility of belief and the ability to absorb within a strictly Christian frame-work elements of traditional belief systems, almost as if to sweeten the pill.

The cultural history of African Christianity can at the moment only consist of a series of loose, interlinked general case studies. This is an area of vast research poten-tial, and the study presented here has only really scratched the surface. Africa is perhaps the major social and cultural force shaping world Christianity at this moment; to understand how this dynamism has come about we need to take our-selves back in our imaginations to the forum of a great city in Roman north Africa, to a small hermitage in the deserts of Egypt, to a magnificent new painted cathedral on the shores of the Nile, to the court of King Ezana at Aksum, to the Kingdom of the Kongo, and perhaps finally to a small mission station in southern Africa. Africa's Christian past has formed the Christian present and Christian future for us all.

Further reading

There are a number of introductions to African art, all considering some of the themes developed in the first half of this chapter. Perhaps the most accessible and readable introduction remains F. Willett's *African Art* 1993 (revised ed. London: Thames and Hudson) although it tends to concentrate rather heavily upon western Africa to the expense of southern Africa. There is a useful small section on modern Christian art in Africa. The magnificently illustrated catalogue to the exhibition of the same name *Africa: The Art of a Continent* (1995, ed. T. Phillips, Munich: Prestel) offers a very fine and detailed survey of African art from the earliest times up until the recent past, although the emphasis is largely upon statuary, and as previously stat-ed Christian art is largely under-represented. A useful survey of African architecture in recent times is N. Elleh's 1997 book *African Architecture: Evolution and Transformation* (New York: McGraw Hill), which has a useful although limited survey of church architecture. Some of the theoretical aspects of the nature and study of African art are covered in the authoritative *A History of Art in Africa* (2000, London: Thames and Hudson) edited by M. Visona, R. Poynor, H. Cole and M. Harris. There is only one detailed work that specifically deals with the history and evolution of Christian art in Africa. J. Theil and H. Helf's 1984 work *Christliche Kunst in Afrika* (Berlin: Reimer Verlag) is a wide-ranging survey (in German) of the whole experience of African Christian artistic expression, from Ethiopian paintings to modern church building. It is an indispensable and very well illustrated work, although unfortunately is not currently in print.

Glossary

The following definitions may help in understanding some of the more technical liturgical and ecclesiastical terminology discussed in this book.

Anchorite: A solitary holy man or hermit who lived his contemplative life alone. The founder of this Eremetic lifestyle was the Egyptian St Anthony (*c.*251-356).

Arius: *c.*250-336, condemned at the council of Nicaea (325) by Athanasius. Arius' outlook denied the divinity of Christ. His creed was especially popular amongst the Vandal groups who attacked the Roman Empire in the fifth century AD.

Coenobite: A monk who settled within a community rather than remain in a solitary lifestyle. This type of monasticism was developed in Egypt by St Pachomius (*c.*290-346).

Monophysites: Monophysites believe that Jesus Christ did not have two distinct natures namely the human and divine, but he only had a single nature which was the divine, it dominated his human nature; this view was first expounded by Eutyches (*c.*378-454) who was the head of a monastery in Constantinople. This perspective was held to be heretical by the mainstream church, and was formally anathematised at the extraordinary council of Chalcedon in 451. The Coptic Church of Egypt, the Jacobite Church of Syria, the Armenian Church, the Ethiopian Orthodox Church and the Nestorians (a diverse Christian community centred on Iraq and the Middle East) all still hold to the monophysite doctrine. These churches are known loosely as the Oriental churches.

Orthodoxy: Meaning the right belief, the modern Greek Orthodox church is essentially dyophysite in outlook recognising that Jesus Christ had two natures i.e. the divine and human. It was this viewpoint that won the day at the council of Chalcedon in 451. Followers of this doctrine were known as Chalcedonians or Melkites. The Orthodox eastern church separated from the western church, represented by the Roman Catholic Church after the Great Schism of 1054.

Protestantism: A broad and generic term representing the various sects that originated from the sixteenth century onwards as a protest against the Roman Catholic Church. Such groups include Anglicans, and so-called Nonconformist groups such as Baptists and Methodists. From the seventeenth century onwards, Protestant mission societies have been active within Africa.

Index

Page numbers in **bold** refer to illustrations